REDEFINING M. ..., RLAM POPULAR MUSIC

Redefining Mainstream Popular Music is a collection of 17 essays that critically examine the idea of the 'mainstream' in and across a variety of popular music styles and contexts. Notions of what is popular vary across generations and cultures – what may have been considered alternative to one group may be perceived as mainstream to another. Incorporating a wide range of popular music texts, genres, scenes, practices and technologies from the United Kingdom, North America, Australia and New Zealand, the authors theoretically challenge and augment our understanding of how the mainstream is understood and functions in the overlapping worlds of popular music production, consumption and scholarship. Spanning the local and the global, the historic and contemporary, the iconic and the everyday, this book covers a broad range of genres, from punk to grunge to hip-hop, while also considering popular music through other mediums, including mash-ups and the music of everyday work life. *Redefining Mainstream Popular Music* provides readers with an innovative and nuanced perspective of what it means to be mainstream.

Sarah Baker is a senior lecturer at Griffith University, Queensland, Australia. She is the author of *Creative Labour: Media Work in Three Cultural Industries* (with David Hesmondhalgh).

Andy Bennett is Professor of Cultural Sociology and Director of the Griffith Centre for Cultural Research at Griffith University, Queensland, Australia. He has authored and edited numerous books including *Popular Music and Youth Culture, Cultures of Popular Music, Remembering Woodstock*, and *Music Scenes* (with Richard A. Peterson).

Jodie Taylor is a Research Fellow at Griffith University, Queensland, Australia. She is the author of *Playing It Queer: Popular Music, Identity and Queer World-making*.

REDEFINING MAINSTREAM POPULAR MUSIC

Edited by Sarah Baker, Andy Bennett, and Jodie Taylor

GRIFFITH UNIVERSITY

Routledge
Taylor & Francis Group

NEW YORK AND LONDON

First published 2013
by Routledge
711 Third Avenue, New York, NY 10017

Simultaneously published in the UK
by Routledge
2 Park Square, Milton Park, Abingdon, Oxon OX14 4RN

Routledge is an imprint of the Taylor & Francis Group, an informa business

Library of Congress Cataloging in Publication Data
Redefining mainstream popular music / edited by Sarah Baker, Andy Bennett, and Jodie Taylor.
    pages cm
Includes bibliographical references and index.
1. Popular music—History and criticism.   2. Popular culture. I. Baker, Sarah, 1977– editor.   II. Bennett, Andy, 1963– editor.
III. Taylor, Jodie, 1980– editor.
ML3470.R425 2013
781.6409—dc23
                                                           2012027433
ISBN: 978–0–415–80780–7 (hbk)
ISBN: 978–0–415–80782–1 (pbk)
ISBN: 978–0–203–12785–8 (ebk)

Typeset in Bembo
by RefineCatch Limited Limited, Bungay, Suffolk, UK

Senior Editor: Constance Ditzel
Editorial Assistant: Elysse Preposi
Production Editor: Emma Håkonsen
Marketing Manager: Jessica Plummer
Copy Editor: Louise Morgan
Proofreader: Jane Canvin
Cover Design: Jayne Varney

Printed and bound in the United States of America by
Walsworth Publishing Company, Marceline, MO.

CONTENTS

PREFACE

Music is a cultural medium frequently described as mainstream – a description most commonly applied to popular forms of music situated in the sociocultural context of a late modern global capitalism. Popular music is also understood as stylistically heterogeneous: it is made and consumed by people of all classes, ages, nationalities, races, ethnicities, genders and sexualities; it is produced using a multitude of acoustic and digital technologies; and it is distributed to multi-scale audiences, spanning mass commercial markets and independent local scenes. Often intersecting with broader cultural trends, the styles, cultures and consumption patterns of popular music have an irregularly combined, contextually varied and fluid effect on our perception of music as either being, or potentially becoming, mainstream.

It is not uncommon to find the music regarded by one generation, local scene or market as obscure or alternative, later adopted or perceived by another group as part of its mainstream cultural vernacular. Even if we take the Top 40 as the quintessence of mainstream popular taste, this perplexity prevails since many different popular styles regularly coexist in the Top 40 charts (Brackett 2002), the logics of which have become increasingly complex in the iTunes era. The inherent variability in taste and heterogeneity of popular music subjectively impacts upon our understanding of the mainstream itself, making it difficult to ascertain a clear, comprehensive and ubiquitous definition of what mainstream popular music is, or even to loosely specify the criteria necessary for inclusion within this category. In popular music studies and popular music cultures more broadly, we find countless references to the mainstream; however, the term itself remains poorly defined and haphazardly applied.

In Sarah Thornton's (1995) *Club Cultures* – a United Kingdom-based study of 1990s dance club scenes, which to date has been one of the most cited interrogations of the term – she argues that 'whatever its exact status, mainstream is an inadequate term for the sociology of culture' (115). She attributes this inadequacy to the ideological distinctions that draw discriminatory lines between the mainstream – which is associated with conformity and artifice, and is accordingly gendered 'feminine' – and the supposedly more 'hip', serious or authentic clubbers. The latter, Thornton argues, are motivated by the acquisition of subcultural capital, which is a kind of cultural asset accumulated by situating oneself as subcultural in opposition to an imagined monolithic mainstream.

Indeed, since the 1970s, the style, meaning and currency of subcultures have occupied the attention of cultural studies and popular music scholars to such a degree that the mainstream appears to have had little cultural value; it has primarily been reproduced in antithetical relation to the more 'authentic' music of subcultural producers and participants (e.g. Hall and Jefferson 1976; Hebdige 1979; Thornton 1995; Muggleton 2000; Hodkinson 2002; Gelder 2007). Since relatively few scholars have sought to critically investigate its meanings, functions and sensibilities, Huber (2007) notes that what constitutes the mainstream appears to be simply taken for granted – even apparently commonsensical. Here, we take the view that mainstream is a term with significant cultural value, and thus one that is in urgent need of detailed consideration. Exploring the relationship between a variety of mainstream cultural practices in contemporary and historical settings, popular music styles, technologies and consumption patterns, meanings and figurations, and the sociocultural context within which they emerge, this volume hopes to conceptually reframe and empirically augment our understanding of the mainstream.

Outline of this Book

Arranged in five overlapping parts, we believe this volume critically innovates popular music studies through the authors' insistence on centralizing the mainstream in popular music discussion and criticism. Rather than simply taking the mainstream as a commonsense term, or subordinating it to subculture, we aim to problematize this concept in multiple historical, cultural and social contexts, incorporating a multi-layered understanding that considers both the most spectacular permutations of the mainstream and the everyday operations of audiences and practitioners.

In Part I: Reappraising the Mainstream, the authors underscore the mainstream's contingent and contextual qualities, presenting a series of revised perspectives on the plurality of meanings, roles and functions of the mainstream, its consumption and production.

Setting the scene for the theoretical work to follow, Alison Huber's chapter provides an updated polemic against the taken-for-granted assumptions and existing figurations of the mainstream – what she calls a metaphorical rendering and 'spatialized imagining of dominant culture'. Troubling the mainstream/

subculture binary, Huber positively reconceptualizes the term, arguing that an understanding of mainstream logics, practices and processes is necessary for a fuller interrogation of the spatio-temporalities of popular music.

Teenybop is a much derided form of mainstream music, but Sarah Baker's chapter highlights some of the more extraordinary particularities of mainstream practice that make up young girls' engagement with this element of Top 40 pop. Baker outlines the tradition of trivializing the popular music consumption of young women, in which teenybop music is regarded as inauthentic and its consumers as inconsequential. To counter this position, Baker provides examples from her ethnographic research with pre-teen girls; these fieldwork snapshots illustrate that the musical lives of teenyboppers are 'far more complex and nuanced' than popular discourse gives them credit for.

Stripping away the mythologies of mainstream music production that emphasize controlling impresarios and entrepreneurial svengalis, Matt Stahl's chapter examines the making of The Archies, an animated pop group that achieved chart success in the late 1960s. In the popular imagination, the man behind The Archies' success is the shrewd music executive Don Kirshner, but Stahl complicates this narrative by highlighting the 'complex divisions of cultural industry labour' involved in the creation of this 'prefabricated' band. This focus on virtual cartoon performers enables Stahl to illustrate 'both the contingent nature of entertainment-industrial ensembles and the (crypto-)diabolism that often populates critical accounts of mainstream music'.

In Part II: Perceptions of the Mainstream, the authors consider the plurality of the mainstream by examining how various popular music audiences and practitioners come to understand the mainstream's relationship to its 'others'.

Looking beyond an implicitly heteronormative perception of the mainstream, Jodie Taylor's chapter points to the intersections of sexuality, gender and popular music discourse. Focusing on lesbian and queer feminist musicalities, Taylor illustrates the multiple and shifting perceptions of mainstream lesbian music and its contingent relationship with feminist and queer political strategies. By examining the emergence of and responses to womyn's music, lesbian chic, riot dyke and celesbiansim, this chapter illustrates some of the various ways in which feminist, lesbian and queer female identities have been constructed and contested in relation to multiple styles and spaces of popular music, and in relation to variable notions of the mainstream.

Borrowing from Durkheim's division of the sacred and the profane, and drawing on his ethnographic work with Swedish and Indonesian punks, Erik Hannerz's chapter focuses on how the meaning of mainstream differs among punks, and the consequences this has for the ways in which the subcultural is staged and authenticated. By outlining two different subcultural frameworks, referred to as *convex* and *concave*, Hannerz demonstrates that the mainstream is not a residual category, but is constantly being redefined and repositioned. In order to understand how punk meaning is constructed and how punk actions are made sense of, this chapter suggests that we must approach the mainstream as existing within articulations of the subcultural.

Murray Forman's chapter addresses the mainstream in relation to hip-hop culture. Drawing on hip-hop lore, rap lyrics, social networking 'battles' and academic discourse, Forman posits that an understanding of how hip-hop culture deals with notions of time, change and age is central to understanding the sensibilities of the hip-hop mainstream and its 'other'. According to Forman, in hip-hop culture the mainstream is indicative of generational divide and conflict, where young contemporary performers continue to pursue other, more radical styles and practices in order to assert their own political agendas, lived experiences and provocations.

The mainstreaming of an alternative and/or underground popular music genre is often seen to go hand in hand with a waning of its authenticity and credibility. In her chapter on the mainstreaming of grunge, Catherine Strong contests such ideas. Drawing on empirical data generated through interviews with Australian grunge fans, Strong demonstrates that the transition of grunge to a mainstream popular music actually broadened its reach to a global audience, which saw no apparent contradiction between grunge's mainstream status and its legacy as a music deeply in touch with the everyday lives of post-industrial youth.

Part III: Historicizing the Mainstream explores British and American popular musics of the 1950s, 1960s and beyond, critically reappraising the dialectics of a co-opted mainstream versus authentic counter-cultures, and considering historical industrial processes and the mainstreaming of music heritage.

The section begins with David Baker's chapter on Elvis Presley's career as a movie star during the 1960s. It is commonly suggested by critics and academic writers that this period in Elvis's career marked a downturn in his credibility – a symbolic betrayal of his earlier identity as a teenage icon. Challenging this perception, Baker argues that a far more complex and nuanced set of circumstances pertain to Elvis's shift from live performer to film actor during the 1960s. Thus, observes Baker, the films of Elvis mark something of a unique moment in film history, coming between the end of the Hollywood star system and the emergence of the blockbuster movie. Within this space, suggests Baker, there was ample scope for Elvis films to explore a broad range of issues, while Elvis himself often played roles that remained close to his roots as a white, working-class male from the American Deep South.

A further consideration of Elvis's position in the mainstream is provided in Mark Duffett's chapter, which emphasizes the temporal specificity of Elvis's mainstream-ness. It does this by focusing on a range of Elvis heritage sites in Memphis, Tennessee, which are in varying states of preservation or decay. Duffett deploys Bahtkin's notion of the 'chronotope' to explain how Elvis fans' 'imagined memories' of the performer 'are encapsulated in a specific time period and geographic setting', which in effect come to 'fossilize' the landscape of Elvis's America. As Duffett argues, 'perhaps stars who once dominated the charts and now linger as part of popular memory need to be considered in the context of a *fading* mainstream formation'.

Looking back to British popular music of the 1960s, Sheila Whiteley's chapter explores the gender narratives that underpinned mainstream pop and rock counter-culture of this era. Although at the time, Whiteley argues, traditional gender roles were said to be weakening off the back of the freedoms promised by the so-called cultural revolution of the 'Swinging Sixties', she goes on to show that the gender discourses underpinning both mainstream pop and rock counter-culture revealed little in the way of change. Predicated on a normative and repressed version of femininity, both the mainstream and counter-cultural spaces were characterized by conservative cultural narratives that continued to frame listeners' experience in gendered terms.

Timothy J. Dowd's chapter shifts our attention to the charts, specifically focusing on the 'burgeoning success of international performers' on the mainstream US charts from the 1960s onwards. Dowd's exploration of the internationalization of the mainstream market in the United States draws on the *Billboard* charts as a way to illustrate the extent to which performers from outside the United States have been able to navigate the US mainstream market and, in some cases, become 'fixtures in the American mainstream'. Dowd argues that the patterns of internationalization he has observed in the charts between the 1940s and 1990s can be attributed to a range of industry gatekeepers, who control the production and distribution of mainstream music and whose varying levels of conservatism influenced the extent to which 'music from abroad flowed into the US mainstream'.

Part IV: Production Aesthetics and the Mainstream examines the aesthetic dimensions of popular music production, changing production values and the increasingly blurred distinctions between the sound of alternative and mainstream popular music.

Adrian Renzo's chapter focuses on the production aesthetics and discourses of online mash-up scenes. Putting some distance between earlier discussions of mash-up producers and consumers as an example of a non- or anti-mainstream scene, Renzo suggests that such scenes are modelled on skilful displays of technical prowess akin to mainstream practices. Drawing on his own participant observation of online mash-up communities and his experience as a creative practitioner, Renzo explains what he calls the *mainstream aesthetic criteria* that amateur producers use to evaluate the success of mash-ups.

In his chapter comparing the production of mainstream popular music from a cross-cultural perspective, Dennis Crowdy observes how understandings of and attitudes towards music technologies and their place in music production are often inherently tied to aspects of locality. Comparing the contexts of Australia and Papua New Guinea, Crowdy notes the importance of locality and context in shaping perceptions of the relationship between sound recording and notions of musical authenticity in mainstream popular music. Crowdy illustrates that while in the Australian context significant emphasis is placed on state-of-the-art recording techniques, a history of limited access to such equipment in Papua New Guinea has led to a more eclectic attitude towards the types of technology applied in the production of local mainstream popular music.

Drawing on interviews with independent rock musicians in Brisbane, Australia, Ian Rogers' chapter explores how these musicians understand their position in relation to the 'global commercial media sphere'. What Rogers teases out from the interview data is the divide that exists between the musicians' engagement with mainstream music as consumers on the one hand, and 'as a viable career' on the other. Their resulting isolation from mainstream career pathways situates them as 'hobbyist' musicians on the margins of the music industry. Yet, as Rogers argues, although hobbyist activity is 'seldom discussed as a fully integrated driver of the mainstream music industries', this is actually where the majority of musicians labour, all the while negotiating the possibilities of achieving something akin to 'mainstream success'.

In Part V: The Mainstream and Vernacular Culture, the authors consider the relationship between mainstream popular music and a variety of listening practices associated with vernacular forms of music consumption and interpretation in everyday contexts.

Michael Brown's chapter focuses on the tradition of 'tramping' (local vernacular for hiking) in New Zealand. As Brown observes, a key aspect of tramping is song – with aspects of traditional folk song being creatively combined with elements drawn from more mainstream popular music. As Brown observes, such is the diverse range of musical influences drawn on by trampers that accepted notions of mainstream and vernacular song easily break down and force new considerations of where such distinctions lie and how they are creatively manipulated.

The chapter by Michael Walsh introduces the term 'mainstream musical listening' to indicate personal listening practices in everyday life that affect cognitive states by way of controlling the immediate audible environment. To illustrate this, Walsh uses the example of workers who listen to music at their place of employment as a way to cope with the particularities of open-plan offices and to control their experience of working in that environment.

In the final chapter, Andy Bennett introduces the concept of 'ironic listening' – adopted from Ang's (1982) work on 'ironic viewing' – to consider a further dimension of the audience's appropriation and enjoyment of mainstream popular music. As Bennett observes, while it has long been acknowledged that the appeal of mainstream popular music hinges on audiences' ability to see through the constructedness of popular music artists but to still regard them as 'real' or 'authentic', the success of certain mainstream popular music suggests a rather different audience dynamic at play. Bennett then goes on to argue that what is key here is the audience's ability to decode the constructedness of particular mainstream popular artists in a non-serious, playful way, thus deriving ironic pleasure from such artists and their music.

In deliberately attending to such a conventional category as mainstream, we consider the contributors to this volume daring in their commitment to challenge what many scholars, makers and lovers of popular music have routinely taken for granted. This collection of essays not only raises insightful reflections, criticisms and redefinitions of the mainstream, but necessarily problematizes the constantly changing array of practices, processes and contexts that determine how we come to think of certain popular music styles and practices as mainstream. Furthermore, by attending to various and, at times, contradictory interpretations of what is or is not mainstream, the perspectives offered up in this volume collectively reveal ideas and observations concerning cultures of popular music that have previously been overlooked, excluded or misunderstood. For these reasons, we hope this edited collection is read as both a pivotal and political mediation on the mainstream and its discontents.

Jodie Taylor, Sarah Baker and Andy Bennett
July 2012

References

Ang, I. (1982) *Watching* Dallas: *soap opera and the melodramatic imagination*, London: Routledge.

Brackett, D. (2002) '(In search of) musical meaning: genres, categories and crossover', in D. Hesmondhalgh and K. Negus (eds), *Popular Music Studies*, London: Arnold.

Gelder, K. (2007) *Subcultures: cultural histories and social practice*, Abingdon: Routledge.

Hall, S. and Jefferson, T. (eds) (1976) *Resistance Through Rituals: youth subcultures in post-war Britain*, London: Hutchinson.

Hebdige, D. (1979) *Subculture: the meaning of style*, London: Routledge.

Hodkinson, P. (2002) *Goth: identity, style and subculture*, Oxford: Berg.

Huber, A. (2007) 'What's in a mainstream? Critical possibilities', *Altitude*, 8: 1–12.

Muggleton, D. (2000) *Inside Subculture: the postmodern meaning of style*, Oxford: Berg.

Thornton, S. (1995) *Club Cultures: music, media and subcultural capital*, Oxford: Polity Press.

ACKNOWLEDGEMENTS

The work that has gone into editing and producing this volume has been the combined and equally shared efforts of Sarah Baker, Andy Bennett and Jodie Taylor. Therefore, as the volume editors, we would like to stress that the order in which our names appear on this book's cover is alphabetical and does not reflect any editorial hierarchy. Sarah, Andy and Jodie would like to acknowledge the support of the Griffith Centre for Cultural Research, Griffith University and their assistance with the production of this volume. In particular, we give thanks to our copy editor Sue Jarvis for her meticulous proofing and typesetting of this volume. We are indebted to our contributors for their willingness to embark on this project with us and for their timeliness in providing content and incorporating revisions. Finally, we thank our publisher Constance Ditzel and her colleagues at Routledge for their professional advice and assistance.

PART I
Reappraising the Mainstream

1

MAINSTREAM AS METAPHOR

Imagining Dominant Culture

Alison Huber

Mainstream Matters

> Proper music fans are doing what they always do when the mainstream
> smells stagnant – visit the tide pools and freshwater burns where new talent
> spawns.
>
> *(Liner notes to* Q Magazine *CD,* Rise and Shine:
> The Best New Music of 2002*)*

This chapter is interested first and foremost in the *idea* of the mainstream.
Mainstream is a particularly important category of value for popular music
cultures, particularly for the reasons exemplified in the quote above, which
rehearses the full range of negative associations stereotypically attached to the
concept. However, the term 'mainstream' is deployed in a variety of contexts,
ranging from politics and social policy to cultural identity and popular culture,
and emerging from academia, journalism, public debate and beyond. Read across
this array of situations, the word has a habit of seeming nonsensical, and probably
fuels the notion that 'mainstream' is a term so nebulous that it has little usefulness
as a theoretical tool. Yet, paradoxically, mainstream's utility continues: start listening
for it, and you'll hear and read it every day. It is even likely to form part of your
own imagining of the world.

My interest in the idea of the mainstream began when I fell in love, rather
unexpectedly, with a Top 40 song. The song was 'Say it Once' (1999) by Ultra, one
of the many groups that joined the seemingly endless parade of boy bands
crooning and shimmying their way into the musical mainstream in the late 1980s
and 1990s. I listened to this CD single incessantly, and was drawn magnetically to

the television whenever its film clip appeared. For someone who had envisaged herself as (having become) anti-mainstream, who felt she had found her natural home in so-called 'indie' music, it came as something of a shock to have such an intensely affective response to this song. How could I love something that was so clearly 'mainstream'? Even though my cultural studies training had repeatedly assured me that I was not, in the words of Stuart Hall, a 'cultural dope' (1981: 232) in the dead-eyed thrall of capitalist mass culture, things still didn't feel right. What we can observe in my confused reaction to this moment of 'mainstream love' is the range of complex relationships between the idea of a mainstream and identity politics, taste and cultural value, entwined as they are with practices of consumption. We can also find a sense of why mainstream matters so much to the articulation of these relationships. I had learned from my peers explicitly and tacitly through the very same cultural studies training that alterity to the mainstream of culture was what should be desired. Yet my love for this song made me start to think seriously about what 'mainstream' might be all about, beyond these normalized, devalued associations.

But try checking for the word 'mainstream' in the index of almost any book published under the broad rubrics of cultural studies or popular music studies, as I began to do, and your search will reveal only a few texts that reference the term.[1] This dearth of indexed reference to 'mainstream' does not mean, however, that the word – and, in turn, the concept(s) it is called upon to describe – do not figure in scholarly work. Indeed, the idea of the mainstream has not only been deployed regularly in cultural and popular music studies, but it is in many ways integral to the understandings and analyses of cultural subjects, practices and products that have been developed by practitioners in these fields. The role of the concept of mainstream, then, has generally been unacknowledged, and it has remained largely undefined and under-theorized. Nevertheless, it has been working quietly behind the scenes, upstaged by the romantic bravado of concepts like 'subculture' and 'resistance' – words that have continued to enjoy much academic interrogation and re-imagination in the years since they emerged as key terms of analysis during the subcultural studies moment of the 1970s (e.g. see Thornton 1995; Muggleton 2000; Hodkinson 2002; Gelder 2007).

To complicate matters further, 'mainstream' acts not only as the undefined, multi-purpose centre to the periphery, the 'other' to subcultural, alternative, underground, outsider, folk and art cultures (which was the way that I had imagined it in my Ultra encounter). Look a little more closely and its use is even more flexible than this. It is sometimes imagined to be a place (when things 'go mainstream' or 'cross over into the mainstream'); sometimes it is a cultural force, a natural energy that 'sweeps' things into its magnetic pull (thus seeming to reify its metaphorical promise); at other times, it is used as a marketing synonym for the 'mass audience' of popular culture's products; frequently, it is used as an adjective, attached to a noun to signify some inherent aesthetic trait; you'll hear it used in place of the word 'normal' or 'normative'; it can also refer to a socio-economic category used by politicians to refer to the majority of their constituency. The mainstream is, in some ways, a schizophrenic category, a cultural imaginary comprising multiple 'inconsistent fantasies', as Sarah Thornton (1995: 93) puts it. Indeed, despite acknowledging the powerful status and broad utility of these fantasies, Thornton ultimately concludes in her *Club Cultures* study that mainstream is an 'inadequate term' (1995: 115). But how did we arrive at a situation where a term so vague, yet simultaneously so potent, appears to describe everything and nothing, in all sorts of contexts? And how might we start to deploy the notion with more precision?

What follows in this chapter is an extended consideration of the cultural imaginary of the category, which works to expose some of the origins of the taken-for-granted assumptions about the term. I begin by revisiting one particularly influential example from the emergent field of cultural studies where mainstream is used as an 'other' to the category 'subculture'. I then connect the negative associations replicated in this work to the function of mainstream as a metaphor, and its spatialized imagining of dominant culture. In other words, this chapter is an exercise that clears some room to begin to think about and use mainstream 'as a substantive category' (Toynbee 2000: 122), instead of as a hold-all term with little or no concrete definition, or that operates purely at an ideological level (Thornton 1995). Like Jason Toynbee, I want to think *with* mainstream, not against it, and I want to avoid replicating the 'relentlessly negative approach' (Toynbee 2002: 149) that often accompanies deployment of 'mainstream' in both academic/critical and popular registers; however, I do want to try to think productively about the origins of this negativity. In working towards a reappraisal of the term in this way, mainstream has the space to emerge from this chapter as a fresh term with the potential to hold a clear utility in cultural analysis because it describes something specific and particular: a space of cultural production and consumption with its own logics, practices and processes.

Mainstream and Hegemony: Mainstream as the Subculture's Other

It is not news that the idea of hegemony was integral to work done at the Centre for Contemporary Cultural Studies (CCCS) in the 1970s, or that the relationships between dominant and subordinate culture, parent culture and subculture, cultural dominance and cultural marginality comprised the foundations of the Birmingham School's world-view. In particular, the many inequalities between the 'haves' and the 'have nots', drawn into high relief by the juxtaposition of these binary pairs, influenced much of the politically charged work from this time. Moreover, the politics at the heart of the modish theories that guided this work (particularly those derived from Karl Marx, Louis Althusser and Antonio Gramsci) drew critics into high-level theoretical considerations of lived experience.

It is in this CCCS context that the connection between the cultural mainstream and hegemony was subtly – yet perhaps definitively – described by Dick Hebdige in his oft-cited, landmark book, *Subculture: The Meaning of Style* (1979), and I want to look briefly at this work to show some of the ways in which mainstream was framed in this influential contribution to cultural studies. Hebdige's work has been critiqued routinely (even relentlessly) ever since it was written. However, it is important for my purposes to revisit it here because it belongs to one of the historical theoretical trajectories that continues to influence cultural studies in general and the study of music cultures in particular, and it is for this reason that it is also the genesis of one of the most enduring usages of mainstream.

Hebdige, like many of the early cultural studies scholars, was particularly *uninterested* in the mainstream. In fact, his interest lay squarely in the mainstream's opposite – the subversive and the marginal – and it was these subjects that formed the basis of *Subculture*. As a consequence of these concerns, Hebdige's focus was the methods by which (specifically) male, working-class youth cultures managed to define themselves as *other than* mainstream. His writing is thus concerned with how resistance to dominant culture might be achieved and how symbolic power might be claimed through, in particular, stylistic differentiation.

Early on in his study, Hebdige defines hegemony as:

> [Referring] to a situation in which a provisional alliance of certain social groups can exert 'total social authority' over other subordinate groups, not simply by coercion or by the direct imposition of ruling ideas, but by 'winning and shaping consent so that the power of the dominant classes appears both legitimate and natural' (Hall 1977). Hegemony can only be maintained so long as the dominant classes 'succeed in framing all competing definitions within their range' (Hall 1977), so that subordinate groups are, if not controlled, then at least contained within an ideological space which does not seem at all 'ideological'; which appears instead to be permanent and 'natural', to lie outside history, to be beyond particular interests . . .
>
> *(Hebdige 1979: 15–16)*

This definition, drawing heavily on Stuart Hall, who in turn finds inspiration in Gramsci, focuses attention on the fact that hegemony appears to be 'natural'. Hegemony's power lies in its consensual nature: both the 'ruling' and the 'ruled' are implicated in the ongoing effectiveness of its control. In every sense, the ideological 'containment' of the subordinated classes is naturalized and thus does not seem like containment at all. In light of this, it is particularly interesting to note how Hebdige goes on to refer to the mainstream. He discusses the overt theatrical and constructed 'display' of spectacular subcultural style, and he describes this stylistic signification as:

[going] against the grain of a mainstream culture whose principal defining characteristic, according to Barthes [1972], is a tendency to masquerade as nature, to substitute 'normalized' for historical forms, to translate the reality of the world into an image of the world which in turn presents itself as if composed according to 'the evident laws of the natural order'.

(Hebdige 1979: 101–2)

Hebdige's connection between the mainstream and hegemony is clear. For him, the mainstream *is* hegemony. Like hegemony, the mainstream 'masquerades as nature'; it appears to be 'normal', it is 'ahistorical'. For Hebdige – in this example at least – mainstream represents everything that the youth subculturalists in his study were trying to subvert: the stifling presence of the majority, complicit in their own subjugation and too complacent to realize their containment, let alone effect any sort of opposition. Underlying this rhetoric is a latent disdain for those who do not choose to oppose the mainstream actively, or who choose to experience (or at least find themselves experiencing) life in its space. In championing the semiotic moves of certain youth subcultures, Hebdige implicitly criticizes what Gary Clarke later identified to be '"straight" working class youth' (Clarke 1982: 1) and their perceived 'normalcy' (2). In doing so, Hebdige's focus has the effect of implicitly devaluing subculture's binary opposite: the 'mainstream'. Problematically, the simple pitting of specific subcultures against a vaguely defined mainstream does little to denaturalize or understand mainstream/hegemony in the theoretical terms to which this approach aspired. In other words, this is an understanding of mainstream (and hegemony) that is achieved in the negative, defined by what it *isn't* rather than what it *is*.[2]

Hebdige also uses the word 'mainstream' in a different way in this wordy discussion of the incorporation of subcultural style:

[T]he succession of post-war youth styles can be represented on the formal level as a series of transformations of an initial set of items (clothes, dance, music, argot) unfolding through an internal set of polarities (mod v. rocker, skinhead v. greaser, skinhead v. hippie, punk v. hippie, ted v. punk, skinhead v. punk) and defined against a parallel series of 'straight' transformations ('high'/mainstream fashion). Each subculture moves through a cycle of resistance and defusion . . . Subcultural deviance is simultaneously rendered 'explicable' and meaningless in the classrooms, courts and media at the same time as the 'secret' objects of subcultural style are put on display in every high street record shop and chain-store boutique. Stripped of its unwholesome connotations, the style becomes fit for public consumption.

(Hebdige 1979, 129–130)

In this instance, 'mainstream fashion' is presented in binary opposition to 'high fashion' – the inference here is less about hegemony and more about low or mass culture. Hebdige's point is that the mainstream eventually – even inevitably – incorporates and subsumes subcultural style. In the act of incorporation, a subculture's power is diffused, and it will need to create new ways of showing its resistance. Eventually, as the moral panic surrounding subcultural style disperses and its shock value wanes, subcultural style is integrated into the mainstream, thus losing its potency and potential to resist. In other words, it is 'watered down' enough to be consumed by the undiscerning, uncreative mainstream masses.

While these are just a few instances of Hebdige's use of 'mainstream' in *Subculture*, we can see the term being used in multiple ways – as Thornton (1995: 93) notes, 'each reference to the "mainstream" in *Subculture* points in a different direction'. In its many guises, mainstream becomes, at various times and sometimes all at once, a synonym for hegemony; a social group; the opposite of art; the epitome of 'straight-ness'; the enemy of creative youth culture; the repository of cultural artefacts ripe for resignification with subversive meaning; the site of artifice; the locus of all that must be resisted. We can also detect in Hebdige's words the tacit derision for anything and everything to do with being or becoming or consuming in the mainstream. These implications give a clear indication of the value judgements and negative connotations that have often – if not always – accompanied the notion, both popularly and academically: here we find an inkling of the mainstream that is banal, homogeneous, unsophisticated, undiscerning, uncultured, low, inauthentic, fake, commercial, conservative, unimaginative, conformist or just plain stupid. In this view – particularly if one shares the political spirit of Hebdige's intent – there seems to be no sensible reason to advocate for mainstream. For these and other reasons, we find that the mainstream of culture remains under-examined, both in a theoretical sense and in terms of the range of subjects that attract cultural analysis.[3] Yet, paradoxically, there is also a serious political reason to stake a claim for knowing more about mainstream, particularly for the cause of denaturalizing hegemony. To leave mainstream as an 'everywhereness' – a kind of all-encompassing and undifferentiated 'everything else' from which, in this view, subcultures mark out and occupy portions of cultural territory – is, in a sense, to give this dominance its power.

At the same time, it is important to remember that this 'mainstream', no matter how multi-purpose its connotations and how slippery its deployment, is at heart a metaphor. While Hebdige's work may well consign mainstream to being the devalued 'other' in the binary pairing of subculture–mainstream, it is the strength of the metaphoric associations of mainstream that give these uses their sense. Therefore, I now turn my attention to the subject of metaphor.

Mainstream as Metaphor

My title ['The main stream of music'] is a metaphor which is useful so long as it is not overworked. It is obviously so loose an expression that it cannot be misunderstood . . . I only wish to make sure that we shall all mean the same thing when we talk of the main stream of music; though you may find food for thought in the fish which I propose to catch in those waters. But you will be disappointed if you expect me to mention other than the most hackneyed musical subjects. The main stream of music is what we all think we know.

(Tovey 1938: 330)

This quote from Donald Tovey, noted scholar of music, pianist and composer, delivered in the opening lines of a lecture presented to the British Academy in 1938, plays with the metaphoric associations of the word 'mainstream', and suggests a number of problems and possibilities for the metaphor.

First, Tovey acknowledges the 'loose'-ness of the term. The challenges set by its non-specificity seem as obvious today as they did to Tovey in the 1930s; however, while the 'main stream' that Tovey describes might be loosely defined and inter-preted, somehow it is still specific enough for his listeners to assume that it is 'what we all think we know'. This is an odd and enduring contradiction – that the main-stream is both vague and specific. It is concurrently an amorphous cultural category without concrete definition, but is simultaneously a cultural category that 'speaks for itself', and that should, in a commonsensical kind of way, be 'under-stood' by all. Second, the music to which Tovey refers as 'main stream' is expected to be 'hackneyed' – in other words, clichéd, commonplace, boring. Even in the 1930s, the term had potent negative associations. Third, and of greatest importance to my argument, Tovey's playfulness with the term's status as a metaphor suggests the power of the spatial and geographical imagery that accompanies its use.

These metaphoric connotations are derived from the word's primary literal definition in the *Oxford English Dictionary* as a descriptor of a potamic phenom-enon: 'the principal stream or current (of a river etc.)'. The metaphor thus invokes connections to 'nature' and 'the natural': the main stream of a river is a natural force, derived from a spring, moving in a powerful and relentless onward flow towards the sea. Pulled along by gravity, the river carves out a path through the surrounding terrain. Yet Tovey goes on to argue against an image of the river's source as pure:

The metaphor is obviously useless if it is extended to speculations as to the source of the stream. The source of a river is usually supposed to be that spring which lies farthest from the mouth; but many tributaries must have been united before the waters were worth calling a main stream, and the title is not earned until, as a pious teleologist once preached, it has pleased Providence to bring large rivers into contact with important towns ...

(Tovey 1938: 330)

While the river in this metaphor might have an 'authentic' source, it is 'contami-nated' by the streams that accumulate to make the mainstream. If anything, it is only the tributaries that can be 'pure' or 'original'. Certainly, the associations can be taken further: there are places when the river bends back on itself, perhaps widening out into a lake; it is not always singular since it is fed by tributary streams along its path which are incorporated into its flow; deviating brooks leave the river's course and end up in swamps and murky bogs; sometimes the river forks into multiple arms but eventually all water meets in the final destination of the sea. The imagery of this metaphor presents the mainstream as all-encompassing, homogeneous and homogenizing: it claims any nearby water, subsuming tributaries into its current; there they are 'watered down', and lose their own 'identity', 'purity', 'originality' and 'authenticity'. To suggest another metaphor, this mainstream is cannibalistic. Moreover, it is the dominant feature of the landscape.

When using the word 'mainstream' to describe cultural and social phenomena, the imagery of the river necessarily resonates. When we hear phrases like, 'joining the mainstream', 'crossing over into the mainstream', 'swept up in the mainstream' and 'watered down by the mainstream', the word is being used as a metaphor, but it is also alluding to the imagery of the river. The river flows behind the word's metaphoric use, so the metaphor alludes to the river. But the river itself is an allegory. In other words, the river is a way of thinking about the mainstream of culture.

To take this further, the river stands for cultural dominance. If we think again about what the main stream of a river does, then a familiar understanding of dominance is revealed. The river is pulled by gravity towards the sea, and when it reaches this destination there is no longer any possibility for deviation at all. In fact, all opportunities to resist the river's control are gone, and the ocean is all there is. So when the metaphor of the mainstream is used to describe dominant cultural and/or social formations, the immediate associations that accompany the idea of the mainstream are a geographic, or visual, representation of the Gramscian idea of hegemony, which Hebdige used to great effect. Just like the river of nature, hegemony 'masquerades as nature' (Hebdige 1979: 102). At the end of the metaphoric river, there is unfettered hegemony; there are no more opportunities for alternatives, and all possibilities for deviation and resistance are gone. In the narrative of the metaphor, hegemony seems to be the aim and the inevitable endpoint of the mainstream's flow: set sail down the mainstream and there is no return. So it is little wonder that 'being (in the) mainstream' is, in so many contexts, accompanied by the negative connotations implied by Hebdige's work (like those of incorporation, contamination, assimilation and weakness): these political implications are written into the word itself.

It seems obvious that an understanding of 'mainstream' as a cultural concept is intertwined with both the literal definition and the metaphoric associations of the word. When the term is deployed, the metaphorical baggage of its associations with the natural world accompanies its use, contributing in very real ways to our understanding of what the word is being used to describe. However, we must remember that mainstream has no relationship with the natural. Rather, mainstream is constructed by practices just as specific as those enacted by subcul-turalists; simply put, it is stuff that people do and say that creates what we call 'mainstream'. Furthermore, mainstream is not amorphous, autonomous or self-perpetuating. It is a space of cultural production and consumption that – like hegemony – might appear to us as inevitable, natural and ahistorical, but is instead produced by a range of historically specific practices and processes. Indeed, it is this range of processes and practices that constitute this space in and for our imagination.

The Future is Mainstream

What emerges from this discussion is a strong sense of the complicated discursive place that 'mainstream' holds, and the kind of rhetorical work that needs to be done before staking a claim for its usefulness. However, in spite of this (and as I hope is clear by now), I disagree with Thornton's (1995) assertion that mainstream is an 'inadequate' term; I don't think it necessary to leave the term (or what it is used to describe) stranded on the shores of the critical mainstream. It is true that the spectre of negativity haunts the mainstream; uncovering the metaphoric asso-ciations of the term helps to understand these connotations. It is also true that the term has been used so far without a consensus on what its use describes. Meanwhile, the function of the term as something approaching a synonym for hegemony in Marxist-inflected cultural studies suggests an attendant political undesirability of mainstream-ness. It is perhaps because of the collision of these histories that the word is proclaimed as unuseful, or irredeemable. Mainstream may well, as Thornton concludes, be a potent ideological category of distinction, but it seems to me to have more potential to describe something 'concrete' (Toynbee 2002: 149).

The reason for this feeling is that, in amongst these many, varied and contradic-tory uses, there is one particular commonality: the desire to imagine, describe and map forms of dominance – be it dominance that is cultural, social, aesthetic, political or otherwise. So, if nothing else, there is a strong case to be made for trying to understand in more complex ways the operations of these modes of dominance. It is in this project that mainstream can find a specific function for the study of popular culture, not least because it can signify something rather different from the term 'popular', which – as Stuart Hall (1981) famously observed – has its own range of rhetorical problems; it can also operate without the overwhelming focus on class that has arguably led hegemony itself to lose traction in cultural studies to some extent (see Toynbee 2002: 151). If, instead, we think about the *specificity* of main-stream and the particularity of its practices and processes, then mainstream becomes an historically contingent category that usefully refers us to modes of dominant (or dominance-producing) behaviours, discourses, values, identities, and so on.

Perhaps this usefulness is best exemplified if I return to where I began this chapter: my short-lived 'mainstream love affair' with Ultra, circa 1999. For a few brief months, Ultra occupied and at times dominated everyday public spaces with its hit single. The acts through which that dominance was achieved are too numerous to list here, but include everything from the full range of commercial and marketing decisions at record companies, radio stations and retail outlets to the banal and quotidian actions of individuals. The confluence of a series of disparate acts made that song 'mainstream'. Yet it was temporarily so. After some months of mainstream appearance, the song fell out of the kind of regular circulation that made it seem mainstream. 'Say It Once' is no longer mainstream, though it remains part of popular music's history. It may well become mainstream again should a similar convergence of acts make it so, but for now it is not part of a dominant music culture.

The material changes in music practice, at all levels of production, distribution and consumption, make similar examples of 'mainstream-ness' appear very differently to us at the time of writing in 2012. Music comes to achieve mainstream-ness not so much through CD singles, hit countdowns and music magazines as it did in 1999, but rather with digital downloads, file-sharing and social media networking – these are the contemporary parameters that enable the massification of certain products of the music industry, but they too are historical. This is where thinking with and through 'mainstream' reveals its usefulness: as a conceptual tool that illuminates the ways in which certain kinds of music (and other aspects of culture) come to temporarily dominate everyday life at certain times and in certain places. It is this sense of a dominant and dominating culture from which the subculturalists of the 1970s sought to differentiate themselves. We know what they did to achieve subversion, but we are still in need of investigating in similar detail the mainstream that inspired their activities.

Notes

1 Some rare examples of work that has explicitly engaged with mainstream include Grossberg (1992), Thornton (1995), Toynbee (2000, 2002) and my commentaries (Huber 2005, 2007, 2008).
2 Toynbee (2000, 2002) also notes the similarities between 'hegemony' and 'mainstream', and suggests the usefulness of thinking about a mainstream's hegemonic tendencies. My intention here is slightly different: to connect the imagination of mainstream-as-hegemony to its negative discursive place in cultural analysis.
3 This is best read in the context of the longer history of cultural studies, and the difficult place that the notion of 'the popular' holds within the tradition – issues that are beyond the bounds of this chapter. For further discussion, see Hall (1981) and Hartley (2003). For a discussion of the particularity of these issues in relation to popular music studies, see the 'Middle Eight' discussion in *Popular Music* (Editors 2005).

References

Clarke, G. (1982) *Defending Ski-Jumpers: a critique of theories of youth sub-cultural studies*, Birmingham: Centre for Contemporary Cultural Studies, University of Birmingham.
Editors (2005) 'Can we get rid of the "popular" in popular music? A virtual symposium with contributions from the International Advisory Editors of *Popular Music*', *Popular Music* 24(1): 133–45.

Gelder, K. (2007) *Subcultures: cultural histories and social practice*, New York: Routledge.

Grossberg, L. (1992) *We Gotta Get Out of This Place: popular conservatism and postmodern culture*, New York: Routledge.

Hall, S. (1981) 'Notes on deconstructing "the popular"', in R. Samuel (ed.), *People's History and Socialist Theory*, London: Routledge & Kegan Paul.

Hartley, J. (2003) *A Short History of Cultural Studies*, London: Sage.

Hebdige, D. (1979) *Subculture: the meaning of style*, London: Routledge.

Hodkinson, P. (2002) *Goth: identity, style and subculture*, Oxford: Berg.

Huber, A. (2005) 'Learning to love the mainstream: Top 40 culture in Melbourne', unpublished PhD thesis, English Department, University of Melbourne.

—— (2007) 'What's in a mainstream? Critical possibilities', *Altitude: an e-journal of Emerging Humanities Work*, 8: 1–14, www.thealtitudejournal.com (accessed 20 April 2012).

—— (2008) 'Top 40 in Australia: popular music and the mainstream', in S. Homan and T. Mitchell (eds), *Sounds of Then, Sounds of Now: popular music in Australia*, Hobart: ACYS Press.

Muggleton, D. (2000) *Inside Subculture: the postmodern meaning of style*, Oxford: Berg.

Thornton, S. (1995) *Club Cultures: music, media and subcultural capital*, Oxford: Polity Press.

Tovey, D.F. (1938) 'The main stream of music', in D.F. Tovey, *Essays and Lectures on Music*, London: Oxford University Press.

Toynbee, J. (2000) *Making Popular Music: musicians, creativity and institutions*, London: Arnold.

—— (2002) 'Mainstreaming, from hegemonic centre to global networks', in D. Hesmondhalgh and K. Negus (eds), *Popular Music Studies*, London: Arnold.

Ultra (1999) 'Say It Once', CD single, East West/Warner.

2

TEENYBOP AND THE EXTRAORDINARY PARTICULARITIES OF MAINSTREAM PRACTICE

Sarah Baker

How can we make the ordinary extraordinary and evoke an ordinariness in such a way that people will see just how extraordinary it is?

(Bourdieu 1998: 21)

Pierre Bourdieu raises an interesting question, one that has direct relevance to a discussion of the popular music mainstream – music that is positioned as the polar opposite of 'authentic' music culture and widely regarded as ordinary. In his examination of symbolic creativity in everyday life, Paul Willis (1996: 2) suggests that: 'It is the extraordinary in the ordinary, which is extraordinary, which makes both into culture, common culture.' It is with the words of Bourdieu and Willis in mind that I approach the idea of the 'mainstream' in this chapter. The popular music mainstream, though often derided and made 'ordinary', is actually a site of diverse cultural practice, and I illustrate this here through an examination of the extraordinary mainstream musical practices of pre-teen girls.

While the notion of the musical mainstream is inherently complex, problematic and contentious (see Huber 2007), it is regularly used to refer to popular music 'characterised as banal, homogenous, unsophisticated, undiscerning, uncultured, low, inauthentic, fake, commercial, conservative, unimaginative, [or] conformist' (Huber 2002: 82). Under these terms, arguably the most mainstream popular music is that loosely referred to as 'teenybop' – that is, highly commercialized Top 40 music marketed particularly to young girls. At the turn of the twenty-first century, artists given this label included, for example, the British group S Club 7, the American boy band *NSYNC, and the Australian singer Nikki Webster. Artists from earlier eras who are associated with the term include The Osmonds and The Bay City Rollers (see Garratt 1984). Correspondingly, the most mainstream members of popular music's audience are the principal consumers of this type of music, with young girls collectively known – and derided – as 'teenyboppers'. Indeed, at the time of my ethnographic fieldwork in 2000, it was estimated that girls aged between 9 and 14 constituted 50 per cent of the record-buying public (Dubecki 2000), contributing to the massive popularity and worldwide success of groups like the Spice Girls and the Backstreet Boys. Though the structure of music sales has changed over the past decade, in 2012 the pre-teen and teen female demographic continues to drive the rapid success of mainstream acts – including, for example, the boy group One Direction. Young girls' contributions to the music industry are therefore enduring. What I find interesting is the place pre- and early-teen girls hold within the structure of the music industry – they are the target market of a hyper-commodified type of 'pop' but are then routinely derided for consuming this same music.

The trivialization of teenybop relates to long-standing assumptions regarding young girls' engagement with popular music. Girls have historically been cast as passive consumers who have been duped into buying the lightweight and worthless commodities of Adorno's 'culture industry' (see Baker 1999). In popular music discourse, this is where the word 'mainstream' operates in its most negative mode. Teenybop and teenyboppers are the denigrated 'other' of so-called authentic, creative, resistant music subcultures. Of course, 'teenybop' has a much wider audience than 8- to 14-year-old girls. However, when other audiences listen to this form of popular music, it is more likely to be described as 'pop', 'Top 40', 'adult contemporary' or even 'easy listening'. This suggests it is the particular ways in which young girls engage with the music that make them teenyboppers, thus separating them from the music's other listeners.

This chapter focuses on young girls' engagement with popular music in order to expose the nuances of mainstream cultural practice. I argue that it is only through an examination of how the mainstream is experienced that we can fully re-evaluate the term 'teenybop/per' and its application so that we may find the extraordinary in what is perceived to be an otherwise ordinary musical form and cultural experience. Unlike Melanie Lowe (2004), I do not attempt to appropriate the notion of 'resistance' in understanding girls' engagement with the mainstream. To reclaim a sense of the extraordinary in mainstream practice does not require either the deployment of the subcultural discourse of resistance or the politicizing of girls' mainstream engagement. Rather, this chapter seeks to better understand how teenybop is lived and negotiated *on its own terms* – for, as Alison Huber (2002: 84) points out, mainstream music and its related cultural practices need to be discussed in their own contexts and outside the forced logic of the subculture–mainstream divide. Huber argues that the mainstream 'is best thought of as specific and particular' and emphasizes its processual qualities, leading her to suggest that 'it is the particularities of these processes that we need to know more about' (2007: 12). To this end, the chapter draws on ethnographic fieldwork with pre-teen girls in Australia, providing a snapshot of the place of the mainstream in girls' popular music practices at the beginning of the twenty-first century. It does so in the hope that a deeper understanding of girls' experiences of this cultural form might further problematize the ways in which a notion of the (or a) 'mainstream' is characterized.

Teenybop: It's a Girl Thing

There are many assumptions that surround young girls' engagement with popular music. For the most part, girls are derided for being passive consumers. Roy Shuker (1998) notes that the term 'teenybopper' first came to be used in the late 1950s and, as a means to separate the young female pop music audience from a masculinized rock culture, the term quickly 'acquired strongly derogatory connotations' (297). A historical account of the culture surrounding teenyboppers is given by Angela McRobbie, who notes that teenybop was a 'long-standing feature of post-war girls' culture' and was 'based around an endless flow of young male pop stars' (2000: 22). McRobbie also draws attention to the explicit commercial origins of this form of popular music, describing it as 'an almost totally packaged cultural commodity . . . [that] emerges from within the heart of the pop music business and relies on the magazines, on radio and TV for its wide appeal' (22). This overt link to commercial popular music production, combined with the notion that it is a feminized musical form, is a key reason why teenybop has never really been taken seriously – except, of course, by the teenyboppers themselves.

In contrasting pop with the perceived seriousness of 'rock' and its male audience, girls' engagement with the mainstream ends up being reduced to the standardized sound-bites of journalists who dismiss this music as 'the toy of teenyboppers', and by inference denigrate women's and girls' engagement with popular music more generally. Writing in the *New York Times*, for example, Jon Pareles laments:

> This season belongs to the kiddie-pop-brigades. Applause is passé; the reaction most eagerly sought by pop culture right now, from music to television to movies, is a high-pitched squeal from a mob of young girls. When it's directed at males, that squeal signifies romantic fantasy while it tests out some newly active hormonal responses. Directed at females, it's a squeal of sisterly solidarity and fashion approval.
>
> *(1999: 1)*

Sue Sharpe asserted in the late 1970s that in their engagement with popular music, girls had popularly been 'cast as the inevitable followers . . . who demonstrate acts of adulation for their idols' (1978: 112). In the 1990s and 2000s, such discourse continues to perpetuate an assumption that girls idolize male performers and ape and imitate female performers in their consumption of popular music. This 'inauthentic' behaviour, which copies already inauthentic pop music, contributes in general terms to teenybop's perceived lack of authenticity, meaning that music and those involved with it – producers and consumers alike – get brushed aside as inconsequential, thus (re-)producing and further contributing to the trivialization of 'girl femininity'.

While rock was masculinized in the discourse, pop became intrinsically linked to the learning of femininity in contemporary society and was characterized as being 'allegedly slick, prefabricated, and used for dancing, mooning over teen idols, and other "feminine" and "feminised" recreations' (Coates 1997: 53). In accounts such as that of Pareles (1999), pop's gender contexts are constructed as strictly heteronormative. As Gayle Wald (2002) observes, Pareles sees teenybop music as being 'governed by the "rules" of heterosexual division . . . where girl-fans want boys and want to be like other girls'. Young men's engagement with rock music is portrayed very differently: as a serious cultural practice linked to notions of resistance, technology, creativity and public spaces. As a feminized cultural form, girls' engagement with popular music is thus never just about the negotiation and constitution of cultural identities because it is always underpinned by its aged and gendered contexts and the assignation of cultural value.

It is important to note the frequent slippage in the literature – and indeed this chapter – between the terms 'mainstream', 'pop' and 'teenybop'. The purpose of this chapter is not to define or clarify the usage of these constructed and discursive terms. Rather, the chapter looks at the 'real-world' practices and articulations of pre-teen popular music consumers that are only ever alluded to, or stereotyped, in the majority of writing on this cultural form. What my research has shown is that girls' popular music practices are not only extraordinary, they're also far more complex and nuanced than previously imagined.

Introducing the Teenyboppers

The 2000s were an exciting time to be conducting research into girls' engagement with popular music. From the late 1990s to the mid-2000s, there was a surge in the numbers of boy bands, girl bands and teen artists charting in the Top 40, and this boom coincided with material changes to the music industry – particularly around music downloading. My research therefore captures a particular moment of 'mainstream' cultural practice at a time of significant historical change for the industry. It also came at a time when public debate was increasing about the sexual content of popular music and its impact on the sexualization of children. Given these contexts, the research set out to uncover the richness of teenybop practice and the depth of girls' engagement with popular music. To do this, I undertook ethnographic fieldwork in an after-school care centre located at a Catholic Girls' School in Adelaide, South Australia (see Baker 2004b). Seven girls aged from 8 to 11 years – Kate, Felicity, Rosa, Emlyn, Amelia, Kylie and Clare[1] – became my key participants. All were engaged, to varying degrees, with teenybop culture.

As I outline in detail elsewhere (Baker 2003b; Bloustien and Baker 2003), the project deployed innovative methods as a way to uncover the complexities of the girls' musical worlds, with each participant using a still camera and portable tape recorder to document her everyday life. The girls' musical practices included the full range of activities commonly associated with girls' appreciation of music: listening to tapes, CDs and the radio; singing and dancing; taking extra-curricular music lessons; recording compilation tapes; reading music magazines; surfing the internet for lyrics and information about pop artists; hanging posters of pop stars on bedroom walls; occasionally attending pop concerts or artists' promotional appearances in record stores and shopping malls; and watching music video programmes like *Video Hits* and the talent television series *Popstars*. In addition to pop, the girls were also exposed to other music genres. At home and in the family car, for example, they routinely negotiated the music played by parents and siblings; Amelia talked about 'the blues' ('The blues is sad music. I know because my mum likes it.'); and Emlyn mentioned the likes of Slim Dusty, Billie Holiday and Bob Dylan, going so far as to describe the latter as being 'a boring old fart'. Apart from the girls' own interest in mainstream music, these were not pop-loving households, and as a result the girls' music preferences were often derided by family members. Emlyn was teased relentlessly by her brothers and father because she liked the Spice Girls, and Clare's mother called *Popstars* 'rubbish'. The girls also perceived other adults in their lives to be 'anti-pop', including the after-school care coordinator who Amelia described as not liking 'happy music' (i.e. pop); in the girls' reasoning, this was why she would often ask them to 'turn their music [volume] down'.

The Mainstream as a Shared Marker for Pre-Teen Identity

Willis (1996: 2) argues that the oft-trivialized and seemingly ordinary interests of many young people are frequently 'crucial to the creation and sustenance of individual and group identities'. Teenybop adheres the girls together culturally as a peer group by becoming a shared marker of their pre-teen identity. In their collective practices around teenybop, the girls activate and appropriate the possibilities opened up by this trivialized form, making the ordinary extraordinary through their music-making and music-listening, their conversations and dancing, and their many other music-related activities.

The place of teenybop in establishing a collective sense of music-related identity can be observed in Clare's friendship book, a notebook she circulated amongst her friends so they could contribute short biographical identity portraits. The book begins with Clare's own entry:[2]

Name:	Clare
DOB:	1989
Age:	11
Family:	Dad, Mum and brother

Pets:	2 dogs, 2 fish
Fav Bands:	M2M, Eiffel 65, S2S, five, Backstreet Boys, SOAP, Sclub7, Real blonds, All Saints, Nsync.
Fav Singers:	Mandy Moore, Britany Spears, Tom Jones, Madasen Avenue, Christina Aguilera, Mariah Carey, Shania Twain, Jessica Simps., Lea haywood.
Fav Actors:	Leo, Melissa Joan hart, Katie holmes & Rebecca Cartwright.
Fav hobbies:	Swimming, singing, drawing, netball.
Notes	

Thankyou for wrighting in my friendship book.
Sig: Clare

Clare is not alone in such a representation of the musical pre-teen 'self'. All the girls who contributed to Clare's friendship book constructed their portraits in an almost identical fashion, calling them 'My Profile' and arguing that these profiles consisted of only the most important things that defined 'who you are'. Pop music was a key element in the profiles, and throughout Clare's friendship book, favourite bands and singers – almost all of whom would be popularly described as 'mainstream' – were always listed at the top, soon after 'name' and 'date of birth'. For some of the girls who contributed to the book, the music list was extensive. Clare, for example, cited a total of 19 artists. The favourites of other girls were more specialized, as they narrowed their preferences to two or three performers.

The privileging of pop artists in the girls' entries highlights the integral place of mainstream music in their simultaneous constitution and representation of identity. In the entries in Clare's friendship book, specific forms of musical knowledge were highly valued. Top 40 chart music is emphasized to the exclusion of all other music and, even more specifically, the artists the girls are citing are those marketed to the young female consumer rather than other chart acts of the time, like Matchbox 20, Powderfinger or 28 Days.

The artists that Clare listed as her favourites also appeared in the entries of other contributors, thereby validating Clare's choices and producing for the book's participants a sense of being 'in-sync' with one another. Take, for example, Kate's entry:

K@te's profile	
full name:	Kate
D.O.B:	1990
Age:	10
Pets:	2 dogs 2 cats 1 Turtle and some fish
Fav bands:	5ive, BSB, Sclub7
Fav Singers:	Britney Spears, Christina Agalira

On the tapes she produced as part of the research, Kate recorded audio versions of 'My Profile'. In the recordings Kate revelled in being an interviewer. Adopting a somewhat serious voice, she would interview her peers. The first interview on her tape began with the announcement, 'Hello, I'm Kate and I'm reporting Rosa'. She then went on to ask, 'Rosa, what is your favourite colour?', 'What is your favourite animal?', 'What is your favourite song?' Kate ended the interview by saying, 'And that was Rosa with My Profile'. These questions, which recur throughout the interviews, might appear trivial, but they lead to a spiralling out of information about things that are the concerns of the girls' peer groups. As was the case with Clare's friendship diary, the audio profiles also gave Kate the opportunity to affirm that her preferences corresponded with those of her interviewees, therefore strengthening her associations with these girls. So she would respond to answers with exclamations like '5ive. Oh, I love that group too!'

With their focus on popular music and other forms of popular culture, the girls' written and audio profiles are a means to momentarily contain the 'self'; a way to manage individual and collective 'becoming' in the context of peer relations. Collective becoming through music has been much discussed in subcultural literature, perhaps to the point that it has almost obscured our ability to see that collective becoming through mainstream pop is equally significant. There is nothing 'ordinary' about mainstream becoming (or becoming-mainstream); the mainstream acts as a cultural space for becoming to be played out, and in the process the mainstream itself – specifically the music and consumption practices of teenybop – is negotiated as a site of struggle.

The Mainstream as a Site of Struggle

Staking a claim on teenybop identity was central to much of the girls' music practice. Singing, for example, played an important role in the girls' social worlds. During my fieldwork, girls would frequently break into song. I heard the girls singing in after-school care, in their homes and even over the phone. The girls' research tapes reflected this interest in singing, including everything from the taunting playground chants of Amelia to a partially self-composed pop ballad by Rosa. In after-school care, the ability to sing was a mark of distinction in the girls' peer group.

As with all other aspects of the girls' musical practice (see, for example, Baker 2004a, 2011), the girls' singing can be understood as 'hard work' (Willis 1996) because it is so deeply connected to a sense of individual and collective identity. In the girls' play with popular song, the pop star identity is momentarily embodied with their singing opening up a sensual space of becoming; a space to question 'who and what "I am" and could become' (Willis 1996, 11). Pareles asserts that teenybop music provides girls with:

> a harmless first crush, an easy transition to adult concerns, which will intrude soon enough in the lives of its younger fans. The music is an intermission

between crises, and it's less troublesome than genuine rejuvenation could ever be. Because in kiddie pop, growing pains never arrive.

(1999: 32)

What such an account fails to realize is that pre-teen girls are already in a process of transition. Pop music enables 'a means for them to "think and feel" their way from girl-child to adult-woman and from the milieu of primary school to high school and the spaces beyond' (Baker 2002: 29). The girls' engagement with popular music is far from trivial; rather, in the words of Willis, 'there is work, even desperate work, in their play' (1996: 2).

One of the photographs taken by the girls during the research depicts 10-year-old Emlyn posing as a pop star – *becoming*-pop star. Her eyes are closed, her head leans to one side and is tilted backwards slightly, and one hand is clenched tightly around an imaginary microphone as she silently belts out a nameless pop song. The pose reminds me of the female singer Anastacia in her music video for 'I'm Outta Love'. In fact, not long before this photo was taken, Emlyn had been to see a live performance of Anastacia when the singer visited Adelaide to give a short promotional concert (see Baker 2003a). But whereas Anastacia performs as a recognized pop star on the global stage, Emlyn poses in her school uniform, standing on the bench under the shade of the school rotunda with only a handful of girls (as well as myself) participating in her performance. What is striking about this photograph is that it has captured one brief moment in which Emlyn's fantasy – a fantasy to be a pop star – was embodied.

Emlyn wanted to be a singer and she wanted to be famous. The expression of Emlyn's desire was encapsulated by the persona she adopted for the school's 'Book Week' parade, in which she dressed up and presented herself as 'the new Britney Spears'. Although she wanted to be a singer, Emlyn was very particular about what she wanted to sing – 'I don't like Opera and that classical stuff'. Unlike other girls in the research, Emlyn did not participate in the school's junior choir because she did not like the choir's repertoire. Emlyn told me:

> I went to choir practice once and it was so boring. All it was was breathing, teaching us how to breathe. And when we actually got to sing something it was only 'Kookaburra sits in the old gum tree', no modern stuff!

Yet in the very early stages of my research, Emlyn mentioned that she attended singing lessons at the school. I asked her what she sang in the lessons and she replied, 'Modern stuff . . . Like the Spice Girls'. 'Would you like to be a singer?' I questioned further. 'Yes, but not wear all that make-up' Emlyn said, adding, 'But I'd like to put out a CD and stuff.'

However, for Emlyn the fantasy of being a famous pop star was cruelly shattered. Not long into the third school term, Emlyn said to me, 'My singing teacher wrote in my report that I was crap, that I can't sing, so now Dad won't let me go to singing lessons anymore.' Emlyn had been receiving lessons for less than six months. She explained, 'It's hard singing with the piano because it doesn't sound like the CD.' I asked Emlyn whether she still sang at home. 'No,' she replied, 'because I don't have a CD player . . . I only have a radio.' However, on a visit to her home I had seen a stereo system in the living room so I queried, 'But you have a CD player in the house?' 'Yeah' said Emlyn, 'I can sing fine when I'm on my own, but I sing crap when there's another person there.'

Being told that she was not a competent singer meant Emlyn had to quickly renegotiate her dreams and desires. A week later she asked me, 'Do you want to be famous?'; 'Do *you*?' I immediately questioned back. 'Yeah, I want to be an actress because anyone can learn to be an actress,' she replied, then added quietly, 'I'd rather be a singer, but I can't sing.' Being told she didn't have the ability to sing did not necessarily mean that Emlyn would discontinue any fantasy of being a pop star. It was more likely that this identity, explored in play, had been repositioned rather than having been given up entirely. But for Emlyn, this fantasy now highlighted the acquisition of 'envied skills and success' (Sharpe 1978: 91). Indeed, after being told her singing abilities lacked sufficient merit, Emlyn began questioning her previous pop aspirations. She said to me, 'I can't believe when I was six I thought I was going to be a pop star. My brother was even my manager. I *must* have been getting desperate. I really believed I would be a pop star. How *stupid* was I?!' Emlyn also became far more critical of the singing abilities of others, including pop stars. She remarked of Christina Aguilera, 'All her songs sound the same – she screeches', and while she thought Britney Spears' voice was 'funky', she commented about the song 'Lucky', 'It's okay, but gets a bit annoying. She can't really sing in it. It shows she has quite a weak voice.'

Although Emlyn had been told she was not a good singer, she continued to enjoy singing. In fact on the final day of fieldwork she confided in me that 'I'm going to leave school when I'm sixteen and join a record company and become a singer.' Over the course of that year's final school term, Emlyn refocused and gained a new confidence in her voice. She began testing out her singing skills around others – and this was where her troubles arose. Most noticeable was the conflict that developed between Emlyn and Rosa over the relative merits of their voices. On one occasion when Emlyn was singing Bardot's 'Poison', Rosa glared at Emlyn, then looked at me with her nose turned up in distaste, then she rolled her eyes before looking the other way. Another time it was Rosa who was singing and Emlyn kept joining in. Each time she did this, Rosa would stop singing and deliver Emlyn a real 'How dare she?' look.

In the final days of my fieldwork, Emlyn – who had been talking to me about a number of newly released songs – began singing Wheatus' 'Teenage Dirtbag'. Sitting on the other side of me was Rosa. She loved this song and couldn't resist joining in. Halfway through the song, Rosa stopped and whispered to me, 'Doesn't Emlyn *know* she can't sing?' Once Emlyn had finished, Rosa started to sing the song again. This prompted Emlyn, with her face screwed up in disgust, to whisper in my other ear, 'Does she *really* take singing lessons?' A year after the fieldwork, I received an email from Emlyn expressing a similar sentiment:

> Rosa must be in the playground because i can't here her vibrating sounds of what she calls SINGING (and i am not joking) and what the rest of us call
> 'SHUT UP'

In their singing and in constructing written and audio profiles, the girls can be observed negotiating, representing and constituting their place in the world through an involvement in the mainstream. Far from being trivial, teenybop enabled the girls to begin making sense of the nuances of music and identity. Though they are stereotyped as passive consumers of an inauthentic cultural form, what my research illustrates is that pre-teen girls are, in fact, aware and critical individuals who actively engage with the products of the cultural industries in complex ways to negotiate their place in the world. A description of the tensions they experienced with the teenybop voice has the potential to disrupt our understanding of young girls as mere consumers of pop music; instead we see (and hear) the girls as active participants in this music culture – producing music, producing meaning and negotiating the spaces of the mainstream from within.

In this chapter 'teenybop' signifies not a passive relationship between girls and the musical mainstream, but rather the extraordinariness of girls' collective and individual experiences of pop in their everyday life. If we look more closely at the particularities of girls' practices in and around mainstream music, we can come to see teenybop, and the mainstream more broadly, as a complex space that encompasses a multitude of practices – all of which are struggled over in the process of girls' cultural and gendered becoming. In doing so, we can then release 'teenybop' from its purely derogatory contexts. Cultural commentators who continue to treat young girls' musical practices with disdain demonstrate an ignorance about girls and pop. Indeed, girls' musical activities challenge those dominant ideologies that construct girls' consumption practices as passive and unworthy of serious critical analysis. So although the music young girls find important is denigrated by journalists and rock-ist cultural commentators via allusions to the many pejorative connotations of 'mainstream-ness' and 'ordinariness', my analysis of their real-world cultural practices reveals, instead, the extraordinariness in and of the mainstream.

Notes

1 The girls have been given pseudonyms.
2 Original spelling and grammar is retained in this chapter wherever the girls' writing is quoted.

References

Baker, S. (1999) 'Selling the Spice Girls', in R. White (ed.), *Australian Youth Subcultures*, Hobart: ACYS.

—— (2002) 'Bardot, Britney, bodies and breasts: pre-teen girls' negotiations of the corporeal in relation to pop stars and their music', *Perfect Beat*, 6(1): 18–32.

—— (2003a) 'The screamers', *Youth Studies Australia*, 22(2): 19–24.

—— (2003b) 'Auto-audio ethnography; or, pre-teen girls capturing their popular music practices on tape – research report', *Context: A Journal of Music Research*, 26: 57–65.

—— (2004a) 'Pop in(to) the bedroom: popular music in pre-teen girls' bedroom culture', *European Journal of Cultural Studies*, 7(1): 75–93.

—— (2004b) 'It's not about candy: music, sexiness and girls' serious play in after school care', *International Journal of Cultural Studies*, 7(2): 197–212.

—— (2011) 'Playing online: pre-teen girls' negotiations of pop and porn in cyberspace', in M.C. Kearney (ed.), *Mediated Girlhoods*, New York: Peter Lang.

Bloustien, G. and Baker, S. (2003) 'On not talking to strangers: researching the micro worlds of girls through visual auto-ethnographic practices', *Social Analysis*, 47(3): 64–79.

Bourdieu, P. (1998) *On Television and Journalism*, London: Pluto Press.

Coates, N. (1997) '(R)evolution now? Rock and the potential of gender', in S. Whiteley (ed.), *Sexing the Groove*, London: Routledge.

Dubecki, L. (2000) 'The knowledge: five things you didn't know about . . . young people and music', *The Age*, Today section, 16 August: 2.

Garratt, S. (1984) 'All of us love all of you', in S. Steward and S. Garratt, *Signed, Sealed and Delivered*, London: Pluto Press.

Huber, A. (2002) 'Learning to love the mainstream', in D. Crowdy, S. Homan and T. Mitchell (eds), *Musical In-between-ness*, Sydney: Faculty of Humanities and Social Sciences, University of Technology, Sydney.

—— (2007) 'What's in a mainstream? Critical possibilities', *Altitude*, 8: 1–12.

Lowe, M. (2004) ' "Tween" scene: resistance within the mainstream', in A. Bennett and R.A. Peterson, *Music Scenes*, Nashville, TN: Vanderbilt University Press.

McRobbie, A. (2000) *Feminism and Youth Culture*, 2nd edn, Houndmills: Macmillan.

Pareles, J. (1999) 'When pop becomes the toy of teenyboppers', *New York Times*, Section 2, 11 July: 1, 32.

Sharpe, S. (1978) *Just Like a Girl*, Harmondsworth: Penguin.

Shuker, R. (1998) *Key Concepts in Popular Music*, London: Routledge.

Wald, G. (2002) ' "I want it that way": teenybopper music and the girling of boy bands', *Genders* 35, www.genders.org/g35/g35_wald.html (accessed 18 May 2012).

Willis, P. (1996) *Common Culture*, Milton Keynes: Open University Press.

3

HISTORICIZING MAINSTREAM MYTHOLOGY

The Industrial Organization of The Archies

Matt Stahl

The entertainment industry institutions conjured up in invocations of 'mainstream' often seem monolithic, endowed with the power to rationalize production, create markets and bend audiences to their will. Particularly when they come up in the context of discussions of 'whatever your favourite music is not' (Huber 2001: 1), the canny producers, impresarios and executives who organize production on behalf of these institutions appear almost diabolical, projecting teen idols, boy bands, girl bands and other seemingly prefabricated pop phenomena into mass media and consciousness. These producers appear cynically to appeal to and manipulate the least sophisticated tastes – especially those of young female fans, who for decades have been dismissed by critics and connoisseurs as 'neither spontaneous nor creative': the ultimate adherents to mainstream music (Goldman 1970: 13). Exploiting pre-adolescents' 'aspirational' media consumption (Mitroff et al. 2004: 10), as well as their anxieties about gender norms and expectations, and about fitting in at school (Wald 2002; Lipsitz 2007: 4–7; Monnot 2010), the mainstream music institutions' 'shrewd commercial operators' (Goldman 1970: 13) seem to hit their young targets with almost uncanny accuracy and frequency. Their products often appear in popular critiques as hordes of glossy, standardized performers, hatched out of the Orlando-Hollywood entertainment-industrial complex, laying waste to revered and fragile 'authentic' music traditions.

Such quasi-diabolism characterizes *Before the Music Dies*, a polemical 2006 documentary film that offers a concentrated example of this kind of critique (Shapter 2006).[1] This film works hard rhetorically to distinguish 'real' from mainstream popular music. In one segment, the filmmakers conduct a derisive 'experiment' in which they assume the roles of the very music industry operators they loathe and fear. They enlist the middle-aged male co-writer of Jewel's 1996 hit song 'You Were Meant for Me' to write a new 'tween' hit, using an idea ('my mum's not home') suggested by the film's director. The filmmakers hire a teenage female model, musicians, a studio, a video crew and (crucially) a sound engineer who can repair the model's poor vocal performance technologically. Without much inspiration or trouble, it appears, the filmmakers have constructed a perfectly viable standard pop star. However, in attempting to demonstrate the ease with which disposable performers may be prefabricated, the filmmakers are revealed as virtually in awe of big-league pop producers. The film implies that the power of mainstream music institutions and executives must be truly overpowering if they can spin this straw into gold, if they can conjure superstars out of good-looking but otherwise unremarkable youngsters and convince millions of their special value.

Yet, far from the striding industrial titans and satanic celebrity mills that populate 'rockist' discourse on pop (such as that engaged in by *Before the Music Dies*), the ensembles involved in the production of mainstream music are often fascinatingly contingent constellations of struggling as well as reputed professionals, new as well as established enterprises and untested as well as familiar symbolic forms. These ensembles come together at particular moments in history, in fields that are structured by governing (if perhaps rapidly changing) legal, economic, political, social and cultural conditions, in ways and with results that could sometimes hardly have been foreseen by the participants.

This chapter takes The Archies as a case study of a successful mainstream music marketing project that sheds light on both the contingent nature of entertainment-industrial ensembles and the (crypto-)diabolism that often populates critical accounts of mainstream music. Hyped in a full-page RCA Records advertisement in *Billboard* on 24 August 1968 as 'the biggest, most explosive multi-media entertainment package of all time', The Archies had two Top 10 hits before achieving the top chart position in 1969. In the fall of that year, The Archies' 'Sugar, Sugar' was number one on the *Billboard* pop chart for four weeks. However, unlike The Rolling Stones or The Temptations – whose songs 'Honky Tonk Women' and 'I Can't Get Next to You' preceded and succeeded 'Sugar, Sugar' in the top chart position that fall – 'The Archies' did not actually exist in any simple way: they were cartoon characters, not human beings. These pop music 'performers' were the main characters in an animated Saturday morning television cartoon series, *The Archie Show*, produced by the animation studio Filmation and appearing on the CBS network in 1968 (and in numerous variations through the late 1970s).

Hit-making musical acts – including The Rolling Stones and The Temptations – usually depend on ranks of creative and technical workers to help produce 'their' music. However, The Archies would not even have existed without such workers. The Archies were the audio-visual manifestations of complex divisions of cultural industry labour that included animators, storyboard artists, in-betweeners, the inkers and painters of animation cels, directors and animation producers, as well as songwriters, musicians, singers, producers and arrangers, and numerous other behind-the-scenes creative and technical workers. In the group's existence as *virtual* performers, The Archies was perhaps the most fully 'prefabricated' pop act of that era, surpassing even television's fictional Partridge Family and the 'groups' assembled by bubblegum pioneers Kasenetz and Katz (Porter 2001).

In most accounts from the late 1960s through the first decade of the twenty-first century, the establishment of The Archies as a top-selling, prototypical mainstream act is attributed entirely to the acumen and power of publisher and producer Don Kirshner. However, a fuller account must move beyond such reduction. The hoped-for but uncertain success of this cartoon group resulted from the fortuitously timed, cross-media concatenation of enterprising professionals, mass-mediated pop cultural forms and entertainment industry institutions in the context of a changing mass media political economy. By retrieving participants and recalling contexts eclipsed by the Kirshner myth, this chapter seeks to fracture polemical conceptions of mainstream popular music that attribute excessive power and agency to such figures.

The received accounts, built on Kirshner's own record of self-mythologizing, as well as on his symbolic deployment by RCA Records in trade journal advertising, contribute to monolithic conceptions of the mainstream. This chapter offers an alternate narrative that complicates such conceptions. By bringing to light the individuals, institutions and historical conditions that together made possible the astonishing (and by no means assured) success of the prefabricated Archies, I aim to advance our understanding of the constituencies and contingencies obscured behind polemical presentations of mainstream.

Received Narrative

As I recount at greater length below, the animation studio Filmation employed pre-eminent pop music publisher, producer and music industry executive-for-hire Don Kirshner to supervise and produce The Archies' music. Yet the fact of his integration into a production apparatus for a project conceived and directed by others is obfuscated by popular discourse that presents Kirshner as the generative mastermind. For example, a 1969 *New York Times* article (for which Kirshner gave an interview) asserts that Kirshner is '[t]he man behind the idea' of this 'nongroup' The Archies (Jahn 1969: 38). In his 1972 explanation of The Archies' genesis, Kirshner told *Rolling Stone* that he had 'wanted to do the same thing with a cartoon series that Ross Bagdassarian had done with the Chipmunks'. 'I wanted my own Alvin, Simon and Theodore,' he averred. 'I figured the country was ready for it and "Sugar, Sugar" sold 10 million copies' (Werbin 1972: 10). Kirshner's self-narrative resonated: Dave Harker (1980: 94) credits Kirshner with the 'manufacture' of The Archies. According to Jake Austen's (2002: 181) account, Kirshner 'came up with the perfect band, one that would do his bidding'.[2]

A second variation of the 'Kirshner did it' story incorporates the well-known 1967 struggle by the prefabricated group The Monkees to overthrow Kirshner, then serving as their music supervisor. This version, while not as obviously reductive or reverential as the earlier ones, still contributes to a conception of mainstream institutions and executives as omnipotent by suggesting that Kirshner had friction-less and authoritative access to numerous production worlds. Thus, even while acknowledging Kirshner's subordinate position relative to those of the Filmation executives, Weingarten accepts Kirshner's questionable explanation of the route 'Sugar, Sugar' travelled on its way to the top of the charts. Weingarten (2000: 201) quotes Kirshner: 'The Monkees laughed at me when I brought them "Sugar, Sugar" ... [b]ut it wound up making millions for Filmation.' According to Weingarten, this supposed encounter took place in 1969, yet The Monkees had ejected Kirshner from their production milieu two years before, with severe acrimony – the conflict resulted in a bitter legal battle. To be clear, I am suggesting that this interaction prob-ably never took place; as far as I know, no former Monkee (or other witness) has acknowledged it. Nevertheless, this story is remarkably durable.[3]

A Contingent Constellation

Don Kirshner's role with respect to The Archies was not as generative, authorita-tive or decisive as the accepted accounts suggest. Kirshner was folded into a contingent arrangement that incorporated numerous actors and factors, no single one of which was either ultimately responsible for – or utterly dispensable with respect to – the commercial success of The Archies. Without a doubt, Kirshner's expertise and professional reputation and connections played a considerable role in the success of The Archies. *Billboard*'s August 1968 advertisements promoting The Archies 'entertainment package' explicitly locate the centre of The Archies' gravity in Kirshner's reputation. Surrounding a photograph of the smilingly confi-dent executive, RCA's text reads 'THIS MAN recently had the industry doing monkey flips and now is readying to turn the whole scene upside down, inside out, and every which way again' with this promising new property. Kirshner's reputation got him the job, and the relationship he had established with RCA to distribute Monkees records provided the basis for that record company's agree-ment to release Archies records on its subsidiary label and justified the company's allocation of resources to Archies marketing and advertising.

Yet the divisions of executive, animation and musical labour (of which Kirshner became a part) that coalesced to produce this 'multi-media entertainment package' were themselves components of contingent entertainment industry projects rather than monolithic, purposive institutions. On one side was the rela-tionship between RCA Records and Don Kirshner; on the other was that between the CBS television network and Filmation, an animation studio producing cartoons for the network. Each of these relationships was still relatively new in 1968, when The Archies' cartoons and music debuted. Moreover, the deci-sions made by CBS regarding *The Archie Show* were conditioned by a changing discourse on and regulatory environment surrounding the production of television for children.

Cartoons, Saturday Morning and Popular Music

In the early 1960s, networks did not consider children to be valuable consumers; advertising rates were low and children were inexpensive audiences for advertisers to reach. The high concentration of children in the Saturday morning viewership, as well as the willingness of cost-conscious and risk-averse advertisers to divide up sponsorship (a departure from an earlier norm of single-sponsor programs), rendered the 'generic [Saturday morning] time slot a comparatively low-risk venture with high potential for long-term profits' (Mittell 2003: 49). The low cost to advertisers of Saturday morning child audiences supported programming experimentation, and children's perceived enjoyment of repetition facilitated constant reuse of programming. As Jason Mittell (2003: 49) writes, 'networks saw the time slot as a cash cow for toy and food sponsors looking to reach the "kidvid" audience'; where until the early 1960s networks had been content mainly to program old theatrical cartoons, they soon 'decided to raise the stakes by including more original Saturday morning cartoons'.

By 1964, these forces had contributed to the creation of a voracious market for inexpensively produced cartoons aimed at children between the ages of 2 and 11. In 1965, the most popular television cartoon was ABC's *The Beatles* (1965–69). This cartoon served to extend The Beatles' property and wring additional value from established Beatles hits. To the younger siblings and neighbours of the teen-agers who were The Beatles' more active consumers, the cartoon offered narra-tives loosely organized around the songs' themes. The Beatles, after all, were an ascendant pop culture force in the United States at the time; their appearances on live television, their hit film *A Hard Day's Night* and their very heavy airplay and radio, press and record store promotion probably did a great deal to interest viewers in the cartoon, each 15-minute segment of which incorporated one full-length Beatles song. The cartoon was produced in the United Kingdom on a shoestring budget; despite its use of Beatles songs as narrative kernels, the series 'didn't deviate too radically from every other Saturday morning cartoon comedy of the time' (Weingarten 2000: 197).

In the wake of the success of *The Beatles* cartoons, Austen (2002: 178) writes, 'a number of cartoon rock 'n' roll bands emerged, but ... their producers had little grasp of rock 'n' roll and were simply making fun of it or exploiting it half-heartedly'. Austen (179) observes that the coming 'cartoon rock revolution' still awaited the development of bubblegum pop music – aimed expressly at the chil-dren and adults ignored by rock music makers, marketers and culture – and the erosion of television animation's technical standards in the drive towards maximum profitability. In addition to Weingarten and Austen, other scholars have traced these broader developments in pop music marketing and culture (e.g. Cooper and Smay 2001; Simpson 2005); my interest at this point is in contextualizing *The Archie Show* and specifying the nature and makeup of the music/animation ensemble out of which The Archies emerged as a prototypical mainstream 'non-group'.

Filmation and CBS

Filmation, the studio that produced *The Archie Show* and hired Don Kirshner to supervise The Archies' music, was formed in 1963 by Lou Scheimer and Hal Sutherland, who had worked together in the animation studio of Larry Harmon (aka Bozo the Clown). Soon after forming the company, Scheimer and Sutherland took on former DJ, record producer and Embassy Pictures vice-president Norm Prescott as a partner. By all accounts the studio struggled to stay afloat in the early 1960s, scraping by on small jobs such as a minimally animated life of Jesus for the Lutheran Church and animated television commercials for Gillette. According to Scheimer, 'Things were so bad that Hal and I used to take turns answering the phone because we would know that anybody calling was asking for money; nobody was calling to give us work to do' (Scheimer 1979). This situation was to turn around in 1965, in the context of the ongoing institutionalization of Saturday morning children's cartoon programming, when fabled network executive Fred Silverman – then new at CBS – began commissioning original animation for the network's Saturday morning slot.

Silverman's first commission would establish the value to networks of low-cost superhero-themed animation, underwrite the establishment of Filmation as a major studio, and raise the stakes in the development of children's TV audience; it was a turning point in American television animation. Rather than compete directly with ABC's *The Beatles* by offering music-themed cartoons, Silverman bought the rights from National Periodical Publications (colloquially known as DC Comics) to broadcast a Superman cartoon, which the publisher would produce and supply to the network. Having no expertise in the production of animated cartoons, DC Comics sought out a trustworthy representative, versed in film production and animation, who could find and vet a studio and supervise the contracting out of the cartoon's production. DC Comics story editor Mort Weisinger nominated Prescott, a show-biz acquaintance, to fill this role. Prescott set an extraordinary gamble in motion: after thanking Jack Liebowitz, president of National Periodicals, for the job offer, he countered that his own studio would do the best possible job on the series. Prescott told Liebowitz, 'I'm not gonna lie to you. We don't have any money. We have the talent, we have the studio, we got the best pencil pushers in the world, but we don't have any money' (author interview 2004). Interviewed in 2004, Prescott stated that the part about being broke 'was the truth. The lie was that we had no studio' (author interview 2004). In a tale famous among animators and aficionados, Prescott called Scheimer from New York, instructed Scheimer to find some unused commercial space and throw together what would look like a busy animation studio, and then told him 'I'm just gonna get drunk as a skunk, and you're gonna surprise me' (author interview 2004). Scheimer borrowed a moviola and space in a production office during a Wednesday lunch hour, recruited friends, neighbours and sympathetic workers in nearby studios to occupy desks and hold pencils, and placed drawings and cels (from a production stalled because of lack of funds) in front of them in order to convince the publisher's West Coast contact that Filmation was indeed a working studio capable of fulfilling a major network order. According to Scheimer, the contact 'called back to New York and said, "It's a little studio, but they seem to run a pretty tight ship down there." ' Liebowitz approved the contract 'without a completion bond [a prohibitively expensive form of insurance] or anything. He gave us the job to do. It was our first network show' (Scheimer 1979). The mocked-up studio trick had succeeded.

DC Comics offered Filmation $36,000 per half-hour programme; the going rate at Hanna-Barbera, the dominant American television animation studio of the mid-1960s, was $45,000 (Scheimer 1979). This cut rate set the low-cost terms on which Filmation would produce animation for the duration of its institutional life: its well-known 'stock system' was an advance in efficiency and cost-cutting even over the 'limited animation' perfected by Hanna-Barbera (Stahl 2010: 15). *The New Adventures of Superman* debuted in the fall of 1966 and achieved unprece-dented Saturday morning ratings, establishing Fred Silverman's reputation and enabling Filmation to enter the field and compete with Hanna-Barbera.

The advantages of using licensed characters such as Superman immediately became apparent: established properties reduce expensive conceptual work and minimize risk in marketing (Stahl 2010: 15). Following the success of *Superman*, Filmation focused entirely on recognizable, licensable properties, tracking down copyright holders, pitching cartoon versions to the networks (whose appetites for such fare were growing rapidly), negotiating licence (and sometimes profit partici-pation) agreements, and producing at low cost using the system it had developed (Stahl 2010: 13). In Lou Scheimer's words, after *Superman*, 'anything that flew and had a cape we did a version thereof' (author interview 2004).

Having come from behind through the exploitation of what one television critic called 'morally repellant pseudoscientific space fantasies' populated by 'cartoon superheroes beating the brains out of supervillains' (Hendershot 1998: 27), CBS and Silverman became primary targets for elite castigation in the early stirrings of the children's television reform movement. As Heather Hendershot (1998: 27–32) explained, 1968 – with its freight of national political violence and assassination – was to be a crucial year in the imagined and real history of US television censorship. Filmation hit upon the Archie comic books as suitable source material in 1967; by 1968, faced with 'pressure group accusations that Saturday morning cartoons were excessively violent', Silverman must have viewed the thematically mild *Archie* prop-erty as a godsend (Erickson 1995: 71). *The Archie Show* was primed to palliate critics and resuscitate CBS's reputation among concerned reformers.

Enter Kirshner

Filmation's *Archie Show* diverged from the Archie comics not only in numerous minor ways – the characters and backgrounds, for instance, were graphically simplified to speed production – but also in one major way: the animation studio decided to put the characters into a pop group. According to Lou Scheimer, 'it just seemed appropriate'; 'we thought it would just be interesting to do something with a musical background' (Stahl 2010: 14). The conditions were optimal: the 1966–67 chart success of music from the television program *The Monkees* was demonstrating the power of cross-media promotion to sell records to kids, and Filmation partner Norm Prescott had been a DJ and record producer with experience 'breaking' (selecting, introducing and helping to build excitement for) new records. Prescott's experience enabled Filmation to treat the songs that its Archies pop group would be represented as playing as music that would and could compete for audiences beyond those 2- to 11-year-olds watching cartoons on Saturday mornings.

Prescott bypassed staff musicians and contract composers, and sought out 'Top 10 writers, people who know bubblegum music, [which] immediately gave us credibility' in the eyes of music industry decision-makers, 'something that our competition, Hanna-Barbera, never did and wouldn't think of doing' (Stahl 2010: 14). Wanting to accomplish with The Archies 'the same thing' that Don Kirshner had with The Monkees, they reasonably enough hired Kirshner as producer (Stahl 2010: 14). In the interviews I conducted, Prescott asserted that he had auditioned the songs and 'spent a lot of time' (author interview 2004) with the songwriters, discussing with them 'the fact that the kind of songs that we wanted were bubblegum-oriented songs; I gave a few examples, they understood immediately' (Stahl 2010: 16). Filmation hired Kirshner because 'he'd already done it' with The Monkees; Prescott 'figured this was a shortcut'. They hired Kirshner 'to do a job and he was hired because he was good. For that job he got X percentage of the publishing rights'; because of Kirshner's existing deal with RCA, 'we had an automatic RCA Victor release on one of their other subsidiary labels' (Stahl 2010: 16).

To Prescott, hiring Kirshner was a 'shortcut' of the same logical kind as Filmation's practices of working exclusively with pre-existing properties and their development of the stock system: it would save time and money and minimize risk. Far from 'creating' or 'manufacturing' The Archies, Kirshner appeared on the scene as a mobile music professional hired for his ability to contribute a distinct form of value (state-of-the-art mainstream pop record production) to the property, and who brought with him industry connections that would virtually guarantee widespread exposure of *The Archie Show*'s musical content in legitimate pop music worlds.

Embroiled in a nasty lawsuit with Screen Gems/Columbia over his firing by the producers of The Monkees' television show, Kirshner was nevertheless available to turn his attention to a new project in 1967. By late summer 1968, RCA Records had hinged its initial Archies promotional efforts on Kirshner's reputation. On 31 August 1968, two weeks prior to the Saturday morning debut of *The Archie Show*, a second, two-page-spread advertisement appeared in *Billboard*. On the right-hand page was a reproduction of the paper picture-sleeve in which The Archies' first single would be packaged; on the left-hand page appeared the image of a freshly unfolded letter, placed at a slight angle on the page, suggesting that the letter was lying on the reader's desk. The text, typed on Kirshner Entertainment Corporation letterhead, enumerated the forces harnessed by this 'total entertainment' project, emphasizing the anticipated rewards for stores selling the records and radio stations playing them. The cartoon would reach 'an estimated audience of twelve million families' and the CBS network demonstrated its confidence 'by contracting now for two full years of "The Archies" program'. The comic books on which the programme was based reached 'a world-wide audience of fifty million annually'; these publications would 'tie in with the records and dances of the show'. The Archies comic strip was 'now in more than 500 newspapers with a circulation of more than 75 million'; moreover, 'A generation has grown up with Archies, and now for the first time, they and their children will enjoy "The Archies" on records.' Finally, 'a complete line of Archie products will be licensed and marketed to consumers'. The letter was signed 'Don Kirshner'. This advertisement simultaneously invokes the range of institutions and individuals and cultural forces involved in the production of The Archies, and obscures them behind Kirshner's image as a formidable hit-maker.

A front-page article appearing in the same 31 August 1968 issue of *Billboard* also hypes Kirshner's reputation as a major selling point for the 'package'. But perhaps more interestingly, in its thinly veiled promotional exhortation to record stores, radio stations and other institutional readers of the journal to get on The Archies' bandwagon, the article 'RCA, Kirshner Enter New Tie' details the truly massive promotional campaign that RCA apparently deemed necessary to support the Kirshner imprimatur. According to the trade journal, the RCA campaign 'is already in full swing with a series of teaser mailings to disk jockeys, distributors and press of the Archie comic books, as well as individual pieces of art work of the "Archies" characters captioned with words of the theme song of the TV show, "Everything's Archie" '. The article enumerates the varieties of advertisements in other publications, of stickers, posters, buttons, balloons, window displays and other paraphernalia to be distributed to retailers, as well as '20-, 30-, and 60-second radio commercial[s]' and a DJ promo kit that 'will include, among other things, a biography of "Archie" '. Furthermore, '[a] radio station "Archie" look-alike contest is being planned and [a] special airplane promotion has been scheduled for the Labor Day weekend, when the "Everything's Archie" theme will be flown over beaches in the New York, Chicago, Los Angeles and Miami areas. During August and September all RCA locations will use a special "Everything's Archie" postage slug on all mail.' Finally, the ad concludes, 'A press/dealer reception will be held to coincide with the debut of the TV series in two weeks' time'. Likely derived almost entirely from an RCA press release, this story (as well as the advertisements excerpted above) demonstrates that while RCA perceived Kirshner's name, likeness and reputation to be a brand useful in driving enthusiastic participation on the part of retailers and radio, the company did not stop there. RCA invoked numerous other institutions, individuals and cultural phenomena, and engaged in a wide variety of promotional activities, in order to ensure massive record sales to the best of their abilities.

Conclusion

This chapter has endeavoured to complicate reductive conceptions of mainstream music institutions and their 'shrewd commercial operators' by peering behind the received narrative of a powerful (but not all-powerful) music industry professional and 'his' 'perfect band'. The image of Don Kirshner in the popular and scholarly imagination has waxed to the point where it eclipses the other very important factors that contributed to the astonishing (but by no means guaranteed) success of The Archies. Drawing on trade journal advertising and reportage, and inter- views with other participants, this chapter has sought to relocate Kirshner to a less Olympian, more true-to-life place in a historical assemblage of institutions, indi- viduals, cultural phenomena and divisions of entertainment industry labour. Kirshner's golden-eared acumen and real, valuable reputation were indeed impor- tant to The Archies, but factors such as the market for, public discourse on and developing regulatory framework around the programming of children's televi- sion, as well as the particular sets of interests, abilities and intuitions of a network executive, the principles of an untested animation studio, and the patterns of investment and marketing of a major record company were equally important.

Notes

1 The idea of rescuing an 'authentic' cultural form (such as 'authentic' rock) from imma- nent extinction is a familiar one, evident in elite discourse dating back at least to the eighteenth century (see Bendix 1997).
2 The reference here is to Kirshner's tenure and dismissal as music supervisor of the televi- sion band The Monkees (see Stahl 2002, 2010).
3 Pre-eminent popular music scholars are not immune from this discourse; Lipsitz (2007: 2–3) also credits the Kirshner-did-it thesis.

References

Austen, J. (2002) 'Rock 'n' roll cartoons', in D. Goldmark and Y. Taylor (eds), *The Cartoon Music Book*, New York: A Capella Books.
Bendix, R. (1997) *In Search of Authenticity: the formation of folklore studies*, Madison, WI: University of Wisconsin Press.
Cooper, K. and Smay, D. (2001) *Bubblegum Music is the Naked Truth: the dark history of prepubescent pop, from The Banana Splits to Britney Spears*, Port Townsend, WA: Feral House.
Erickson, H. (1995) *Television Cartoon Shows: an illustrated encyclopaedia, 1949 through 1993*, Jefferson City, MO: McFarland.
Goldman, A. (1970) 'Portnoy in the playpen: bubblegum music', *Life* magazine, 30 January 1970.

Harker, D. (1980) *One For the Money: politics and popular song*, London: Hutchinson.

Hendershot, H. (1998) *Saturday Morning Censors: television regulation before the V-chip*, Durham, NC: Duke University Press.

Huber, A. (2001) 'Learning to love the mainstream', paper presented at the biennial meeting of the International Association for the Study of Popular Music, Turku, Finland, July.

Jahn, M. (1969) 'The Archies are fictional but their success is not', *New York Times*, 5 November.

Lipsitz, G. (2007) *Footsteps in the Dark: the hidden histories of popular music*, Minneapolis: University of Minnesota Press.

Mitroff, D., Christenson, P., Roberts, D., Strange, J. and Wild, D. (2004) *Prime-Time Teens: perspectives on the new youth-media environment*, New York: William T. Grant Foundation.

Mittell, J. (2003) 'The great Saturday morning exile: scheduling cartoons on television's periphery in the 1960s', in C.A. Stabile and M. Harrison (eds), *Prime Time Animation: television animation and American culture*, London: Routledge.

Monnot, C. (2010) 'The female pop singer and the "apprentice" girl', *Children and Media*, 4: 283–97.

Porter, J. (2001) 'Kasenetz and Katz and their super-duper rock & roll kavalcade', in K. Cooper and D. Smav, *Bubblegum Music is the Naked Truth*, Port Townsend, WA: Feral House.

Scheimer, E. (1979) 'My Dad, the trendsetter', http://web.archive.org/web/20040322033845/http://www.louscheimerproductions.com/erikaloubio.htm (accessed 22 October 2011).

Shapter, A. (2006) *Before the Music Dies* (documentary), Austin, TX: Roadwings Entertainment.

Simpson, K.J. (2005) 'Hit radio and the formatting of America in the 1970s', PhD thesis, University of Texas at Austin.

Stahl, M. (2002) 'Authentic boy bands on TV? Performers and impresarios in *The Monkees* and *Making the Band*', *Popular Music*, 21: 307–29.

—— (2010) 'The synthespian's animated prehistory: The Monkees, The Archies, Don Kirshner, and the politics of virtual labor', *Television and New Media*, 12(1): 3–22.

Wald, G. (2002) ' "I want it that way": teenybopper music and the girling of boy bands', *Genders*, 35, www.genders.org/g35/g35_wald.html (accessed 13 April 2012).

Weingarten, M. (2000) *Station to Station: the history of rock 'n' roll on Television*, New York: Pocket Books.

Werbin, S. (1972) 'Monkee man does Fillmore of the air', *Rolling Stone*, 12 July.

PART II
Perceptions of the Mainstream

4

LESBIAN MUSICALITIES, QUEER STRAINS AND CELESBIAN POP

The Poetics and Polemics of Women-Loving Women in Mainstream Popular Music

Jodie Taylor

In general terms, heterosexuality is mainstream; queer sexualities are not. The anecdotal evidence is unequivocal: whether tuning your radio to the weekly Top 40 countdown, watching the chart-toppers on MTV or browsing the 'most downloaded' listings on iTunes, images and narratives of heterosexual love and desire dominate mainstream popular music. With few exceptions, the repetitive performances of hetero-norms manifest as qualities that contribute to the potential mainstream appeal of popular music artists. Following this, the natural province of queer music and those who make it is the cultural fringe.

Given the marginalization of queers within the mainstream, a phrase like 'mainstream lesbian music' is likely to be read as a contradiction in terms – dubious at the very least. Yet a quick scan of the music forum pages on the lesbian pop culture website After Ellen (www.afterellen.com) reveals that 'mainstream lesbian music' is clearly a 'thing'; to what or whom the phrase refers is less clear. On many of the publicly accessible music forum pages at which I looked, members would frequently refer to loving or hating various kinds of 'lesbian music', insisting that some lesbian music was more mainstream than others. For example, in a specific thread dedicated to the topic, one member commented: 'I'm not a fan of mainstream, stereotypical lesbian music . . . there is a thriving, underground music scene of queer musicians that get overlooked . . . because they aren't being [sic] in the mainstream spotlight' (posted 11 February 2011). Such a comment begs numerous questions, not least about what lesbian music is and how it is positioned in relation to categories such as the mainstream and what this forum post terms the 'queer underground'. However, answering these questions is not a straightforward matter because the parameters of 'the mainstream' itself are all too commonly ill-defined.

Music simply described as 'mainstream' (not unlike describing music as 'lesbian') eludes identification of explicit musical characteristics, a discrete style or genre of expression. Rather, the mainstream is a value-laden category that frequently – and problematically – derives its meaning in association with its multiple corollaries such as counter-culture, subculture, underground, indie, folk, alternative, experimental and avant-garde. When situated in binary opposition to the politically resistant stylized rituals of a potent subculture (e.g. Hebdige 1979), the mainstream garners negative connotations, unhelpfully implying a lax association with an inauthentic, commercialized, normative and depoliticized form of cultural hegemony (Huber 2007). Furthermore, incorporating this figuration of the mainstream into lesbian music, which I do in the last section of this chapter, takes us quite some distance from the notion of mainstream lesbian music referred to in the above forum post.

As Alison Huber argues in Chapter 1, for a nebulous term like mainstream to function critically in studies of popular music, we must first acknowledge that the – or rather, a – mainstream is always an historically situated, contingent and contested term. In this chapter, through the lens of lesbian and queer feminist musicalities, I draw further attention to the limitations of the binary structuration of the mainstream *vis-à-vis* its subcultural 'other'. I argue that lesbian identity is (re)produced across multiple sites of popular music, concomitantly revealing the multiple strategies, politics, communions and contentions that figure in the musicalized representations of queer female intimacies. Furthermore, I consider the various ways in which these representations are positioned in relation to notions of the mainstream, thus revealing the multiple discourses and connotations of the mainstream within lesbian and queer female music cultures, as well as particular abstractions of lesbianism with mainstream pop music. Progressing chronologically, I begin this chapter by outlining the emergence of womyn's music in the 1970s. I then consider how select lesbian artists situated themselves within the mainstream during the late 1980s and early 1990s, enshrining their status as mainstream lesbian musical icons. To follow, I discuss the riot dyke critique first propelled by post-punk feminist musicians in the mid-1990s and ornament this discussion with localized ethnographic data illustrating the contemporary polychromatics of lesbian and queer musicalities. Finally, I point to what some have termed 'celesbianism' or 'fauxmosexuality' in the mainstream pop arena of the twenty-first century.

Womyn's Music and Lesbian Musicality

Developing alongside lesbian feminism[1] of the 1970s, womyn's music – 'womyn' in this instance implicitly meaning 'lesbian' (Lont 1992) – was a reaction against the heteropatriarchy and the sexist power politics that dominated the rock and pop styles championed by the mainstream music industry of the time. During the late 1960s and early 1970s, popular forms of rock music such as hard rock (later dubbed 'cock' rock due to its overtly phallic imagery) symbolically excluded women from both the making and consumption of rock, relegating them to the status of sexual object, groupie or encumbering nag. Cock rock espoused an aggressive male sexuality made audible via an emphasis on volume, rasping vocal production, misogynistic lyrics and driving rhythmic structures 'built around techniques of arousal and climax' (Frith and McRobbie 1990: 319). Quintessential purveyors of this style included The Rolling Stones, The Who and Led Zeppelin. Set in contrast to rock's masculine authenticity were the 'fabricated' – ergo feminized – styles of pop music such as teenybop, bubblegum and dolly-bird pop. Pop was the (hetero)normalized site of girl-fandom where balladeering men such as Donny Osmond wooed his female fan-base with romantic love songs. Although pop was slightly more accommodating to female performers than rock, with a few exceptions (Suzi Quatro being one), women were seen as second-rate artists and rarely as instrumental performers, with the available female musical roles being limited to vocalist (Whiteley 2000). Both mainstream popular music and main-stream society of this time represented a hostile place for progressive women to occupy.

Distancing themselves from the mainstream cultural industries of rock and pop, the early proponents of womyn's music, such as Alix Dobkin, Cris Williamson, Holly Near and Meg Christian, insisted that the stylistics of folk be its vehicle. A traditional site of minority cultural production with strong ties to protest music, folk was already imbued with leftist and egalitarian political themes, and less bound to the rigid gender roles ascribed to rock and pop. In the feminist imagin-ary, folk's emphasis on acoustic instrumentation, its 'softer' (ergo less masculine) sound and its earnest and confessional singer-songwriter narratives evoked the essence of womanhood. Accordingly, folk was seen as the most suitable musical platform from which to launch a movement and promote a 'serious', emotionally committed and sexually contained image of woman-identification (Bayton 1993; Kearney 1997; Peraino 2006). Part of a conscious effort to institutionalize lesbian culture and generate a degree of lesbian visibility within public culture, in 1973 the group Lavender Jane – which consisted of womyn's music pioneer Alix Dobkin, flautist Kay Gardner and bassist Patches Attom – released the first 'out' lesbian album, *Lavender Jane Loves Women*. With an express desire for 'lesbians to have tangible musical proof of their existence' (Dobkin 1979: 12), *Lavender Jane Loves Women* was a musical revelation. Its lyrical themes spoke explicitly to lesbian experiences and its DIY lesbian separatist approach to music production – which 'used women sound engineers, photographers, and studio musicians, and . . . their lesbian underwriters as chorus and distribution agents' (Peraino 2006: 161) – promoted alternative values of collectivism and anti-corporatization. Murray (cited in Sport 2007: 354) suggests the feminist musical discourse to follow would reassure women that lesbian 'feelings and actions are not the oddity that main-stream society has assumed [them] to be'.

The rampant masculinist capitalism of the 1970s meant that record labels were hesitant to sign female musicians, thus few female artists were able to cross over into the mainstream. Exemplifying women's power to mobilize their own systems of music production and promotion outside the industry, feminist collectives established a number of record labels and music festivals that excluded all forms of male participation. Among others, these included the now iconic Redwood Records (founded by musician and activist Holly Near in 1972), Olivia Records (founded in 1973), Ladyslipper (founded in 1976) and the highly successful Michigan Womyn's Music Festival (first held in 1976). However, the lesbian feminist ideology of womyn's music, which attempted to universalize the lesbian experience, grew problematic – particularly in America. Racial critiques posed by women of colour (e.g. Lorde 1984) questioned the implicit whiteness of woman-identification, while a younger generation of feminists took issue with the exclusion of bisexual women and transgender people.[2] Despite the impact of womyn's music, a number of lesbians also began to seek broader audiences and alternative genres of expression. The rivulet of womyn's music was drying up and, taking a swift change in course, lesbian music steered towards faster-flowing tributaries.

During the late 1980s and early 1990s, lesbians who had previously approached womyn's record labels and played the womyn's festival circuits began dropping anchor along the banks of mainstream popular music. In 1988, singer-songwriter Tracy Chapman charted in the Top 10 in America, Australia and the United Kingdom with 'Fast Car'. Releasing albums in 1988 and 1989 (with many more to follow), rock guitarist and songwriter Melissa Etheridge garnered mainstream appeal and numerous Grammy nominations with rock songs such as 'Bring Me Some Water' (1988). Also in 1988, k.d. lang began making waves in the country music charts with her debut solo album *Shadowlands*, and in 1992 appeared in mainstream music charts with her now iconic lesbian ballad 'Constant Craving', winning a Grammy for her vocal performance of this song the following year. Other lesbian and bisexual singer-songwriters such as the Indigo Girls, Michelle Shocked, Phranc, Two Nice Girls, Ani DiFranco and Sophie B. Hawkins also had some success in the mainstream during this time. Reflecting on this cultural shift towards the mainstream, Stein posits:

> Though influenced by feminism, and frequently women's music, they were convinced that it was necessary to work within the constraints of the industry to get their message across, and saw mainstreaming as an act no less subversive than the feminist disaffection from the industry a decade earlier.
>
> *(Stein 1995: 420)*

Of course, the mainstream was (and remains) a hostile environment for lesbian and bisexual women, with marketability requiring certain compromises at the political level – namely, sexual ambiguity. The likes of Phranc and DiFranco chose to be politically and sexually bold, concomitantly lessening their mainstream impact. While other musicians such as Etheridge, Lang, Chapman and the Indigo Girls – perhaps taking their lead from the likes of Joan Jett, who had a No. 1 hit with 'I Love Rock and Roll' in 1982, or even the much earlier successes of closeted women like Janis Joplin and Dusty Springfield – put their music, rather than their sexuality, first and refrained from 'coming out' early on in their careers for fear that it would hinder their commercial acceptance.[3] Further to her point above, Stein (1995: 421) insists that 'the classic dilemma persisted' – this dilemma being that if a woman was to come out she would be marketed first as a lesbian artist and thus 'doomed to marginality'. Otherwise, 'she watered down her lesbianism in order to appeal to a mass audience'. As Phranc's lyrics from the song 'Folksinger' (1989) imply: 'Just don't wear a flat-top and mention sexuality, and girl you'll go far, you'll get a record contract and be a star.'

While iconic 1970s lesbian folk songs like Dobkin's 'View from Gayhead' (1973) narrated the 'pleasure to be a lesbian . . . in no man's land', and 1980s mainstream lesbian music like Etheridge's 'Like the Way I Do' (1988) asked, in a gender-ambiguous way, 'does she stimulate you, attract and captivate you?', both divorced the music from any association with lesbian eroticism or genitally orientated sexual pleasures. The former did so by privileging lesbians' emotional, social and political bonds, and divorcing the idea of lesbian-identification from sexual desire. The latter did so by Etheridge's then refusal to acknowledge her own lesbian identity, thus within a mainstream framework of 'compulsory heterosexuality' (Rich 1980) the question posed in Etheridge's lyrics appears directed towards an ex-male lover. Indeed, one of the main criticisms leveraged against the corpus of lesbian music – in both the marginal traditions of 1970s womyn's music and the increased mainstream appeal of lesbian music in the late 1980s/early 1990s – has been its lack of sexual explicitness. Accordingly, Belcher argues that lesbian musicality is often seen as repressed, unsexy and shameful, and lesbian music 'comes to figure as [a] locus of that frigidity' (2011: 413).

You might even go so far as to call it the soundtrack to 'lesbian bed death'.[4] A good example of this association can be seen in Lisa Cholodenko's mainstream film release, *The Kids are Alright* (2010). In a bedroom scene early on in the film, the looming lesbian bed death of the lead characters – two monogamous cohabitating lesbian mothers – is fortified later in the film when one of the women breaks into an a cappella rendition of Joni Mitchell's 'All I Want' (1971) only moments before she comes to realize her female partner is having an affair with a man. While Mitchell is not a lesbian-identified musician, her mainstream success in the early 1970s made her commercially available to a generation of feminists and lesbians unable to tap into the marginal world of womyn's music. Moreover, just as the symbolic appropriation of heterosexual artists such as Judy Garland and Madonna have, at different times, been analogous with mainstream gay male music taste (Musto 1995), Mitchell's 'confessional' singer-songwriter style places her firmly within the parameters of lesbian musical aesthetics.

In terms of both gender and genre, lesbian music often evokes a kind of mainstream ordinariness, suggesting melancholy confessionals sung by dowdy androgynous women strumming acoustic guitars in the neo-folk style or, like Etheridge, standard rock formation. As a brief personal aside, I can honestly say that for me, and many of my musically inclined peers, the phrase 'lesbian music' has often seemed tedious. Dubious about the sex-negative musicality of womyn's music and the sexual reservations of the lesbian mainstream, the sexually assertive queer women I'm about to discuss searched for aesthetic and political rejuvenations in the mainstream's 'other' – which in the 1990s was post-punk musical forms.

Riotous Dykes and Queer Strains

Riding feminism's third wave, the 1990s generation of in-your-face, angry, out and sex-positive dyke punks ushered in a new era of queer feminist music affiliated with the intertwined cultural phenomena of riot grrrl and queercore (Ciminelli and Knox, 2005; Peraino 2006).[5] Reminiscent of the grassroots activism and DIY business model of womyn's music, riot grrrl and queercore reactivated a strident critique of the capitalist heteropatriarchy's symbolic, economic and physical violence against women and queers. Although often depicted on the periphery of riot grrrl due largely to heterosexist erasure of lesbian subjectivities in the mainstream music press (Kearney 1997), North American dyke punk bands such as Tribe 8, Fifth Column, Team Dresch, The Butchies, Bitch and Animal, Lesbians on Ecstasy and the Gossip fused riot grrrl's punk rock feminism with a reinvigorated, queerer form of lesbian musicality.

These 'riot dykes' as Halberstam (2005) names them, 'set themselves up against an earlier conception of white lesbian community, which included elements of sex negativity, gender separatism, cultural feminism, and womanism' (180). However, they did not reject the efforts of womyn's music in totality, but instead simultaneously interrogated and paid tribute to them, producing an arrhythmic moment of subcultural lesbian/feminist/queer musicality. 'Build[ing] a bridge between the raucous spirit of rebellion and the quieter, acoustic world of women's music from the 1970s and 1980s' (18), a number of riot dykes have stylistically recontextualized womyn's music. An example of this offered by Halberstam is The Butchies' album *We are Not Femme* (1998), which features a cover of Cris Williamson's iconic womyn's anthem 'Shooting Star' (1975). Other temporal disjunctures in the narrative of lesbian music include the electro band Lesbians on Ecstasy, who re-recorded a range of iconic lesbian favourites by the likes of the Indigo Girls, Melissa Etheridge and k.d. lang on their 2004 self-titled debut album (see Halberstam 2007). To this, we can also add folk-punk duo Bitch and Animal's album *Sour Juice Rhymes* (2003), which was co-produced and co-recorded with June Millington. Millington came to fame as the guitarist in Fanny – one of the first all-female rock bands to achieve notoriety in the early 1970s. As I have argued previously (see Taylor 2012), this musical pairing can be seen as building a stylistic bridge in the opposite direction: from queer melodic neo-folk to a pioneering form of feminist rock. Implicit in the idea of queerness is, to use musical terms, a sense of discord and arrhythmia: where musical voices don't always combine to create harmonious affect and culture may be made with a sense of it being unfashionable or out of time (see Freeman 2010). Moreover, queer feminist music is not hermeneutically sealed from so-called mainstream lesbian music, nor is it necessarily sealed from the commercial mainstream. As the above examples suggest, since the 1990s, riot dykes have frequently cited both womyn's music and mainstream lesbian artists while also embracing other non-traditionally lesbian musical devices. Accordingly, the corpus of queer feminist music is increasingly heterogeneous, as is its relationship to the mainstream.

Take, for example, a local site of queer feminist music-making in Australia. Brisbane and its surrounding regions of South-East Queensland and Northern New South Wales have birthed numerous lesbian/dyke/queer/feminist and allied bands, DJs and solo performers. Collectively, this translocal[6] scene reveals that the musical sensibilities of women-loving women are stylistically complex. Artists with ties to this scene include, for example, electropop-punk duo Toxic Lipstick, folk-pop duo Women in Docs, power-pop band Lesbian Super Group, acoustic solo artists such as Kristy Apps and Melania Jack, electro-rock artist Zia, punk rockers The Ovaries, DJs Ish and Neroli, roots artist CC the Cat, Polynesian soul singer Ofa Fanaika, country folk duo Hussy Hicks, the self-proclaimed electro-flash duo Shiny Shiny, quirky ukulele comedy duo The Ukulele Sisters, all-girl grunge outfit The Boys, indie rock band Love Like Hate and five-piece funk, reggae and ska band Bertha Control to name a few.[7]

As part of an ethnographic project on popular music and queer world-making (Taylor 2012), since 2005 I have attended live performances by the majority of these artists, spoken to many of them *in situ* and formally interviewed others. Although the goal of my original ethnography was not to interrogate this scene's relationship to the mainstream, my experience of this scene revealed that within a queer/lesbian framework, the mainstream is an inherently flexible and pluralistic concept whose meaning is derived via complex relations with economies of music production, genre of expression and gender/sexual identity politics – relations which are continually contested and reconfigured. For example, some women may define themselves as outside of the mainstream because they produce music independently and in some cases within separatist collectives. Others may ascribe their anti-mainstream sensibility to their indie, punk, roots or electro sound, or simply due to their perceived stylistic distance from lesbian acoustic folk and soft rock. Others (DJs in particular) still see their femaleness as a boundary to acceptance within the mainstream club scene, which is dominated by men. For many, explicitly politicizing one's music as either lesbian or queer is an act that is interpreted as anti-assimilationist and anti-mainstream.

Celesbianism[8]

There is one final example where lesbian identity intersects with the mainstream in the latter's most pejorative – inauthentic, commercialized, normative and depoliticized – figuration. As I indicated in this chapter's introduction, incorporating an understanding of the mainstream as 'inauthentic' into a reading of lesbianism takes us quite some distance from the notions of mainstream lesbian music I've discussed thus far. Since the 1990s, mass media and consumer culture have made a number of attempts to capitalize on the so-called 'pink economies' (see Binnie 2004) by mainstreaming certain images of lesbians and gay men. However, the types of 'queerness' served to audiences have frequently been a conformist and desexualized image of white, middle-class, monogamous homosexuality. Such images only reinforce the dominant norms of white heteropatriarchy, privileging this limited rendering and making it the only version of 'queerness' intelligible to the hetero-mainstream.

August 1993 saw k.d. lang appear on the cover of *Vanity Fair* with supermodel Cindy Crawford, marking the beginning of the mainstream media's fascination with lesbians. This cultural fad – or, more accurately, the fashionable exploitation of lesbian culture – became known as 'lesbian chic' (see Aaron 1999). Cultural artefacts such as prime-time television show *The L Word* (2004–09) are also indicative of this trend towards the mainstreaming of lesbian culture. According to Chambers (2006: 86), the cast of the lesbian TV drama *The L Word* exhibits:

> practices that reify the structures of heteronormativity – by either mimicking the heterosexual norm or upholding patriarchal visions [and] assumptions [of women] – these practices, may and should, be criticised for their conservative and freedom-limiting effects.

In what is perhaps an even more monstrously commercial rendering of lesbian chic, during the 2000s the pop industry offered up numerous musical episodes that likewise point to the mainstreaming of lesbianism, but this time in an overly glamorized and explicitly hetero-feminine guise. In 2008, singing her hit song 'I Kissed a Girl', the self-declared hetero pop star Katy Perry sat at the top of the ARIA[9] charts for six weeks and in the US charts for seven consecutive weeks. We can add to this list the infamous Madonna and Britney kiss at the 2003 MTV Awards, plus the rejuvenation of faux-lesbian Russian duo t.A.T.u, who in 2008 replaced Victoria Beckham as the face of Marc Jacobs' latest fashion collection. Also in 2008, a frenzy of rumours surrounded Lindsay Lohan and DJ Samantha Ronson, plus one member of the teen pop duo The Veronicas and MTV VJ Ruby Rose who made tabloid headlines for their lesbian escapades. In fact, girl-love was so fashionable that the *Sydney Morning Herald* actually listed 'lesbian culture' in the number one position of its top ten list of trends sweeping the globe in August 2008 (Whitelaw 2008).

While some scholars (e.g. Rupp and Taylor 2010) have provided a more lenient account of female 'heteroflexibility', the queer press has tended to take a harsher view. 'Fauxmosexuality' or 'celesbianism' (fake celebrity lesbianism), as it has been tagged by some journalists (e.g. Duggan 2008b), has been described as a mutation of lesbian culture: the mainstreaming of 'girl-on-girl love' driven largely by the cultural industry's publicity machines and phallic gaze. Articles in the lesbian and gay press have shown great disdain towards the emergence of Katy Perry-style celesbianism within mainstream pop. In an article titled 'Lesbianism: The New Black', Duggan (2008a) slams the celesbian craze, saying that 'with Madonna too busy working on her new face to spend time culturally raping minorities any more,[10] it's up to the new breed of singers like Katy Perry to take what they can from the lesbian scene and milk it for all it's worth before its value runs out'.

Ending on a Positive Note . . .

Of course, this doesn't mean that the commercial music industry is anathema to women-loving women. It remains disappointing that candid queer confessions amass less mainstream attention than fauxmosexual flights of fancy. Yet it could be an indication that mainstream pop may be more amenable to lesbians and queer women than at previous times.

Looking beyond the oft-cited polemics of pink marketing by major media corporations, the mere existence of subsidiaries such as Sony/BMG's label Music With a Twist, which focuses on signing and selling LGBT artists, and Viacom's American LGBT cable television channel Logo, indicates that the contemporary intersections of mainstream pop culture and queer sexualities are more complex that ever before. Moreover, the recent mainstream success of a new generation of out female artists such as Tegan and Sarah and fat-positive femme riot dyke Beth Ditto of Gossip fame, suggests that some women no longer feel it is necessary to pit themselves against the mainstream, or to closet themselves for the mainstream, or even oppose the mainstreaming of lesbian culture. In fact, the rising mainstream appeal of indie-dykes like Ditto is cause for celebration, or at the very least optimism.

Returning to my opening statement, while heterosexuality is the purview of the mainstream, in musical terms at least, the mainstream is not immune to queer affect. Acknowledging both the plurality of the mainstream and the plurality of lesbian identities is to acknowledge the more complex realities of identity, politics, music-making and consumption in the twenty-first century, and hopefully an increasingly pluralistic view bespeaks more pluralistic lesbian, dyke, queer and feminist musicalities and futures.

Notes

1 Lesbian feminism attempted to reconstruct the category of lesbian, shifting it from a category of sexuality to a political position that any woman who rejected men, regardless of whether they had sex with other women or not, could assume.
2 For example, Holly Near (founder of Olivia Records) has since admitted to concealing her bisexuality from her lesbian feminist peers while the Michigan Women's Festival has long been criticized for its transphobic attendance policy, which stipulated that participants must be women-born women.

3 Lang came out publicly in 1992 and Etheridge in 1993. During the 1990s, The Indigo Girls also gradually revealed their persuasion and Chapman has never publicly declared her sexual identity.

4 'Lesbian bed death' is a contentious phrase that supposedly originated in the socio-logical study *American Couples* (Blumstein and Schwartz 1983) and continues to be used colloquially. It implies an incrementally waning interest in sex between committed lesbian couples the longer they have been partnered, eventually resulting in the death of sexual intimacy.

5 Some argue that the radical critique of (heterosexual) grrrl power was eventually contaminated by the onslaught of mainstream pop sensations like the Spice Girls, who appropriated and repackaged a sanitized version of girl power signalling the commod-ification of girl sexualities and the acquisition of agency through consumerism (Freeman 2010; Sheridan-Rabideau 2008).

6 Translocal refers to the cultural exchange and hybridization – the ways in which music and styles produce affective communities that, while situated within the local, interact and connect with other culture-makers and sites (see Bennett and Peterson 2004).

7 I am mentioning these artists here to exemplify the diverse styles of queer and feminist music-making in this local context. However, unless explicitly stated, I caution the reader against making assumptions about the personal politics of these artists.

8 'Celesbian' is a recent addition to the queer vernacular, a portmanteau of 'celebrity' and 'lesbian'. While the term is sometimes used to refer to lesbian-identified celebrities (e.g. Ellen DeGeneres), in this context I am using it to refer to faux/publicity-generating displays of lesbian affection by heterosexual-identified celebrities. Here, it has similar value to other idiomatic terms such as fauxmosexual.

9 Australian Recording Industry Association.

10 Here, Duggan is presumably referring to Madonna's hit song and music video 'Vogue' (1990), the idea for which was pillaged from the Black and Latino gay men and trans people who participated in the Harlem drag balls and house culture of the 1980s.

References

Aaron, M. (1999) 'Till death us do part: cinema's queer couples who kill', in M. Aaron (ed.), *The Body's Perilous Pleasures: dangerous desires in contemporary culture*, Edinburgh: Edinburgh University Press.

Bayton, M. (1993) 'Feminist musical practices: problems and contradiction', in T. Bennett, S. Frith, L. Grossberg, J. Shepherd and G. Turner (eds), *Rock and Popular Music: politics, policies, institutions*, London: Routledge.

Belcher, C. (2011) ' "I can't go to an Indigo Girls concert, I just can't": *Glee*'s Shameful Lesbian Musicality', *Journal of Popular Music Studies*, 23(4): 412–30.

Bennett, A. and Peterson, R. A. (eds) (2004) *Music Scenes: local, translocal, and virtual*, Nashville, TN: Vanderbilt University Press.

Binnie, J. (2004) *The Globalization of Sexuality*, London: Sage.

Blumstein, P. and Schwartz, P. (1983) *American Couples: money, work, sex*, New York: William Morrow.

Chambers, S.A. (2006) 'Heteronormativity and *The L Word*: From a Politics of Representation to a Politics of Norms', in K. Akass and J. McCabe (eds), *Reading the L Word: outing contemporary television*, London: I.B. Tauris.

Ciminelli, D. and Knox, K. (2005) *Homocore: the loud and raucous rise of queer rock*, Los Angeles: Alyson Books.

Dobkin, A. (1979) *Adventures in Women's Music*, New York: Tomato Publications.

Duggan, T. (2008a) 'Lesbianism: the new black', *Same.Same*, 18 August, www.samesame. com.au/features/2864/Lesbianism-The-New-Black.htm (accessed 20 August 2008).

—— (2008b) 'The dangers of fauxmosexuality', *Sydney Morning Herald*, 10 October, www. smh.com.au/articles/2008/10/09/1223145536075.html (accessed 12 October 2008).

Freeman, E. (2010) *Time Binds: queer temporalities, queer histories*, Durham, NC: Duke University Press.

Frith, S. and McRobbie, A. (1990 [1978]) 'Rock and sexuality', in S. Frith and A. Goodwin (eds), *On Record: rock, pop and the written word*, New York: Pantheon.

Halberstam, J. (2005) *In a Queer Time and Place: transgender bodies, subcultural lives*, New York: New York University Press.

—— (2007) 'Keeping time with Lesbians on Ecstasy', *Women and Music*, 11: 51–8.

Hebdige, D. (1979) *Subculture: the meaning of style*, London: Routledge.

Huber, A. (2007) 'What's in a mainstream?: critical possibilities', *Altitude*, 8: 1–12.

Kearney, M. (1997) 'The missing link: riot grrrl, feminism, lesbian culture', in S. Whiteley (ed.), *Sexing the Groove: Popular Music and Gender*, London: Routledge.

Lont, C. (1992) 'Women's music: no longer a small private party', in R. Garofalo (ed.), *Rockin' the Boat: mass music and mass movements*, Cambridge, MA: South End Press.

Lorde, A. (1984) 'Age, race, class, and sex: women redefining difference', in A. Lorde, *Sister Outsider: essays and speeches by Audre Lorde*, Berkley, CA: The Crossing Press.

Musto, M. (1995) 'Immaculate collection', in C. Creekmur and A. Doty (eds), *Out in Culture: gay, lesbian, and queer essays on popular culture*, Durham, NC: Duke University Press.

Peraino, J.A. (2006) *Listening to the Sirens: music technologies of queer identity from Homer to Hedwig*, Berkeley, CA: University of California Press.

Rich, A. (1980) 'Compulsory heterosexuality and lesbian existence', *Signs: Journal of Women in Culture and Society*, 5(4): 631–60.

Rupp, L.J and Taylor, V. (2010) 'Straight girls kissing', *Contexts*, 9: 28–32.

Sheridan-Rabideau, M.P. (2008) *Girls, Feminism, and Grassroots Literacies: activism in the girl-zone*, Albany: SUNY Press.

Sport, K. (2007) 'Below the belt and bleeding fingertips', *Australian Feminist Studies*, 22(53): 343–60.

Stein, A. (1995) 'Crossover dreams: lesbianism and popular music since the 1970s', in C. Creekmur and A. Doty (eds), *Out in Culture: gay, lesbian, and queer essays on popular culture*, Durham, NC: Duke University Press.

Taylor, J. (2012) *Playing It Queer: popular music, identity and queer world-making*, Bern, Switzerland: Peter Lang.

Whiteley, S. (2000) *Women and Popular Music: sexuality, identity, and subjectivity*, London: Routledge.

Whitelaw, A. (2008) 'The new black?', *MCV*, 17 September, http://mcv.e-p.net.au/opinion/the-new-black-4029.html (accessed 12 October 2008).

5

THE POSITIONING OF THE MAINSTREAM IN PUNK

Erik Hannerz

Whether we take as our point of departure the Chicago School or the Centre for Contemporary Cultural Studies (CCCS) in Birmingham, difference has been a key element within subcultural studies from its beginning. Subcultures, it has been argued, exist outside of and in opposition to a mainstream culture that threatens to rob the subcultural of its subversive and creative character (Hall and Jefferson 1976; Hebdige 1979). For subcultural researchers, punk has been the prime example of this subcultural resistance against the mainstream through style, politics and actions. However, recent work in subcultural studies has questioned this clear boundary between a normal mainstream and the deviant subcultural, instead pointing to the plurality of subcultural authenticities and mainstreams (Muggleton 2000; Williams 2006). Furthering this idea of subcultural plurality, this chapter aims to investigate how punks enact different interpretations of the binary subcultural/mainstream and to explore the consequences these enactments have for subcultural performances of style and practice.

From 2002 to 2010, I conducted ethnographic research focused on punks in the three major Swedish urban areas of Stockholm/Uppsala, Gothenburg and Malmoe/Lund. During this time, I also spent five months in Indonesia doing fieldwork and interviewing punks in Java and Bali. In both of these cases, I sought to investigate and explore different styles, actions, articulations and definitions of punk. In addition to fieldwork, I interviewed some 30 punks in Sweden and fifteen in Indonesia, mostly in group interviews with two to three interviewees. Group interviews have the advantage of taking place within the cultural context, encouraging the participants to make use of subcultural representations instead of merely commenting on them (Alasuutari 1995). In short, I wanted what Nash (1980) refers to as 'scene talk': topics discussed among participants as members of a group rather than as individuals. Given that I wanted to pursue differences, my informants performed a variety of styles and objects, yet they all self-identified as punk and saw their own version of punk as *the* authentic one. The full findings of this project are reported elsewhere (Hannerz forthcoming); this chapter focuses on the differences among punks in defining the mainstream, but also the similarities between Indonesian and Swedish punks in positioning this mainstream as either external or internal to punk.

Drawing from the work of Durkheim (1915), I argue that it is only through the recognition of collective representations of the subcultural – established through the division of the world into the sacred as opposed to the profane – that meaning can be attributed to action and validated. I will outline two different frameworks, to which I refer to as *convex* and *concave* frameworks due to their differences in positioning the mainstream. A convex bends outwards against an external mainstream, whereas a concave bends inwards, positioning the mainstream within the subcultural. The subcultural rests upon the binary distinction between the subcultural and the mainstream – between the set-apart and the undifferentiated. The prefix 'sub', then, refers to the conceived and performed distance and distinction towards what is referred to as the mainstream. These collective representations of the mainstream, when externalized through style, action and in space, have different consequences.

Punk and the Mainstream Other

The argument that punk rests upon a distinction from a mainstream is far from new. Following Dick Hebdige's (1979) classic claim that subcultural style goes against the mainstream – against the normalization of the dominant culture – punk's alleged opposition to the mainstream has frequently been addressed (Leblanc 1999; Moore 2007). Further, this distance from the mainstream has also been used in order to address both commitment and differences, mainly in terms of style and practice. Participants' actions, as well as their appearances and styles, are assessed in terms of how radical they are: the further detached from the mainstream, the more committed the participant (Baron 1989; Fox 1987). Not only has this resulted in a focus on conspicuous style; it has also meant that the meaning of punk has been rationalized: punks dress and act in a certain way to resist the mainstream society. When different fractions, styles and definitions of punk are touched upon, they are related to and explained in terms of having or lacking this commitment. Unfortunately, this has meant that the relationship between the mainstream and the subcultural has largely been left untouched, even though this dichotomy is claimed to be the basis of real commitment. If authentic punk indeed resists the mainstream, this makes the creation of the 'mainstream' just as important as the creation of the 'authentic'.

More contemporary work on subcultural authenticity (Haenfler 2004; Hodkinson 2002; Thornton 1996; Williams 2003) criticizes this previous focus on commitment and the negligence of the meaning of the mainstream. Instead of taking the mainstream as a given, it is approached as a subcultural construct used to highlight participants' distinct identities. The view of these authors is that, depending on who it is that we are investigating, we will find different views on what constitutes the core as well as the inauthentic mainstream. Consequently, the mainstream as well as the authentic becomes plural.

What is still missing in subcultural theory is how the mainstream is being subculturally constructed, as well as its relation to the subcultural ideal. In short, what consequences do plural mainstreams have for subcultural meaning and performances of style and objects? I will start by describing how the punks I studied defined the mainstream. Far from being merely a residual category, it was something that was constantly outlined and fought.

The Subcultural Sacred and Profane

It would be simple to argue that everything that is not punk is mainstream. Certainly my data would confirm this to some degree. My informants' definitions of the mainstream included everything from their peers to the capitalist system. But at the same time, there were plenty of things in their daily lives that were articulated as neither punk nor mainstream. They shopped for food, drinks, under-wear and books. They watched TV, ate, slept and went to the bathroom. Of course, at times these actions were highly charged in terms of the distinction from the mainstream. For vegan punks, for example, food was subculturally charged, yet even for them everything was not either punk or mainstream.

Durkheim (1915) argues that what is held as being the sacred is that which is set apart from the profane through prohibitions. The ideal is kept separated from that which threatens to pollute it and render it ordinary. Objects have no intrinsic meaning as either sacred or profane, but are made to objectify the collective representations of the sacred or as a sign of the polluting profane. Similarly, in my data, the binary subcultural/mainstream was constantly being worked as the meaning of the mainstream was disputed and reaffirmed, drawing boundaries between participants, actions and spaces. The only thing the punks I followed agreed upon regarding the mainstream was that it had to be fought and kept at bay. The regulations and prohibitions defining both the subculturally sacred and profane, however, differed significantly depending on who I asked.

I will begin by approaching these differences in terms of how the mainstream is positioned as either internal or external to the subcultural. I will refer to these as 'frameworks', as they are used by participants to order objects and actions (Goffman 1986). They are the subcultural background text of performances and validations; the subcultural patterns of meanings that precede these acts (Alexander 2004). Punks in Indonesia and Sweden both used these frameworks to authenticate objects and actions. Even though the objects and actions that were performed sometimes differed between Swedish and Indonesian punks, the frameworks that were used as the back-ground for these were similar. In some cities, there was a clear boundary between spaces dominated by either a convex or a concave framework, while in others they coexisted alongside each other, making it possible for participants to make use of both, depending on the situation. Hence, *these are not categories referring to punks or to objects*, but rather to the subcultural meanings made use of by punks, which enable and constrain the possible outcome of any performance that draws upon them.

A Convex Framework

The majority of the punks I studied in Indonesia and Sweden defined the mainstream as something concrete and direct, and as being outside of punk. It consisted of the people at your school or job, teachers, bosses, parents, the mass media, cops and so on. It was the ordinary society from which punks were set apart:

> I felt that it was me against my whole high school . . . I felt that all the others were losers, this may sound very punk but they were pawns in the game; they're going to school and then they're gonna get a job . . . I felt like I'm not a part of the ordinary, I felt that I don't have to be a part of the whole ordinary system, that's punk to me.
>
> *(Interview, Sweden 2008)*

> I don't want to be mainstream, I don't want to follow and consume what the TV tells me to, I don't want to be like that. I just want to be free.
>
> *(Interview, Indonesia 2004)*

The mainstream was 'the usual system'; ' going to school and getting a job'; being 'a pawn in the game'; passive followers who consumed what mass media told them to – summarized in the claim 'all the others were losers'. This as a *convex* framework, as it bends outwards: the boundary between the subcultural sacred and profane is specified and works through prohibitions and regulations regarding what is conceived of as *external* to the subculture:

> A: It feels like the lyrics mean so much more than just a regular song, you know. If I hear a song on the radio, let's say Pirelli's 'Hero', I cannot hear what the song is about, I cannot grasp it in the same way as I can with a punk song, as for example Rise Against. They have these really deep lyrics that make me wonder whether they mean this or that, I can grasp it, but Pirelli that's just pure shit.
>
> B: It's fake you know, she's standing there singing something someone else wrote.
>
> A: And that's what the mainstream is. And that's what separates us from them. 'Cause we go with our own lyrics, write what we want, we write what we want people to understand, right?
>
> B: Yeah.
>
> *(Interview, Sweden 2008)*

The mainstream as outlined above is equated to the fake, the dependent and the shallow. Further, it is positioned as outside of punk – in this case, radio and especially Charlotte Pirelli's song 'Hero' – the Swedish entry for the Eurovision Song Contest in 2008. This shallow mainstream is then contrasted with the depth of punk – here the American band Rise Against. The boundaries between the subcultural and the mainstream are worked in terms of articulating this fake mainstream as the ungraspable, 'regular' and 'just pure shit'. In contrast, the subcultural is set apart from this mainstream: 'we go with our own lyrics, write what we want'. Instead of being told what to do, the subcultural ideal becomes 'going your own way'.

A Concave Framework

The second framework of the mainstream among the punks I studied positioned the mainstream as being internal to punk. The subcultural sacred was to be protected from polluting forces *within* the subcultural boundaries rather than external to them. This framework, which I refer to as a *concave* framework as it bends inwards, highlighted neither mass media nor friends and family, but rather mindless punks who had turned the subcultural sacred into a commodity:

> The main reason [for not sporting Mohawks] is that we don't wanna be labelled as punks by everybody and thus become connected to those mainstream punks, we're tired of getting mixed up with people who have transformed symbolism into fashion.
>
> *(Interview, Indonesia 2005)*

> It's either you're on the surface layer and you know 'I live among punks, I listen to punk, I drink beer in the parks', but then as you go deeper, attending demonstrations against things, then you're getting closer to this culture of action, where it is not only about punk any more but about a whole life. You are taking stands against a whole system, and that can be scary to many.
>
> *(Interview, Sweden 2008)*

The binary subcultural/mainstream is here worked internally, separating between the dedicated and aware punks and the fashion-centred and hedonist punks who merely consume the subcultural instead of living it. This positioning of the mainstream was accordingly defined as punks selling out the scene, punks not caring, punks bringing drugs into the scene. Similarly, anti-capitalism, anti-racism and veganism were articulated and explained in relation to protecting the subcultural from the actions of mainstream punks. The mainstream was the meaningless and careless – that which failed to recognize the sanctity of the set-apart, and as such guidelines regarding actions and objects were drawn in relation to internal boundaries rather than external ones.

These extensions of the binary subcultural/mainstream through individual acts refer to working the boundaries between the set-apart and the polluting profane

(Lamont 2000). In doing this, the meaning of these individual acts is dependent on the frameworks of meanings within which they are performed. If validated by other participants, these acts work to extend these meanings to the performance (Alexander 2004). This fusion between the performance, the audience's validation of it and the framework is what mobilizes subcultural identities. The separation between the subcultural sacred and profane defines and structures what can be said and how it is said. To argue that actions and objects are subcultural is to say that they are based on, refer to and contribute to this collective understanding of a group identity. Consequently, enacting different frameworks means different extensions of meaning to actions and objects. In contrast to Thornton's (1996: 96) claim that the binary pair subculture/mainstream mainly refers to a means for subcultural participants to imagine their social world, I argue that this binary has real consequences for how and where the subcultural is performed.

Performances of Punk Within a Convex Framework

The mainstream within a convex framework is not only external to punk in the sense of the 'normal' and undifferentiated; it is also a mainstream that is encountered every day and everywhere. Thus the boundary between the mainstream and the subcultural is drawn publicly, as true punk is conceived of as standing out in the midst of this mainstream:

> Punk should be something that sticks out. And you will grow stronger as everyone else will pick at you. That's something all punks probably can agree on; we're all misfits.
>
> *(Interview, Sweden 2003)*

This comment validates difference by drawing on a definition of the mainstream as the ordinary mass: 'everyone else'. Further, this difference is extended to a personal emancipation – breaking free from the mainstream, 'sticking out'. This was by far the most common definition of punk in relation to an external mainstream. Punk was a means of realizing yourself, of living out a difference against a normative and restricting mainstream that surrounded the subcultural. Punk became a means of staying different from what participants perceived as an undifferentiated mass. As one Swedish punk put it, 'Punk is the absence of all rules, just fucking being who you really want'.

But these performances of objects and actions through the working of the subcultural/mainstream binary require the validation by other participants of both the performed object as well as the performer in relation to these background representations (Alexander 2004, 2010). Drawing from these patterns of meaning becomes 'an act of recognition' (Geertz 1973: 215) that involves recognizing the background text that surrounds the action, as well as being recognized by other participants for doing so.

Similarly, stylistic objects were related to the binaries subcultural/mainstream and freedom/complacency. Being recognized as looking different was crucial in the distinction from this external mainstream. This relation between personal freedom and being different worked to fuse what might otherwise be seen as opposite or contradictory logic – that is, constructing a conspicuous style at the same time as claiming to be true to oneself. Having tattoos, spiked hair, dreads, and studded and patched clothes was easy to validate in relation to personal freedom, as punks sporting these objects were simply expressing who they really were. To withhold from doing this would be to betray yourself, and as such be inauthentic. It would be to yield to an external mainstream.

Looking different was a symbolic representation of being punk, as the spatial boundary between the subcultural and the mainstream was constantly blurred. Positioning the mainstream as external had the inevitable consequence of constantly encountering this mainstream. The spatial dimension of this distinction refers to punk as being public: dressing punk in school, at work or in the street; showing your disgust with the external mainstream that shares the same space. Objects, actions and styles that were authenticated followed from this positioning. Accordingly, the *mise-en-scène* of these performances most often took place in public places such as city squares, parks and carparks. Shows, for example, were often held at spaces that were open to non-punks, such as bars, festivals and youth clubs. The conceived mainstream was invited only to be visually and verbally dismissed:

> Sofyan, Bambang and Akbar appeared on Hard Rock Radio yesterday. There was a show about punk featuring [a local punk band considered by these punks to have sold out]. Sofyan and the others were drunk and kept on interrupting and making fun of the hostess and the band . . . A couple of days before Bambang had told me that radio was mainstream, so I asked him if he was mainstream now as well. He answered, 'No, because we fucked them.'
>
> *(Interview, Indonesia 2005)*

The interaction with the mainstream is validated, as it clarifies the subcultural boundary in relation to that mainstream. It is the enactment of a drama in which the performer takes on the outside, resisting and reacting, aiming to maintain an image of authenticity and exclusivity in the encounter with an external mainstream.

The stress on individualism and freedom in punk is well documented (Lewin and Williams 2009; Muggleton 2000), and so is this meeting between punk and the mainstream (Baron 1989; Leblanc 1999; Lull 1987), yet this is never associated with the positioning of the mainstream. What is interesting here is not that a convex framework included the stress on personal freedom and being different, but rather how these were related to the positioning of the mainstream and worked to (re)produce the subcultural. As it was only in relation to what was seen as external to punk that its distinctive character was defined, the stress on a visual difference became crucial for working the boundary to the mainstream. This play between the subcultural and the mainstream, this public performance of subcultural adherence, worked to fuse the performance with the feeling of being different. It validated the distinction between the punks and the external mainstream surrounding it through a visual disassociation with the mainstream: being yourself and being different. Thus the border between the mainstream and the authentic was drawn symbolically as it was blurred spatially.

. . . and Within a Concave Framework

As we have seen, within a convex framework stylistic difference was validated as the positive side of the binaries depth/surface, freedom/complacency and action/passivity. Within a concave framework, on the other hand, such a performance did not fuse. Instead, conspicuous style was placed on the negative side of these binaries and refuted:

> As you might know, shows at that time were sponsored by multinational corporations, even McDonald's sponsored. I think me and B and the other people . . . we who had that kind of idealistic side of punk, felt like this is wrong, this is not how punk is supposed to be . . . I felt maybe we should gather people who actually believe in the DIY-ethos and you know and form a community-centered scene instead of a fashion-centred.
>
> *(Interview, Indonesia 2005)*

The distinction towards an external mainstream is here refuted as fake, shallow, dependent and passive. The mainstream is defined as the punks who sold out the scene, who invited the multinational corporations, and who care more about mindless consumerism. The stress on depth – referred to earlier as 'the idealistic side of punk', 'community-centred' and 'people who actually believe in the DIY-ethos', was the set-apart – that which had to be protected to counter the mindlessness that is seen as polluting the sacred.

Thus, whereas a performance of conspicuous style was easy to fuse within a convex framework, it failed within a concave one. To openly flaunt a punk identity, provoking and confronting passers-by was constantly invalidated. Instead, it was described as the inauthentic, a sign of the apolitical, shallow and ignorant punks. As style and action were performed to strengthen internal distinctions, there was no need for a public display of being punk; instead, performances were private and largely invisible to non-punks. The *mise-en-scène* of performances within a concave framework mostly occurred in private settings – at home, a political café, squats or at shows. Most of these places were shielded from the public. Shows were advertised internally, usually not even including the epithet 'punk' but rather euphemisms such as 'D-Beat Mayhem' and 'melodic HC'. Similarly, style was validated in terms of practical consequences as opposed to the discernible aesthetics of the commercial and mindless punks. As one Swedish punk commented on his dress:

'The ultimate thing would be that you looked like a hobo – you know, people wouldn't know what you were, but you would at least not be conceived of as caring about dress and appearance.' Hence, mohawks, bondage pants or highly visible tattoos were invalidated as being fake and unnatural, referred to as 'masquerade costumes'. On occasion, the same stylistic objects were employed in both contexts but with significant differences. Having dreads, for example, was performed and validated within a convex framework as being radical and different; within a concave framework it was validated as being natural: 'Having dreads is practical, you never have to wash your hair or comb it, you just cut in front so that you're able to see what you're doing' (Interview, Sweden 2007). This is not to say that either of these is a reason for having dreads. What is interesting is rather that the performance of style – as natural and practical, or as deviant and provocative – worked to validate the objects used in relation to either an external or internal mainstream.

As Mary Douglas (1984) notes, calling into being the sacred is introducing order to the otherwise formless and potentially dangerous, in this case, style. By specifying what the appropriate and the obvious way of interpreting this situation is – natural as opposed to style conscious – style becomes a symbolic representation of this naturalness rather than being dressed up. Further, what constitutes this mainstream is that which has to be dealt with. Whatever is beyond that is subculturally mean-ingless. For example, parents, mass media and non-punk peers were never associated with the mainstream within a concave framework. As the subcultural boundary to the mainstream was worked internally, participation was surrounded by regula-tions regarding how to behave in relation to other punks. As we saw above, being recognized as punk within a convex framework did not require much more than standing out from the mainstream and being different. Drawing from a concave framework, on the other hand, often included a narrative of development – of going beyond the shallow and stylistic to political action and seriousness.

Thus punks who were not recognized as political enough, or who were seen as being too focused on style, were rejected as being mainstream. In contrast to the convex definition of freedom as the absence of rules, performances within a concave instead stressed compliance with rules as a means to a higher goal. Shows often involved the bands and organizers reminding the audience of urgent polit-ical matters as well as how not to behave. Consequently, personal freedom became subordinate to collective and equal freedom, surrounded by prohibitions meant to secure this distinction. As one Indonesian punk pointed out, 'Everyone is welcome as long as they are into the DIY ethos and non-sexist, non-racist, non-homophobic and that's it.'

Conclusion

In this chapter, I have argued that subcultural objects and actions have no intrinsic meaning as subcultural; rather, they are made into symbolic representations of the binary subcultural/mainstream. As such, they can only be explained in reference to the representations of this binary and its extensions to include some objects and actions, while excluding others. Subcultural acts and objects are performed and validated within these frameworks. The emphasis in previous research on objects as either punk or mainstream hinders us from seeing that the extension of the binary subcultural/mainstream renders most objects open to (re)definition, as the same object can be defined differently depending on what framework is being used. What makes these objects punk are not some innate features but rather how they are used and validated to appear as such. To paraphrase Durkheim (1915), their subcultural character is therefore not real, but rather assumed.

This chapter has also pointed to the fact that both Swedish and Indonesian punks used these frameworks in similar ways and with similar consequences. Further, the focus on convex and concave frameworks has meant that subcultural differences have been assessed and explained without having to resort to either commitment or external structures such as class or socio-economic changes. This sets these categories apart from previous attempts to capture differences within the subcultural. The model of the convex and the concave is not equivalent to the old distinction of subculture and counter culture (Hall and Jefferson 1976) or the autonomous against the heteronymous pole (Bourdieu 1996; Moore 2007), as the focus is neither on production nor on the subcultural being dependent on external structures, but rather on the framing of the subcultural sacred and the positioning of the mainstream. It also breaks with the previous research on punk, which has explained differences in relation to commitment or years of involvement (Andes 1998; Fox 1987; Leblanc 1999) or in relation to time and societal changes (Moore 2004; Roberts and Moore 2009). Further, in contrast to previous research on mainstreams (Muggleton 2000; Thornton 1996), this model goes beyond merely viewing mainstreams as arbitrary by exploring the subcultural consequences that emerge when acknowledging the plurality of mainstreams in the context of punk. Hence the mainstream is far from a residual category; instead, it is an integral part of the subcultural. It is the contrariness between the sacred and the profane that makes this distinction meaningful. Through the prohibitions that surround the sacred, the subcultural takes a physical and concrete form that works to remind participants of these collective ideals (Douglas 1984). Whereas Leblanc (1999: 169) states that 'subcultures are embedded in mainstream culture', I would turn it around and suggest that the mainstream is embedded within the subcultural: it is given its meaning by the prohibitions that set it apart.

References

Alasuutari, P. (1995) *Researching Culture: qualitative method and cultural studies*, London: Sage.

Alexander, J.C. (2004) 'Cultural pragmatics: social performance between ritual and strategy', *Sociological Theory*, 22(4): 527–73.

——— (2010) *The Performance of Politics*, Oxford: Oxford University Press.

Andes, L. (1998) 'Growing up punk: meaning and commitment careers in a contemporary youth subculture', in J.S. Epstein (ed.), *Youth Culture: identity in a postmodern world*, Oxford: Blackwell.

Baron, S.W. (1989) 'The Canadian West Coast punk subculture: a field study', *Canadian Journal of Sociology*, 14(3): 289–316.

Bourdieu, P. (1996) *Rules of Art: genesis and structure of the literary field*, Oxford: John Wiley and Sons.

Douglas, M. (1984) *Purity and Danger: an analysis of the concepts of pollution and taboo*, London: Ark.

Durkheim, É. (1915) *The Elementary Forms of Religious Life*, London: George Allen & Unwin.

Fox, K.J. (1987) 'Real punks and pretenders: the social organization of a counterculture', *Journal of Contemporary Ethnography*, 16: 344–70.

Geertz, C. (1973) *The Interpretation of Culture*, New York: Basic Books.

Goffman, E. (1986) *Frame Analysis: an essay on the organization of experience*, Boston: Northeastern University Press.

Haenfler, R. (2004) 'Rethinking subcultural resistance: core values of the straight edge movement', *Journal of Contemporary Ethnography* 33(4): 406–36.

Hall, S. and Jefferson, T. (1976) *Resistance Through Rituals: youth subcultures in post-war Britain*, London: Routledge.

Hannerz, E. (Forthcoming) 'Plural authenticities, plural mainstreams', PhD thesis, Department of Sociology, Uppsala University.

Hebdige, D. (1979) *Subculture: the meaning of style*, London: Routledge.

Hodkinson, P. (2002) *Goth: identity, style and subculture*, Oxford: Berg.

Lamont, M. (2000) *The Dignity of Working Men*, Cambridge, MA: Harvard University Press.

Leblanc, L. (1999). *Pretty in Punk: girls' gender resistance in a boys' subculture*, New Brunswick, NH: Rutgers University Press.

Lewin, P. and Williams, P.J. (2009) 'The ideology and practice of authenticity in punk subculture', in P. Vannini and P.J. Williams (eds), *Authenticity in Culture, Self, and Society*, Farnham: Ashgate.

Lull, J. (1987) 'Thrashing in the pit: an ethnography of San Francisco punk subculture', in T.R. Lindlof (ed.), *Natural Audiences*, Norwood: Ablex.

Moore, R. (2004) 'Postmodernism and punk subculture: cultures of authenticity and destruction', *The Communication Review*, 7: 305–27.

—— (2007) 'Friends don't let friends listen to corporate rock: punk as a field of cultural production', *Journal of Contemporary Ethnography*, 36(4): 438–74.

Muggleton, D. (2000) *Inside Subculture: the postmodern meaning of style*, Oxford: Berg.

Nash, J.E. (1980) 'Lying about running: the function of talk in a scene', *Qualitative Sociology*, 3(2): 83–99.

Roberts, M. and Moore, R. (2009) 'Peace punks and punks against racism: resource mobilization and frame construction in the punk movement', *Music and Arts in Action*, 2(1): 21–36.

Thornton, S. (1996) *Club Cultures: music, media and subcultural capital*, Middletown, CT: Wesleyan University Press.

Williams, P.J. (2003) 'The straightedge subculture on the internet', *Media International Australia*, 107: 61–74.

—— (2006) 'Authentic identities: straightedge subculture, music, and the internet', *Journal of Contemporary Ethnography*, 35: 173–200.

6

KILL THE STATIC

Temporality and Change in the Hip-Hop Mainstream (and Its 'Other')

Murray Forman

Obama's iPod

US President Barack Obama listens to Jay-Z. He demonstrated this on the 2008 campaign trail with a knowing gesture, wiping 'Dirt Off His Shoulder' to the crowd's amusement. The President of the United States also admits to enjoying Kanye West, Ludacris and Nas on his iPod; he has officially hosted the Chicago MC Common at the White House; and he demonstrates at least a passing familiarity with Lil Wayne, a fact he revealed on the 100th anniversary of the National Association for the Advancement of Colored People (NAACP) in 2009 when he exclaimed, 'They might think they've got a pretty good jump shot or a pretty good flow, but [they] can't all aspire to be LeBron [James] or Lil Wayne.'

While there is much that is unique about Obama's ascendancy as a black man in the United States, his reputation as a knowledgeable hip-hop fan is also significant. Coming of age in the hip-hop era (he was 18 years old in 1979 when the Sugarhill Gang's 'Rapper's Delight' was released), Obama is well attuned to rap music's lyrics and rhythms, and to the politics and cultural issues that inform hip-hop. This not only associates the nation's Commander in Chief with the tastes of the country's black, Latino and youth constituencies (creating a fascinating flash-point for Republican ire as they castigate the President for his musical choices as much as his policies); it also throws new light on rap and hip-hop. While it might be a stretch to claim Obama as the first hip-hop president, there is no denying that he is the first US President to openly declare his affinities for the music and the culture from which it emanates, and vice versa. Within the contexts of hip-hop culture and media, when the President is name checking artists and feeling their flow, it is a mainstream moment.

By opening with this particular scenario, I want to offer a perspective on the contemporary status of rap and hip-hop in terms of general social awareness and mainstream popular culture. I remain aware, however, that the mainstream is not a singular, uniform concept against which alternatives are easily defined, as Sarah Thornton (1996) has convincingly argued; rather, it is an unwieldy construct conceived within specific historical junctures across the social spectrum. How norms or standards are defined (and ultimately enforced) will inevitably vary across differing sectors at different moments.

In what follows, I address hip-hop and the mainstream in relation to its 'other', focusing on notions of time, change and age that are common to discussions of hip-hop lore and that are increasingly prevalent in rap lyrics, YouTube and Facebook 'battles' (as well as in hip-hop studies). It is my contention that to fully understand the hip-hop mainstream – and its 'other' – it is crucial to include an analysis of the arc of time and the evolution of cultural forms and practices.

The Hip-Hop Mainstream: Neither Monolithic Nor Unchallenged

When describing mainstream aesthetics or practices, there is an implicit sense of a cultural norm attached to the term. The mainstream is inscribed in relation to general, common standards that contrast with alternative expressions forged within a radical milieu (cultural or political), marginal creative endeavours that are challenging, progressive or aligned with an artistic avant-garde, or work that is dismissed for being deemed in poor taste and offensive to standards of propriety. The texts or cultural artefacts associated with the mainstream are ritually engaged, and tend to reflect and reinforce the culturally dominant forms (which, despite this singular term, actually comprise an array of apparatuses that cohere in multiple sites and are extended via multiple practices). Their relative ease of access and ubiquity – in commercial contexts or not – position them within the domain of everyday life as well as within that of conflict and political contestation.

Emphasizing media rituals and social patterns, Nick Couldry (2008: 168) explains that, 'Rituals work not so much through the articulation, even implicitly, of beliefs, as through the organization and formalization of behaviour that, by encoding categories of thought, naturalize them.' For Couldry, 'everyday actions oriented towards media' (169) are of considerable importance, inviting close analysis of the ways in which individuals navigate the mediascape, enacting common and entirely mundane activities and traversing banal conditions while shifting between different media, moments and events. Traditional notions of mainstream authority and influence are, of course, revised with the increased mediatization of everyday experience and the emergence of somewhat new media routines (such as impulse-checking one's Facebook page or texting). Whereas the pursuit of obscure music and other unconventional cultural materials was traditionally restricted and comparatively difficult, contemporary audiences engage with popular culture through many more interfaces that facilitate and ease connections with a variety of artists and scenes, providing new means for circumventing the mainstream as much or as little as one wishes.

Within such ritualized practices, individuals still generally weave between media content and events in quite undisciplined ways, swinging between both popular and esoteric material according to taste preferences and affective intensities. Indeed, for all of its popular influence and ubiquity, the mainstream may not hold much sway at all for some people, registering as only a very partial factor in their daily media practices and experiences. Keith Negus (1999: 359) acknowledges an interwoven, non-binding relationship when he states that 'industry produces culture and culture produces an industry'. He explains that industry produces culture in the ways in which it sets up 'structures and organization and working practices to produce identifiable products and "intellectual properties"' (359). Conversely, culture produces an industry in the sense that 'production does not take place simply "within" a corporate environment created according to the requirements of capitalist production but in relation to broader cultural formations and practices that may not be directly within the control or understanding of the company' (359–60).

With this in mind, it is appropriate to reflect on the mainstream's 'other', for if the 'corporate environment' of the mainstream comprises the cultural dominant, what lies below? In hip-hop, this 'other' generally is referred to as 'the underground'. The construct of the underground provides a rich and pertinent symbolic spatiality that simultaneously acknowledges the mainstream's cultural dominance and the submerged marginality of non-mainstream works – a creative and cultural demi-monde. The term implicitly references multiple aspects of what might be termed *underground-ness* that can be situated within a historical frame. It has deep resonance in African American cultural history, notably in reference to the 'underground railroad' under slavery and its conduits of escape and liberation that were often obliquely encoded in songs such as 'Follow the Drinking Gourd'. In the African American arts and culture (i.e. the Black Arts Movement) and Black Power politics of the 1960s and 1970s, the term 'underground' conveys a submerged creativity fused with radical politics of resistance encompassing struggle against cultural marginalization, systemic racism and class oppression, and coordinated state violence. Within this frame of black power politics, the underground also conjures images of space where strategies of resistance were planned and mobilization was enacted, yet it was also where revolutionaries and insurrectionists retreated upon threat of incarceration or death.

Hip-hop's provocations have varied over the period of its existence. In the earliest stages, rap music, b-boying and graffiti were regarded as disruptions associated with a boiling youth crisis (exacerbated by deep and painful urban malaise in New York) due to their capacity to appropriate and transform public spaces, upending mainstream perceptions of proper decorum and undermining the rules and regulations pertaining to access and use of public spaces (Rose 1994; Forman 2002). As hip-hop's diverse practices converged, the New York subway system constituted a crucial aspect of urban mobility, a site for creative expression as well as a zone of sociability and communal dialogue. Such is the legacy of the underground.

Remaining attentive to its lived realities (that is, real people who inhabit real places), Emery Petchauer (2012: 30) defines the underground as 'an adjective to describe a do-it-yourself, grassroots brand of multicultural hip-hop that centers active participation in hip-hop elements, blurs the line between performer and audience, and often demonstrates some critical consciousness against its dichotomous counterpart, the commercial mainstream'. Through long and widespread use, 'underground hip-hop' (together with accompanying titles such as 'conscious rap') has attained a sub-generic status mainly among music practitioners and audiences (and, to some extent, industry representatives), addressing content/themes and meanings/values that differ significantly from those associated with the commercial, industrial sectors.[1]

In the particular contexts of black cultural politics and expressivity, underground hip-hop resembles an oppositional force whereby artists and small-scale creative enterprises offer a means of challenging representational violence (such as media stereotyping) while developing new forms of communication of black experience and consciousness that are often absent in mainstream media. Since the 1980s, even as corporate commodification of black music has expanded, artists and independent entrepreneurs have strived to ensure the continuation of hip-hop as a vital facet of black culture and political articulation.

It is customary to approach the issue of the active industrial processes of hip-hop's mainstreaming via analyses of authenticity claims (centred on notions of 'the real') and the nexus of meaning, value and legitimacy. The distinctions between mainstream and the underground are based on both material and symbolic characteristics, and the contours of such distinctions fall within a general consensus forged among artists, audiences and industry gatekeepers (record label executives, artist agents, producers, TV producers, radio program directors and DJs, independent entrepreneurs, and so on). Many purists will also cite distinctions between rap and hip-hop music, suggesting that *rap* is of a slightly lower order associated with commercial pop-oriented music of the mainstream whereas *hip-hop* is regarded as the legitimate expression of the culture, fulfilling various aesthetic, lyrical and performance criteria or expectations.[2]

Though the final word has surely not yet been written on the relationship between the standardized practices and aesthetics of the mainstream and hip-hop authenticity, this is an avenue that has been well traversed by a host of astute scholars and cultural critics. While values of hip-hop authenticity frequently cohere within place-based associations of the 'hood (Forman 2002) and as a form of cultural capital expressed within black cultural identities (Clay 2003), most critical hip-hop scholars remain cognizant that 'the real' is a discursive and symbolic construct, and that there is consequently a great deal of selectivity involved in summoning such forms of authenticating experience. As Imani Perry

(2004: 87) explains, 'the frequent calls in the hip-hop community to keep it real not only require the maintenance of an authentic black urban identity; they also constitute a theoretical space that functions as a living testimony to African American experience ... Being "real" is a call to authenticity that becomes a political act.'

These interpretations position 'the real' between the material conditions of lived experience and the symbolic spaces within which such experiences are rendered meaningful; this necessarily includes the terrains of popular culture, encompassing the regime of media representation as well as media narrative. Within the frame of authenticity, the stakes are indisputably high for hip-hop-identified youth, and whether or not one is believed to be 'keeping it real' among a peer group could have serious consequences indeed.

Up to this point, I have been careful not to paint the hip-hop mainstream as a construct with a rigid and negative reputation; popularity and audience appeal, corporate involvement, media amplification, commercial success, artistic integrity, 'hood status, and progressive politics are not necessarily at odds in hip-hop, with interesting convergences and contradictions occurring over many years.[3] The underground may be construed as a specialized domain of hip-hop skill that is characterized further by an adherence to values and principles that distinguish 'true' artists from mainstream rappers (thus winning them accolades and audiences), yet underground MCs saddled with the 'conscious' label frequently disown it, as it carries considerable symbolic baggage, segregating them within the larger hip-hop scene (Dyson 2007).

Mainstream Encroachment and the Hip-Hop Battle Stance

What are we to make of the processes by which cultural objects that are – or once were considered to be – radical (for example, in terms of aesthetics, lyrical content, performance, style or the culture or scene from which the art emanates) acquire greater acceptance over time? How do we account for the ways in which public familiarity and acceptance gradually nudge marginal phenomena closer to what we conceive as mainstream status? This is not an easy matter of inexorable, deliberate incorporation or strategic assimilation by powerful forces; underground or alternative music and culture are not simply absorbed into an opposite and antagonistic entity called 'the mainstream'. Indeed, for hip-hop music, the reverse has also been true, as DJs and producers have long appropriated mainstream pop hits as the bed tracks for hip-hop recordings.

Kembrew McLeod (1999: 134) writes that 'recurring invocations of authenticity are not isolated to hip-hop culture. They also take place in other cultures that, like hip-hop, are threatened with assimilation by a larger mainstream culture.' McLeod's specific focus is on a defensive or preservationist stance that accompanied hip-hop's wider successes, analyzing the discursive articulations of 'the real' in hip-hop while presenting a model for understanding the patterns through which authenticity is defined. As he suggests, 'the real' acquired urgency in the 1990s as a response to the sudden explosion of mainstream corporate involvement in hip-hop and the 'contradictory position that other subcultural groups confronted with widespread acceptance previously faced: being "inside" a mainstream culture they had, in part, defined themselves as being against' (136).

KRS-One exemplifies an anti-mainstream protectionist instinct, intensely articulating aspects of hip-hop's history, values and guiding principles through his lyrics (for example, 'Represent the Real Hip Hop' with Das EFX; '(The Real Hip-Hop is) Ova Here' Pts I and II) and numerous public speaking engagements. His own strengths as an artist lie in his wily lyricism and his reputation as a fierce battle MC (something that is reinforced by a booming voice) – skills that are highly valued among the hip-hop cognoscenti and that bestow him with a degree of authority within hip-hop circles. With the moniker 'The Teacher', he offers spirited lessons about hip-hop's emergence, validating key transitional moments and valorizing the pioneering artists whose influence on the culture is deemed most important, while denouncing hip-hop's sharp commercial turn and mainstream tendencies since the mid-1990s. As reflected on the cover of his influential 1988 release *Boogie Down Productions: By All Means Necessary* (the title of which resonates with a Malcolm X quote about revolutionary insurrection and on which he adopts a pose looking out a window while holding an Uzi pistol, mirroring the mid-1960s iconic image of Malcolm X holding an M1 carbine rifle), KRS-One aligns himself, and by extension hip-hop culture, with a politics of resistance that is unbending and incendiary within the mainstream system of values.

Among his grievances, KRS-One is critical of casual rap fans and indifferent artists who fail to 'do the knowledge' – an expression that addresses one's effort to learn the details about hip-hop's formation and trajectory, and to locate the culture within a broader frame of black culture and history. For him, a failure to 'do the knowledge' obscures an individual's capacity to connect with deeper values that hip-hop can convey, leaving one without the proper information to differentiate between 'real hip-hop' and mainstream rap. The mainstream does not readily or regularly connect with the 'real' or 'underground' hip-hop that has the greatest legitimacy in KRS-One's view; this makes it necessary for individuals to exert additional effort in order to locate and then comprehend hip-hop to the fullest capacity. Ultimately, he is calling for people to reinforce their cultural capital, partly as an authenticating tactic so that they are ideally enabled to evaluate hip-hop in historical terms as well as assessing the distinctions across the spectrum of contemporary hip-hop creativity. KRS-One's promotion of hip-hop knowledge presents a rationale for fans to step away from mainstream rap and corporate commercial product (which Thornton explains is frequently associated with a feminized attitude or sensibility), returning to something that might be understood as being somehow more true, *harder* and perhaps more manly.

Displaying a perspective that is widely shared in hip-hop circles, KRS-One suggests that the mainstream forces of capital have grievously compromised hip-hop by imposing a restricted range of representational and communicative options. This is accompanied by a critique of commercial self-interest among artists and entrepreneurs that has ostensibly eroded hip-hop's potential as a change agent and a means of genuine cultural expression. Identifying narrow industry predilections for established forms with proven market success, Yvonne Bynoe summarizes this perspective:

> What the music industry has done through rap music is to frame the 'authentic' Black American not as a complex, educated or even creative individual, but as a 'real nigga' who has ducked bullets, worked a triple beam, and done at least one bid in prison.
>
> *(2004: 149)*

Like many other underground artists, KRS-One argues for a broadened range of representation, which includes identities that accurately reflect black community and experience. He presents the view that the mainstreaming of hip-hop is a form of cultural assault warranting firm opposition in a classic hip-hop battle stance, protecting the culture from predatory corporate incursion while castigating commercially successful upstarts (such as the St Louis rapper Nelly with whom he has publicly exchanged barbs) for their cultural bankruptcy.

KRS-One subsequently assumes responsibility for hip-hop surveillance and monitoring, occupying the role of self-appointed cultural 'keeper' and manifesting his authority within the Temple of Hip Hop, 'an international ministry, archive, school and society (M.A.S.S.) movement that teaches Hip Hop beyond entertainment' that he founded in 1996 (see www.templeofhiphop.org 2011). While he is commonly described as one of the most steadfast proponents of politically engaged message rap, KRS-One's preservationist discourse ultimately reflects a tacit conservatism and an essentialist bent as he idealizes an earlier period when hip-hop was supposedly more pure, more creative and more firmly rooted in black arts and culture.

Past/Tense: Hip-Hop Origin Tales and the Mainstream

Locating hip-hop's emergence within a specific socio-political environment (encompassing changing affiliations and cultural sensibilities in the shift from the 'soul' generation to the 'post-soul' generation), Mark Anthony Neal (2002: 11) acknowledges the relationship between temporality and transformation: 'While hip-hop publicly came out in the mid-1970s plugged into inner-city lampposts and youth culture and was later embraced for its postmodern sensibilities by "avant-garde" critics, by the end of the century it was the best-selling genre of popular music.'[4] For Neal, the evolutionary arc from informal social sites of production to commercialized mainstream consumption can also be regarded as recalibration of power – not necessarily a dilution of hip-hop authenticity, but a shift 'from margins to center' (11) that refutes notions (such as those held by KRS-One) that hip-hop's mainstreaming is altogether negative.

Michael Bérubé (1992) elaborates on this phenomenon, asserting that:

> the rhetoric of marginality can be a powerful enabling device, even though marginality itself is synonymous with disempowerment: to claim to speak from the margin is paradoxically to claim to speak from the position of authority, and to describe a margin is to describe an authoritative challenge to hegemony . . . Margins are real, but they are always relational.
>
> *(16–17)*

Seen in this light, hip-hop's industrial rise and gradual popular acceptance potentially mitigates the marginalization of a powerful form of black cultural expression. Despite the attendant risks of its popular appeal and commercial successes, rap music's mainstream status ensures that black voices are more distinctly audible within the broader social dialogues and in multiple public venues, even if their subordinate status is not fully evacuated.

As Neal's account indicates, however, even with hip-hop's 35-year trend towards mainstream status, the positive values invested in the original scene – the street, the hijacked electricity, the free-spirited black and brown youths – remain palpable. Indeed, creative expressions of the past are frequently sustained in multiple ways (including via memory and lore) as a residual within the contemporary mainstream. 'Back in the day' has consequently evolved as a standard phrase for addressing hip-hop in retrospect, discursively isolating its emergence within a non-mainstream ideal in a manner that may be historically accurate or emotionally reverential, recalling the thrill of an initial emergent moment while nostalgically fetishizing the past. In each mode, hip-hop's origins are invested with an array of symbolic values that are taken up and debated, contested, defended and quite literally fought over.

Notwithstanding the occasional romanticized notion of hip-hop's origins in the rough and tumble urban locus (which is, in such tales, an important factor in distinguishing an anti-mainstream sensibility that valorizes the 'underground' at the nexus of race, class and locale), such reflections illustrate that hip-hop was unambiguously public early in its formation, and thus popular in the sense that it encompassed collective politics, experiences and pleasures that were entirely within the ambit of the mainstream. The 'mean streets' and city byways from which hip-hop emerged were also traversed by mothers and fathers, grannies and granddads, and by children who grew up with the sonics of soul, funk, R&B, rock, pop, reggae, salsa, disco and eventually hip-hop inflecting their local environment. This is to say that the cultural crucible within which hip-hop was forged was at once the product of a dynamic and evolving African American and Latino youth culture at the margins *and* the quotidian rhythms of established neighbourhoods and their citizens. Put another way, hip-hop was born of conditions that were substantially informed by mainstream attitudes and practices.

A crucial facet of hip-hop's 'creation myth' involves a party on 11 August 1973 in the recreation room at 1520 Sedgwick Avenue, an innocuous apartment building in the Bronx.[5] While it proved to be an auspicious event, it was at the time a relatively standard gathering of teenagers displaying a DIY approach to their own leisure. Hip-hop's various creative forms had not fully congealed at this point, yet the process of normalization took hold surprisingly quickly, linked to myriad routine experiences of community existence. Testimonials, news reports and photographic evidence confirm that by the late 1970s and early 1980s one simply could not walk the streets of the Bronx (and, quite soon afterwards, Harlem and Brooklyn as well) without encountering hip-hop's expressive forms, sounds and style; although hip-hop was not yet part of a wider national conversation, it was already a regular facet of black teen leisure practices in New York.

Contemporary laments for an organic, pre-commercial moment in hip-hop's evolution notwithstanding, hip-hop was unambiguously commercial from the start (as the handwritten flyer for the aforementioned Sedgwick Avenue party hosted by the Campbell siblings indicates). The free public 'jams' in public parks and on the streets that are so fundamental to hip-hop lore were soon augmented by DJ gigs (privately hosted or booked by established club promoters) with admission fees; these latter club events generally included at least a modicum of marketing and promotion, security, quality sound systems and other features that conformed to the standards of a professional mainstream music event. While the purist argument seeks to delimit this fact, negating the taint of commercialism, the argument can also be made that these rudimentary professional impulses more quickly established the foundations for a sustainable set of practices within a wider context of art, culture, leisure and commerce.

In many of these origin tales, there is a notable discourse of innocence and discovery as hip-hop's early innovators moved between localized family dwellings, public spaces and commercial outlets, gradually constructing an encompassing network of like-minded individuals with shared tastes, displaying what Jeff Chang (2005: 85) refers to as 'a new logic – the circumference of a worldview'. As hip-hop developed its own inherent patterns, its core creative minds subsequently encountered other established systems and structures in New York's downtown art world and in the entertainment industries, suggesting a simultaneous convergence across artistic underground and commercial mainstream contexts (Hoban 1999; Forman 2002; Chang 2005). Late-1970s avant-garde art and graffiti art, punk and post-punk music and rap music, modern dance and break dancing collided, in some instances leading to creative cross-pollination and collaboration. Together, these intersecting means of innovative expression attracted the attention of key patrons and cultural influencers, including mainstream media critics, ultimately reaching new audiences and the general public as the words, beats and images circulated outwards. In this frame, as an example of hip-hop's early mainstream status, it is entirely significant that b-boys were featured prominently on the world stage at the closing ceremonies of the 1984 Olympics in Los Angeles or that The New York City Breakers performed for President Ronald Reagan in 1984 and 1985.

Universities and colleges were – and remain – key locales in the establishment of a hip-hop underground and in the processes of mainstreaming; hip-hop and rap music's connections to academia are deep and enduring. In the late 1970s, City College of New York student Russell Simmons immersed himself in the burgeoning hip-hop scene, navigating between his college and the clubs where hip-hop was still a relatively new phenomenon as he initiated his Rush Management Company (Simmons 2001). Simmons' eventual business partner Rick Rubin famously started the rap record label Def Jam in his New York University dormitory room in 1984 (Simmons 2001; Gueraseva 2005) and in 1988 David Mays and Jon Shecter produced a photocopied newsletter called *The Source* (which is still published as a glossy magazine under the heading 'the bible of hip-hop music, culture and politics') while living in their ivy-covered dormitory at Harvard University. Chuck D, the stentorian voice of Public Enemy, also had college ties, blasting hip-hop as a campus/community radio DJ at Long Island's Adelphi University, where he met his future producer and Bomb Squad collaborator Hank Shocklee.

These early affiliations between hip-hop and campus life are noteworthy since they challenge the oft-cited divisions between the 'the streets' as a locus of authenticity and the comparatively mainstream values associated with academia's 'ivory tower'. Indeed, today campus radio playlists diverge sharply from those of larger and more powerful commercial stations that promote standard mainstream rap and R&B, with college outlets occupying a legally mandated complementary role. They tend to feature recordings with a much more explicit political or 'conscious' lyrical content, as well as profiling local artists whose access to mainstream media is severely restricted. Similarly, university and college campuses are crucial tour stops for underground and politically oriented hip-hop artists, as student clubs and various campus organizations book them for orientation events, end-of-year celebrations and for symposia or cultural events such as those associated with February's Black History Month.

Conclusion: Generational Dissonance and the Mainstream

As the preceding emphasis on temporality and transformation indicates, age comprises a key site for the negotiation of meaning and value in hip-hop, since the contours of the mainstream are not precisely the same among youths today as they were among their parents' generation. Acknowledging aesthetic and lyrical characteristics that inform distinctions between mainstream and underground hip-hop, Anthony Kwame Harrison describes audience partiality as a significant factor:

> [M]any longtime hip hop followers – scorned by the thought of 'their music' going mainstream – sensed the invisible hands of Music Industry image crafters at work and were thus primed to celebrate competing versions of hip hop authenticity, particularly those which to a certain extent harkened back to an earlier hip hop era. In this respect, the development of a distinct underground hip hop subgenre was a DIY response to the unsatiated demands of many one-time ardent hip hop consumers.
>
> *(Harrison 2009: 30)*

While Harrison's project is concerned primarily with issues of race, culture and identity (within a specific region) and the evolution of an underground hip-hop scene, the temporality that he cites is highly pertinent to a discussion of the mainstream/underground divisions. Along with the reference to an enduring audience formation – 'longtime followers' – and their identification with 'an earlier hip-hop era', he isolates several temporal markers that indicate a break of sorts, suggesting that by 2000 underground hip-hop 'was thoroughly distinct from its mainstream counterpart' (31).

Aesthetic preferences, modes of production and reception, and industrial patterns have changed substantially over hip-hop's roughly 35-year history, and the ways in which it is perceived or understood are distinctly marked by generational variations. The evidence of this gap is everywhere – for example, the November 2011 issue of *XXL* magazine features an interview titled 'Hey Young World' between Tyler the Creator (the 20-year-old founder of the rap act Odd Future) and Nas, who – celebrating the twentieth anniversary of his recording breakout – is described as an 'elderly spokesman', and mainstream music magazines tout the age angle with headlines such as 'The Changing Face of Hip-Hop' (*Spin*, December 2011) or 'Coming of Age' (*The Source*, March 2012). While the new breed of hip-hop artists is profiled widely, on 8 February 2012, Jon Caramanica of the *New York Times* reviewed hip-hop veteran Jay-Z's charity concerts at Carnegie Hall, a bastion of US mainstream musical achievement, with photos portraying the MC sartorially bedecked in a white dinner jacket with a diamond Cartier lapel pin, accompanied onstage by a string orchestra.

The sense of hip-hop's socio-political relevance (as a medium for the articulation of social ills and an expressive form employed in the contexts of political struggle) also differs according to generational sensibilities. Whereas Bakari Kitwana (2002) and Todd Boyd (2003) noted generational distinctions between the civil rights generation and the hip-hop generation, M.K. Asante, Jr (2008) subsequently introduced the designation 'post-hip-hop generation' in his analysis of inter-hip-hop dissonance. These more recent classifications reveal that, while there may be generally shared values within the general hip-hop culture, the political and cultural priorities among primarily black and Latino urban youths frequently diverge from older/adult 'hip-hop heads', as do the socio-political discourses, strategies and ideals that are enunciated in and through hip-hop's creative expressivity. The development of contemporary responses to localized crises that inordinately impact young citizens (such as failures in the education system, police brutality and racial profiling, criminal justice policies, bleak employment options, gang and street violence, and so on) further exacerbates the divide between younger hip-hop heads and adults who seem incapable of understanding the urgency of their condition.

Adults – especially those 45 years of age and older (some of whom are parents, and some of whom are already grandparents) – who recall hip-hop's formative stages extol their insider knowledge about hip-hop's gradual gravitation from marginal to mainstream status. They witnessed first hand the ways that hip-hop communities adjusted to its successes and negotiated threatening cultural antagonisms (Fricke and Ahearn 2002). They mobilize the term 'Golden Age' to identify one of hip-hop's more productive and creative phases between approximately 1987 and 1994, discursively constructing an aesthetic ideal when the talent was ostensibly richer, the scene more supportive (and safer), the aesthetic range more diversified, and a sense of cohesiveness more pronounced. Younger hip-hop artists and aficionados are, by extension, discursively defined as being comparatively lacking in talent and cohesiveness and, as a result, are deemed to be lesser.

Still, for many younger hip-hop audience members and artists, hip-hop's evolution as a series of artistic practices is largely irrelevant. And why wouldn't it be? For them, invocations to 'know the culture' or 'respect the architects' represent an appeal to backward perspectives that inordinately value the innovations of earlier artists – the pioneers, founding fathers, veterans or OGs (original gangstas) of hip-hop – while diminishing the potentials of today's young artists. The once radical aesthetics, discourses, performances or styles that so troubled the social waters a decade or two earlier are now well known across the general social spectrum, safely ensconced within mainstream sensibilities for most youths; as the 22-year-old MC Tyga explained on the eve of his debut solo album release, 'Most of my fans are from 12 to 25. About 75% are that high school kid fan base' (Brown 2012: 57). For hip-hop youth, the disapproving finger-wagging of an older hip-hop generation is not well received; when rap veteran Ice-T famously berated the teenage internet sensation Soulja Boy Tellum, preposterously suggesting that he 'single handedly killed hip-hop', the young rapper responded in typical fashion – via YouTube – with a barrage of hilarious age-based disses, describing Ice-T as an irrelevant anachronism 'born before the internet', 'old as fuck', who should quit the rap game.

Among a younger cohort, the negative tinge of judgemental nostalgia underrates contemporary creativity and under-values the inevitable aesthetic and lyrical shifts that define contemporary hip-hop, creating a sharp schism of taste and animosity across the generations. The mainstream is the purview of older, established artists, and among many younger MCs, DJs and producers who revel in their own brand of provocation and social irreverence, the response is 'they can have it'.

Notes

1 Anthony Kwame Harrison (2009) adds a further nuance with the term 'commercial underground', referring to somewhat successful 'underground' artists and a 'stratum in which relatively affluent, mostly white audiences predominate' (10). *Spin* magazine also offers a temporal demarcation between 'the industry' and 'the new underground' in its December 2011 issue.
2 KRS-One is commonly cited as the source for the clarifying statement, 'rap is something you do; hip-hop is something you live'.
3 For instance, Public Enemy, one of hip-hop's more iconic acts, successfully navigated the line between art and commerce and between progressive politics and market appeal, as do contemporary artists such as Common or Yasiin Bey (Mos Def).
4 Importantly, Neal (2002) completes this idea by distinguishing the diverse composition of hip-hop audiences, noting that the successes were 'in large part because of its relevance to the lived experience, both real and imagined, of white and Asian youth' (11).
5 The party was conceived by a teenager named Cindy Campbell. It was billed as a 'back to school jam', and the DJ was Campbell's teen brother Clive, whose DJ moniker was 'Kool Herc'. He is generally acknowledged as hip-hop's first/founding DJ.

References

Asante, M.K. Jr (2008) *It's Bigger Than Hip Hop: the rise of the post-hip-hop generation*, New York: St Martin's Press.

Bérubé, M. (1992) *Marginal Forces/Cultural Centers: Tolson, Pynchon, and the politics of the canon*, Ithaca, NY: Cornell University Press.

Boyd, T. (2003) *The New H.N.I.C.: the death of civil rights and the reign of hip-hop*, New York: New York University Press.

Brown, C. (2012) 'Into the wild', *The Source*, March: 57.

Bynoe, Y. (2004) *Stand and Deliver: political activism, leadership, and hip hop culture*, New York: Soft Skull Press.

Chang, J. (2005) *Can't Stop, Won't Stop: a history of the hip-hop generation*, New York: St Martin's Press.

Clay, A. (2003) 'Keepin' it real: black youth, hip-hop culture, and black identity', *American Behavioral Scientist*, 46(10): 1346–58.

Couldry, N. (2008) 'Form and power in an age of continuous spectacle', in D. Hesmondhalgh and J. Toynbee (eds), *Media and Social Theory*, New York: Routledge.

Dyson, M.E. (2007) *Know What I Mean?: reflections on hip hop*, New York: Basic Civitas.

Forman, M. (2002) *The 'Hood Comes First: race, space and place in rap and hip-hop*, Middletown, CT: Wesleyan University Press.

Fricke, J. and Ahearn, C. (eds) (2002) *Yes Yes Y'All: oral history of hip-hop's first decade*, Cambridge, MA: Da Capo Press.

Gueraseva, S. (2005) *Def Jam, Inc.: Russell Simmons, Rick Rubin, and the extraordinary story of the world's most influential hip-hop label*, New York: One World.

Harrison, A.K. (2009) *Hip Hop Underground: the integrity and ethics of racial identification*, Philadelphia, PA: Temple University Press.

Hoban, P. (1999) *Basquiat: a quick killing in art*, New York: Penguin.

Kitwana, B. (2002) *The Hip Hop Generation: young blacks and the crisis in African-American culture*, New York: Basic Civitas.

McLeod, K. (1999) 'Authenticity within hip-hop and other cultures threatened with assimilation', *Journal of Communication*, 49(4): 134–50.

Neal, M.A. (2002) *Soul Babies: black popular culture and the post-soul aesthetic*, New York: Routledge.

Negus, K. (1999) *Music Genres and Corporate Cultures*, New York: Routledge.

Perry, I. (2004) *Prophets of the Hood: politics and poetics in hip-hop*, Durham, NC: Duke University Press.

Petchauer, E. (2012) *Hip-Hop Culture in College Students' Lives*, New York: Routledge.

Rose, T. (1994) *Black Noise: rap music and black culture in contemporary America*, Hanover, NH: Wesleyan University Press.

Simmons, R. (2001) *Life and Def: sex, drugs, money, and God*, New York: Crown.

Thornton, S. (1996) *Club Cultures: music, media and subcultural capital*, Hanover, NH: Wesleyan University Press.

7

THE CONTRADICTIONS OF THE MAINSTREAM

Australian Views of Grunge and Commercial Success

Catherine Strong

The mainstream has often been conceived of in negative terms in discussions on popular music, and is frequently used as the 'other' to which marginal musical forms are compared positively. When previously underground music gains commercial success and becomes part of the mainstream, it is often portrayed as a problem, and as a corruption or destruction of the scene or movement that the music came from. This was certainly the case when the Seattle music scene gained massive commercial success in the early 1990s with a form of music that came to be known as grunge. Grunge's success generally is described as being doubly problematic, in that it not only supposedly had a negative effect on the Seattle scene, but also increased the exposure of other types of underground music to the mainstream, as record companies became more aware of the commercial viability of diverse forms of music.

The data presented in this chapter are drawn from interviews with 43 people who self-identified as having been fans of grunge during its heyday in the early 1990s, and who volunteered to be interviewed 10 years later for a PhD project (Strong 2011). These data will be used to explore fans' perceptions of the apparent transition of grunge to the mainstream in order to challenge some of the negative notions that exist around the concept. The idea that there is a meaningful division between the mainstream and the subcultural will be examined, along with the way the 'subcultural' discourses inscribed in grunge are reproduced through its 'mainstreaming' – that is, its appropriation and dissemination at a global level. I will argue that the interviews I conducted with grunge fans, asking them to look back on the movement, reveal a much more complex and dynamic relationship with the concept of the mainstream than has been understood to date. Accounts that focus on the problems that commercial success presents to localized scenes and the 'true fans' neglect the benefits that globalized audiences gain from these same processes. Taking this approach opens up space to examine how audiences see more going on with the music they like than the simple 'subcultural = good; mainstream = bad' equation that is often presented to us.

Considering commonsense definitions of mainstream popular music, Toynbee (2002: 149) observes that:

> It suggests a type of music which is standardised, popular and easy to listen to ... like junk food, the mainstream has been produced as a commercial product, and foisted on the undiscriminating consumers by an industry concerned only with making a profit.

Similarly, Huber (2007: 6) describes it as 'the sort of music that "most people" enjoyed ... accompanied by familiar connotations of conservatism, "sold-out" conformity and inferior cultural value'. In everyday discourse, the mainstream is often connected to ideas of conformity, and is also contrasted to realness, genuine creativity, independence and so on. This makes it a notion that touches on many of the main debates around popular music, from the very meaning of the word 'popular' to the notion of authenticity. In short, the concept of the mainstream is central to the strategies that are often employed by journalists, fans and academics – and even musicians themselves – when they are trying to make claims about the value of popular music. This ties in closely with other types of claims-making in discourses on rock music, including the way a number of dichotomies have been established, and how the worth of a band or album is constructed in relation to these. For example, one of the longest standing myths of the mainstream – which can be traced at least back to the late eighteenth century in the context of painting and other more 'high brow' art forms (Frow 1995: 17) – is that commercial success and true 'artistry' or creativity cannot exist alongside one another. In close relation to this, music is often judged as being 'real'/authentic or fake. To call something 'mainstream' is a shorthand way of aligning it with the 'bad' side of these pairs, as the mainstream is to do with artifice, capital and a lack of true creativity.

The utilization of these forms of value judgement must be understood as serving strategic purposes for those using them. As Bourdieu (1984, 1993) has demonstrated, hierarchies of culture are socially constructed and are connected to power structures and struggles for power in wider society. In the case of music journalists, the adoption of discourses that valorized some forms of music and bands at the expense of others also served to help legitimize their own newly established profession (Gendron 2002; Jones and Featherly 2002). Fans also gained access to new ways of creating distinction among themselves and acquiring (sub) cultural capital (Thornton 1995).

Academics, in a similar fashion to journalists, have used the idea of the mainstream to allow them to make stronger claims for the worth of more marginal or subcultural music. This was particularly strategic in the early years of popular music studies, when the idea that popular culture should be the object of serious academic analysis was still controversial. By highlighting areas of popular music that could be constructed as political or resistant in some way, academics could make claims for their worth both as culture and as objects of study – for a more in-depth discussion of this point, see Laughey (2006) and Phillipov (2006). There is a long line of academic literature – from Clarke (1982), onwards via Morris (1988), Frith (1992), Harris (1992), Maxwell (2002) and others – that has called attention to the role that researchers' identification plays in choices that are made about what is worthy of study, and how it is then portrayed. This identification is usually either with the (perceived) political aims of the group, or on a more personal level with the people being studied.

As a result of this, it is still often the case that, despite studies of popular culture now having (mostly) gained acceptance in the academy, popular music studies continue to focus on the fringes and margins, despite increasing critiques of this approach. This is where academics find activity that is more easily framed as positive from a position that is informed by left-wing politics, as is often the case in sociology and cultural studies (Harris 1992). The corollary of this, however, is that commercially successful music – the mainstream – along with its audience, can still be used in the same dismissive way as it is by fans and journalists, and framed as the 'bad' music that stands in opposition to the 'good' music being studied (for examples of the mainstream being used in this way, see Matula 2007: 19; Nehring 2007: 6). It is the influence of such factors that has led to a situation where grunge – undeniably one of the biggest cultural phenomena of the 1990s – has been all but ignored in academic analysis, along with many other commercially successful musical forms. What writing exists is almost universally dismissive or critical, portraying the success of grunge as a betrayal or cooption of the politics of punk – see Santiago-Lucerna (1998) and Shevory (1995) for examples of this. The commercial success (or mainstreaming) of grunge negated it as an object of serious academic analysis, and was also portrayed as destructive by critics and journalists.

Theorizing the Mainstream

When academics have directly confronted and attempted to theorize the mainstream, there has been debate about whether it exists in any real sense, or is simply a set of ideas. For example, in her study of UK clubbers, Sarah Thornton (1995) concludes that the mainstream should not be treated as an empirical reality by researchers, and is more a construct (encountered through the media and music industry) that the young people in her study on club cultures employ to define themselves and their place in the world. She sees not one mainstream, but the possibility of many mainstreams – a view that supports the ideas of Grossberg (1987), who sees a postmodern mass of different tastes that no longer has an identifiable centre: 'the centre is a constantly floating configuration of marginality' (148). Thornton agrees with Grossberg's reading of contemporary youth culture as fragmented, but emphasizes the continued importance of the idea of the mainstream. It is, as noted above, important to many people as a foil against which the positive qualities of the music they support can be highlighted. It is even more important to members of musical communities because it gives them something to be opposed to, and as such increases their sense of community, status and identity. This maintains a modernist dualism – 'us' (or the good, active consumers) versus 'the mainstream' (the bad, passive consumers) – while masking the fact that the reality is more complex, embracing a collection of different communities.

In contrast to this, Jason Toynbee has suggested that saying there is no such thing as the mainstream is going too far. He has proposed the following definition:

> A mainstream is a formation that brings together large numbers of people from diverse social groups and across large geographical areas in common affiliation to a musical style. Looked at in this way it is best conceived of as a process rather than a category.
>
> *(2002: 150)*

Huber (2007) also adopts this notion of the mainstream as a process in examining cultural objects such as *Australian Idol*, which are aimed at cultivating as large an audience as possible, and employs the useful notion of 'thinking with the mainstream', rather than against it, in order to be able to understand what it really means (see also Karja 2006). According to this model, the cultural dominance of a particular form of music is produced as a result of the practices of fans, musicians and the record industry at a particular point in time (meaning other cultural, political, social and economic factors will also be at play). As Huber points out, the 'unanticipated results' of these processes can include the mainstreaming of music that does not fit in with the dominant ideas of what the mainstream is, or that were not created with the mainstream in mind (as arguably was the case with grunge).

Using these types of definition, grunge could certainly be classified as having become mainstream, and defining it in this way may allow us to approach it differently. In particular, the study that I have carried out is of the mainstreamed version of grunge, as it was focused on fans of grunge who were almost all located in Australia, and therefore needed to rely on global communications and mass media to even know what grunge was. Furthermore, the retrospective nature of the study (speaking to grunge fans many years after the movement reached its commercial peak) meant that its mainstreaming had become integral to the way people related to and thought about it. As Huber (2007: 12) notes in her study of *Australian Idol,* 'acknowledging it as "mainstream" might enable a more productive engagement with such a form of dominant culture, which need not begin from the premise that it requires redemption because of its populism and massification'.

However, grunge is a case that raises very different questions from *Australian Idol* insofar as, rather than being something that can be examined purely as a mainstream object, the mainstream/subcultural divide is always present in discourses around grunge. In this way, Thornton's (1995) ideas about how the mainstream is used are relevant. Because of this, grunge is an excellent case study for thinking about the mainstream, because of the role it played in making some of these debates more visible. What is often examined, and has been the focus of work on grunge, is the effect that becoming part of the mainstream has on previously 'underground' or 'marginal' music (e.g. see Kirschner 1994; Middleton and Beebe 2002). What is looked at far less is the effect that the mainstreaming of something previously little known has on other forms of culture, and on our very idea of what constitutes the mainstream. Similarly, mainstream *audiences* have been the subject of far less inquiry than subcultural audiences, so speaking to mainstream (in Toynbee's sense) grunge fans adds another perspective to our understanding of the mainstream that, as will be demonstrated below, is less negative about it than subcultural audiences.

Grunge Fans and the Mainstream

The accounts of respondents discussing grunge show that they are well aware of the processes associated with mainstreaming; for many of them, such processes are central to how they discuss and understand grunge. There is a general acceptance that grunge became mainstream, but the *becoming* is vital to what is said about the effects this had. For example, Chris[1] said, 'With Nirvana it just brought the attitude that we had all lived by into the mainstream.' There are two themes that emerge when respondents are talking about grunge becoming mainstream. In the first, there is an emphasis on the damaging effect becoming part of the mainstream had on grunge. Missy said that 'there was a bit of a swing against grunge once it hit the mainstream', and Adrian commented that:

> The irony of it is that now it's become that mainstream that it's, I suppose swallowed itself up . . . I think the only reason people were sick of Nirvana was because the mainstream played them so much, I think it still would have had more of a long-term lasting effect if it wasn't played as much as it was. Granted they sold squillions of records, but I think if they didn't quite have as much and stayed a little bit quieter they probably would have had the continuing substance, if Kurt Cobain had managed to stick around that long.

This type of account has a lot in common with the 'commonsensical' notions of the mainstream as destructive. In particular, this account from Adrian picks up on the idea of success being detrimental to creativity, which will be discussed further below.

The other narrative presented, and which came up more often in interviews, was that grunge influenced the mainstream, rather than simply being taken over by it:

It just really helped kind of breach this gap between what counts as mainstream and what counts as alternative and nobody's ever heard it. I think it was really good, it gave a lot of people an opportunity to hear stuff they wouldn't have heard before and it gave bands an opportunity to reach an audience they wouldn't have reached before.

(Ginny)

Grunge seemed to come and go, didn't it, it seemed to die out, but to me grunge was sort of like, it seemed to have brought down the barriers between mainstream and independent, whereas now you have bands who used to be on [government-funded alternative/'youth' radio station] Triple J now play on [commercial radio station] Triple M, and very few bands from Triple M ... or whatever do come on to Triple J. But it seems to have brought down, I suppose, the thick set wall that seemed to segregate the two styles, independent and, nothing is really independent anymore, it's sort of like a fusion of, you know, acid jazz or all these weird categories for different bands. Yeah, I think, I don't know, I think grunge did break down that barrier where you had all the mainstream people start to listen to this new style of music, which was actually old but to them it was new.

(Roger)

One of the big changes I think it made was the merging of mainstream and independent music, that was stuff that had always been independent before and was never going to chart, I don't know if that was a good thing or a bad thing, but there really isn't, I mean there must be some kind of underground independent music going on now, but it just feels like more of a blur, more of a continuum, that the Top 40 is going to have a lot of that kind of music or music influenced by it, stuff like, you know, Linkin Park or whatever, as well as stuff like Britney. It's harder to pull it apart, but I guess, maybe that's only bad if you're trying to get street cred for yourself and say 'I like indie music' – I don't know.

(Julie)

This idea of grunge as having collapsed the distinction between the mainstream and independent or 'alternative' music is one that is repeated frequently in accounts of grunge in books and media reports, and it is also present in academic accounts of the movement, where this generally is presented as a negative aspect of grunge that shows the ability of the forces of capital to absorb any type of culture and find a way to repackage it for profit, including cultural forms that are actively critical of capitalism in the way grunge often was (see Santiago-Lucerna 1998). However, it needs to be kept in mind that this apparent breaking down of the distinction between the mainstream and alternative often 'betrays ... a continuing conflation of "alternative" music with cultural value, that is superior to music from the "mainstream", while simultaneously reasserting the potency of the mainstream–alternative paradigm as a way of making sense of contemporary cultural forms' (Huber 2007: 8).This is particularly apparent in Roger's statement, where he identifies a category of 'mainstream people', from whom he distinguishes himself by way of his knowledge about the music.

One of the other things that is apparent in Julie's account is respondents' awareness of the ideological connotations of the mainstream and the way oppositional categories are employed by music fans to make claims about themselves (as also documented by Thornton 1995). In the same manner that most of the respondents reject the idea that mainstream success ruined grunge, they also show scepticism towards using a love of underground music as a strategy for claiming (sub)cultural capital for oneself – or, in Julie's words, 'trying to get street cred'. Respondents actively rejected the notion that you would turn your back on music that you liked because other people liked it:

> But I don't know . . . at least it [the success of grunge] made it accessible to people like me. Some people get a bit funny about things like that and they kind of, you know . . . I'm not one of those people who kind of hates commercialism, you know what I mean, some people are very possessive about their bands and they don't want them to get out and they don't want them to be known by the world, but I don't really feel like that.
>
> *(Janie)*

> I think it's a bit elitist to say that [the success of grunge is] a bad thing and it shouldn't have been popular, it's such a shame that it got corrupted, because I think that's a silly thing to say often.
>
> *(Kaye)*

> While [commercial success] does sort of push it into the mainstream realm that's alright, I'd like to see lots of mainstream good music. If you thought this music was for the exclusive use of your friends and your friends alone then that would be lame.
>
> *(Max)*

It must be noted that the position of my respondents as part of the globalized audience for grunge has a strong influence on their rejection of this method of creating distinction. In other accounts of grunge, where the focus has been on people who were part of the music scene in Seattle in the years leading up to the commercial success of albums like Nirvana's *Nevermind*, strong claims are still made for the higher status of early participants – see Prato's (2009) oral history of the Seattle scene for numerous examples of this.

In association with this, despite the contradictions that appear in how the respondents characterized the relationship between grunge and the mainstream, it is notable that they were quite positive about the commercial success of grunge. Only three respondents made statements that suggested they unequivocally saw the success of grunge as a negative. Other respondents gave a range of reasons for why they saw its success as being beneficial, and these were again often connected with their own position as part of a globalized audience.

To begin with, respondents saw the success of grunge as being beneficial to their own access to music, in that:

> If it hadn't been successful I would never have heard it. I don't live in Seattle and I wasn't connected to that underground scene, so I wouldn't have heard any of this at all, and you know, if it hadn't have been successful then a lot of the stuff that's come later wouldn't have.
>
> *(Donald)*

Leading on from this, respondents saw grunge's success as necessarily being beneficial to other people's access to music and listening habits:

> The fact that for a lot of people it opened their minds to so much other music, and, I don't know, because Nirvana were such a good band, regardless of wherever the fuck they came from, but people who had spent their whole lives listening to Kylie Minogue, or, I think at school we were listening to Guns n' Roses and stuff – who I also think were an awesome band – but even people who were really closed-minded to stuff went 'What's this?' and started listening to other bands.
>
> *(Lily)*

While this account can in some ways again be seen to be a reinscription of the mainstream/alternative divide – especially in the way Lily still needs to define a group of people who were 'worse' than her in their listening habits, those 'who were really closed minded to stuff' – it is noteworthy that Lily is quite happy to identify as one of the people who had their mind 'opened' by grunge. Her account indicates greater fluidity between different categories of audience than is often found in audience studies, and a willingness to identify as part of a mainstream audience.

There were other times when respondents made statements that showed the breakdown of some of the dualisms that have been constructed around the idea of the mainstream, particularly the way in which commercial success is framed as destructive to creativity. While some respondents, as demonstrated in Adrian's quote above, still characterized grunge's success in this way, it was more common for respondents to talk about ways in which success actually fostered creativity:

> I guess it would have been nice to, you know, keep the bands to myself, you know, but on the other hand, like, Soundgarden wouldn't have been able to make those amazing albums that they did make 'cos, you know, they had lots

of money to make great records, so it was, that was good. And it also meant, because they were reasonably large, they actually did get to tour here and you did get to see them, and that was really cool.

(Dylan)

Ginny also agreed with this, saying, 'I think it meant there were more bands that were able to get recording contracts who I would listen to as a result of the big grunge explosion.' These accounts recognized that financial backing can be enabling for musicians, especially in terms of helping them reach a larger audience. Other respondents focused on what success meant for popular music more broadly:

Music was shit in the 80s, it was at a totally bad point, and it would just have gone worse and worse and worse. But this sort of came along and opened the way for all these new guitarists and whatever, new people playing in bands. So, totally, yeah, it was really good.

(Percy)

Some also suggested that the success of grunge led to an enhancement of their own creativity, insofar as the greater range of music accessible to them broadened their ideas about what could and could not be done as a musician:

I was already playing music, but not even thinking about alternative, not even aware of alternative music, and not even aware of considering the idea of writing original music etc. Music was something just that I thought you relayed to other people, that they wanted to hear hits and memories and stuff.

(Gordon)

A further interesting perspective emerged from the interviews – one that was more obviously influenced by the fact that the interviews were held over a decade after the mainstream success of grunge. Many audience studies, particularly those that are ethnographic in nature, are done while people are immersed in, or highly involved, with a scene or type of music (e.g. see Schippers 2002; Thornton 1995). Talking to these grunge fans so much later meant there was an opportunity for the respondents to create narratives that encompassed more of their experiences as grunge fans – including, for most, the experience of losing the intense emotional attachment that characterized their earlier experiences with the music. This provided the opportunity to reflect on what grunge had meant over its entire life-cycle. A small minority of respondents thought the popularity of grunge 'ruined' it for them. However, more typical responses were either to explain that while there may have been a period of rejecting grunge because of its commercialization, this rejection had since been re-evaluated:

I guess it weirded me out a bit to see something so quickly picked up, and I guess it's that thing of when you're younger you have special things that are your own ... you sort of, you've got this incestuous little group of people and you think you've discovered a band or whatever, and then you have that teenage thing of being cut when it gets popular, but it was kind of good too, because in hindsight, when it did get huge it sort of paved the way for a whole bunch of kids to be influenced by music, and it was like the next generation of bands.

(James)

This suggests that some of the more positive attitudes towards the mainstream displayed in these interviews may have developed over time (and may have come about partly because of respondents wanting to disassociate themselves from who they were when they were younger, as with James' dismissive comment about 'that teenage thing').

Conclusion

The accounts of these grunge fans show that audiences have a more complicated, and in many ways a much more pragmatic, relationship with the mainstream than has often been suggested in popular music studies. While in some ways respondents reflect the commonsense notions of the mainstream as being negative and destructive, particularly to creativity, in other ways they show a breaking down of the dualisms associated with the mainstream, and a recognition of the benefits that commercial success can bring to artists and audiences alike. This is connected to their own position as part of the mainstream, globalized audience for grunge. The mainstream/alternative divide still holds currency as a way of talking about musical value, but respondents are not averse to positioning themselves on either side of this divide, and more often than not reject the idea that music loses something when it becomes available to a mass audience. Opening up this idea and trying to re-evaluate what the mainstream means (and the 'uncool' and commercially successful more generally) may ultimately lead to greater reflexivity on the part of researchers and a widening of the field of study and the approaches that it is 'acceptable' to take as a researcher. This will hopefully lead to a situation where we can jettison the baggage associated with the mainstream and facilitate the greater understanding of all forms of music and their effects.

Note

1 All respondent names used are pseudonyms.

References

Bourdieu, P. (1984) *Distinction: a social critique of the judgement of taste*, 11th edn, trans. R. Nice, Cambridge, MA: Harvard University Press.

Bourdieu, P. (1993) *The Field of Cultural Production*, London: Columbia University Press.

Clarke, G. (1982) *Defending Ski-jumpers: a critique of theories of youth sub-cultures*, Birmingham: Centre for Contemporary Cultural Studies, University of Bimingham.

Frith, S. (1992) 'The cultural study of popular music', in L. Grossberg, C. Nelson and P.A. Treichler (eds), *Cultural Studies*, London: Routledge.

Frow, J. (1995) *Cultural Studies and Cultural Value*, Oxford: Clarendon Press.

Gendron, B. (2002) *Between Montmartre and the Muddclub: popular music and the avant-garde*, Chicago: University of Chicago Press.

Grossberg, L. (1987) 'The politics of music: American images and British articulations', *Canadian Journal of Political and Social Theory*, 11(1–2): 144–51.

Harris, D. (1992) *From Class Struggle to the Politics of Pleasure: the effects of Gramscianism on cultural studies*, London: Routledge.

Huber, A. (2007) 'What's in a mainstream: critical possibilities', *Altitude*, 8, www.thealtitudejournal.com (accessed 20 May 2012).

Jones, S. and Featherly, K. (2002) 'Re-viewing rock writing: narratives of popular music criticism', in S. Jones (ed.), *Pop Music and the Press*, Philadelphia, PA: Temple University Press.

Karja, A.-V. (2006) 'A prescribed alternative mainstream: popular music and canon formation', *Popular Music*, 25(1): 3–19.

Kirschner, T. (1994) 'The lalapalooziation of American youth', *Popular Music and Society*, 18(1): 69–89.

Laughey, D. (2006) *Music and Youth Culture*, Edinburgh: Edinburgh University Press.

Matula, T. (2007) 'Pow! to the people: the make-up's reorganisation of punk rhetoric', *Popular Music and Society*, 30(1): 19–38.

Maxwell, I. (2002) 'The curse of fandom: insiders, outsiders and ethnography', in D. Hesmondhalgh and K. Negus (eds), *Popular Music Studies*, London: Arnold.

Middleton, J. and Beebe, R. (2002) 'The racial politics of hybridity and "neo-eclecticism" in contemporary popular music', *Popular Music*, 21(2): 159–72.

Morris, M. (1988) 'Banality in cultural studies', *Discourse*, 10(2): 3–29.

Nehring, N. (2007) 'Everyone's given up and just wants to go dancing: from punk to rave in the Thatcher era', *Popular Music and Society*, 30(1): 1–18.

Phillipov, M. (2006) 'Haunted by the spirit of '77: punk studies and the persistence of politics', *Journal of Media and Cultural Studies*, 20(3): 383–93.

Prato, G. (2009) *Grunge is Dead: the oral history of Seattle rock music*, Toronto: ECW Press.

Santiago-Lucerna, J. (1998) '"Frances Farmer will have her revenge on Seattle": pan-capitalism and alternative rock', in J.S. Epstein (ed.), *Youth Culture: identity in a postmodern world*, Oxford: Blackwell.

Schippers, M. (2002) *Rockin' Out of the Box: gender maneuvering in alternative hard rock*, New Brunswick, NH: Rutgers University Press.

Shevory, T.C. (1995) 'Bleached resistance: the politics of grunge', *Popular Music and Society*, 19(2): 23–48.

Strong, C. (2011) *Grunge: music and memory*, Aldershot: Ashgate.

Thornton, S. (1995) *Club Cultures: music, media and subcultural capital*, Cambridge: Polity Press.

Toynbee, J. (2002) 'Mainstreaming, from hegemonic centre to global networks', in D. Hesmondhalgh and K. Negus (eds), *Popular Music Studies*, London: Arnold.

PART III

Historicizing the Mainstream

8

ELVIS GOES TO HOLLYWOOD

Authenticity, Resistance, Commodification and the Mainstream

David Baker

Since what we might call its originary moment in the mid-1950s, rock music and its discourse have demonstrated a profound and often anxious awareness of its circulation within a capitalistic system of economic exchange. This historically determined situation has created considerable unease, most clearly observed in the complex interplay between rock's knowledge of itself as a commodity (defined by sales of recordings, films, concert events, ancilliaries, and so on), and its deep investment in various forms of resistance (subcultural, stylistic, political, sexual). Mainstream success in the commodity sphere (measured by sales and popularity) wrestles with rock's desire and capacity for resistive forms of engagement. Rock discourse continually negotiates a familiar paradox: the more widely an artist is able to model and disseminate particular forms of resistance, the more this success risks engulfment by the very mainstream forces the artist seeks to oppose. Successful rock artists – or at least those critics who speak for them – traditionally have sought to avoid the stigma of 'selling out' by positing various forms of 'authenticity'. This chapter considers the way in which this opposition between mainstream and resistance circulates in recent critical discussion of the career of Elvis Presley. Presley is mythologized as both rock's original iconoclast *and* its founding cautionary tale.

Why Do Pop Culture Scholars Despise Elvis Movies?

Douglas Brode is one of the very few popular culture scholars who have attempted to defend Elvis movies.[1] Brode (2006: 279) suggests that Elvis could have, but did not, opt to make movies for suburban audiences; instead, he 'made movies which, following brief popularity with 1950s teens, settled down to comfortably enter-tain a target audience of farming folk in the rural South and blue collar workers in the industrial North – *his* people; Elvis' people'. In terms of the mainstream versus the margin, this argument suggests that Elvis didn't so much 'sell out' and become mainstream, but rather, by remaining true to his Southern 'self', ultimately 'countrified the entire country' (280). In its strong form, this argument probably draws rather a long bow: Elvis clearly did not single-handedly 'countrify' the entire United States. However, in its weaker form, the argument is persuasive: by remaining true to his Southern 'self' in his movies, Elvis was one factor in the rise of interest in country music (due to its perceived authenticity) among rock performers and their audiences in the late 1960s and early 1970s.

However, Brode's position remains a minority one. Here are four representative examples of what might be the more 'mainstream' critical response to Elvis movies (the first three are quotations):

1. '[Consider] the essential trajectory of Elvis' career: from sexy rock 'n' roll revolutionary in the 1950s to bloated, bespangled legend in the 1970s, with the tame tepidity of his 31 theatrical films coming in between.

    'The great paradox of Elvis' career is that the man who did so much to trigger "the sixties" spent that decade on the sidelines in Hollywood cranking out three movies a year: "their specious, monotonous 'youthfulness,' " as David Thomson has written, "so wholesome, so bouncy, and so riotously clean," standing in flaccid contradistinction to everything the sixties represented' (Feeney 2001: 53).

2. 'It was the career of Elvis Presley, who starred in more than 30 films from 1956 to 1969, which typified most acutely the predictability and complacency of an industry which saw no reason to deviate from a policy of creating movies which were 'poor pop vehicles, all resembling each other, all about having fun, falling in love, boy makes good, with Presley using the same screen persona with a different name in a different setting' (Inglis 2003: 79).

3. 'Here is a man who, as a nineteen-year-old . . . sparked a transformation of American culture, of culture world-wide – a transformation we are still living out . . . far more certainly than it would have seemed to anyone in 1962 . . . when Elvis Presley disappeared into his own Hollywood movie factory . . .

    'As an agent of transformation Elvis did something new . . . he gave voice to emotions that couldn't be contained. And then he was himself contained, in the oldest, stupidest, most obvious straightjackets of fame and success' (Marcus 2000: 182–3).

4. In her fascinating book, *Elvis Culture: fans, faith and image*, Erika Doss sympathetically and perceptively analyses all sorts of quirky and kitsch Elvis phenomena: Elvis fly-swats, Black Velvet Elvises, Elvis bubblegum cards and so on. She writes sensitively and compassionately about fans who have a deeply personal relationship with both Elvis *and* Jesus. She concludes her book by appropriately pointing out the 'intellectual fallacy that there are any simple sound bites about Elvis culture, or easy assumptions to be made about

his fans, his post-mortem popularity, or popular culture in general' (Doss 1999: 258). Doss won't have a bar of the films though, dismissing them with the curt phrase 'truly wretched B-movies'. Her main argument against the 1960s films is their stereotypically 'macho', 'red-blooded American' masculinity, which she negatively contrasts with the androgyny of both the pre-army as well as the post-Hollywood live-on-stage Elvis of the 1970s (138–42).

We can roughly tabulate the key tropes and oppositions from these examples (see Table 8.1).

By making this rough tabulation, we can easily see the way in which rock criticism tends to function as a romantic, ethical and evaluative discourse. The elements of the virtuous discourse of rock are lined up on the left-hand side of the table: freedom, authenticity, individuality, *genuine* sexual expression, unrestricted emotion. The Hollywood movies, by contrast, stand as metonym for all that is *anti*-rock: containment, inauthenticity, predictability, *specious* youthfulness and so on.

I suggest that the blanket disapproval of Elvis movies rests upon a *grievance*. Rock critique routinely acknowledges youthful 1950s Elvis as *the* central figure facilitating the conditions that paved the way for wave after wave of liberatory and emancipatory rock discourse – articulating social issues around class, race, sexuality and lifestyle. Such critique also appears to have no trouble with the suggestion that 1970s overweight, jump-suited but resolutely 'live' Elvis represented a return to some sort of authenticity. The bitter grievance against Elvis is that in the 'middle period' he *betrayed* the very rock discourse he was so instrumental in facilitating. Elvis allowed himself to be *contained* by mainstream forces – first by the army and then by his Hollywood movie career.

I suggest that the very power of rock discourse as an ethical commitment has a seriously distorting effect. In each of the earlier quotations, Hollywood is understood as a movie factory that produced nothing other than complacency and conformity: of pictures, lifestyle and masculinity. Hollywood is here understood entirely in 1960s liberatory rock terms as a failure of authenticity and as a

TABLE 8.1 Key Elvis tropes and oppositions

Rock 'n' roll Elvis	Hollywood Elvis
Sexy.	Specious monotonous youthfulness; 'flaccid'.
Androgynous.	Stereotypical macho.
Revolutionary.	Tame tepidity; predictability; complacency.
'Triggers' the social, sexual and ethical transformation of the 1960s.	Sidelined in Hollywood (1960s); cranking out 'wretched' B-movies.
Gives voice to emotions that can't be *contained*.	*Contained* by Hollywood (raw capitalism).

metonym for 'selling out'. This conceptualization of Hollywood is highly prob-lematic. Far from complacency, Elvis' film career falls precisely into a particularly *anxious* period in Hollywood history. The old-style monopolistic practices of the Hollywood studio system were broken up after 1948. By the mid-1950s, Hollywood no longer controlled the relationship between film production, distribution and exhibition, and simply didn't know how to systematically make profitable films any more – it didn't really figure out how to run a profitable industry until around 1975, with what is now often called the blockbuster or conglomeratization era, instigated by such films as *Jaws* (Spielberg, 1975) and *Star Wars* (Lucas, 1977) (e.g. see Bordwell and Thompson 2010: 299–323, 472–94; Gomery and Pafort-Overduin 2011: 230–90).

The Industrial Context for Elvis Movies

Elvis' movie career was too late for the certainties of the classic studio system, where the major film companies monopolized the film industry by owning all aspects of the theatrical business – production, distribution and exhibition. As a result of this monopoly, companies could make their films with a relatively sound knowledge of what the eventual profits would be, and could budget them accord-ingly. Elvis' movies, were too early for the relative certainties of the conglomera-tion era, with its reliance on the blockbuster and the ability to sell blockbusters through multiple media platforms – movie, television and, through the 1980s and 1990s, music video, computer games, video and DVD release – as well as the new opportunities for vertical integration that conglomeration offers. The movies were routinely profitable in a period when it was very difficult for Hollywood to make profitable movies, and made their profits by mixing various Hollywood genres, in particular the traditional MGM musical, with something very close to an independent, 'exploitation' approach to filmmaking. Thomas Doherty (2002: 7) describes the production strategy of 1950s exploitation cinema as typically utilizing three elements: '(1) controversial, bizarre, or timely subject matter amenable to wild promotion; (2) a substandard budget; and (3) a teenage audience'.

Peter Guralnick (1994) supplies a highly detailed account of the industrial aspects of Elvis' movie career. In March 1956, Colonel Tom Parker signed a lucra-tive three-picture contract with the veteran film Producer Hal Wallis, working out of his independent unit at Paramount Studios (260).[2] There are four significant points to make about this contract. First, the initial idea was explicitly to utilize Elvis to tap into the newly discovered 'youth' market. To this end, Elvis was seen as a kind of song and dance James Dean (260). The three Presley backstage musi-cals of the 1950s thus all present Elvis as rebellious and, in the cases of *Jailhouse Rock* and *King Creole*, as being in close proximity to youth delinquency.

Second, part of the motivation for transforming Elvis from 'performing' the 'movie' star was in order to improve his career prospects. Both Parker and Wallis recognized that Elvis was an extraordinary phenomenon, and that rather than allying his career with this or that musical trend – which might disappear at any moment – his career could be extended indefinitely by turning him into an all-round entertainer and movie star (261). From our current vantage point, it is easy to forget that there was no guarantee in 1956 that rock 'n' roll would have any lasting value whatsoever.

Third, by 1956–57, the controversy that rock 'n' roll had generated, and that basically had fuelled Elvis' rise to fame, was seen – particularly by Parker – as becoming a negative. Criticism of Elvis and rock 'n' roll by church, press and even Congress was, in Parker's eyes, becoming too intense, and his response was to get Presley out of performance and away from the glare of negative publicity (Guralnick 1994: 384).

Fourth, the terms of the 1956 contract were incredibly favourable to Elvis, and Wallis would have been perfectly within his rights to expect that this would mean an exclusive signing of the star. However, Parker simply didn't work in this way: he kept his options open by reserving the right to make one outside picture a year for whatever amount of money he was able to negotiate – for example, *Jailhouse Rock* made by MGM in 1957 (Guralnick 1994: 262). He maintained this practice right through the 1960s. This is the main reason why, over the course of his career, Elvis movies were made by a range of different film companies – the majors, Paramount, Twentieth Century Fox, MGM and United Artists (though curiously never Warner Bros); smaller companies such as Allied Artists and National General; and independent producers who had production deals with major companies – in particular the Mirisch brothers, working with United Artists, and Sam Katzman, working with MGM.

Elvis was drafted into the army in March 1958 and discharged in March 1960. It was during this time that Parker learnt the value of scarcity, and developed the policy that defined Elvis' career in the 1960s: there was to be virtually no public circulation of Elvis apart from the films. Also during this time, the Wallis formula for Elvis movies was developed. In short, the elements of the Wallis formula for what he called the 'mature Elvis' (Wallis and Higham 1980: 152) were: bright, fast-paced, good-humoured musical comedy, always a fist fight, a little bit self-mocking; a formulaic Hollywood approach with a good – but not good enough to over-shadow Elvis – supporting cast playing stock characters; and a romance with *at least* two women vying for Elvis' affections. The setting was spectacular and used semi-exotic locations – tourist destinations like Hawaii, Acapulco and Germany – and decent enough production values (Guralnick 1999: 103). Although Wallis didn't actually write the Paramount Elvis screenplays himself, they were written explicitly to his specifications (170). *G.I. Blues* (Paramount, 1960) was the first film featuring this 'new' Elvis.

Although Wallis' view of Elvis was incredibly influential, it was not an exclusive one. We can see this from the two Twentieth Century Fox movies made early in the 1960s, *Flaming Star* (1960) and *Wild in the Country* (1961). These were 'worthy' films dealing with difficult social issues – race issues in *Flaming Star* and issues of family crisis, delinquency and violence in *Wild in the Country*. Wallis' view, however, was powerfully reinforced by the fact that the two films he made in 1960–61 – *G.I. Blues* and *Blue Hawaii* – were extremely successful at the box office, whereas by comparison the two Fox films were only moderately so. At a time when Hollywood was unsure about how it was going to make profitable films, the Wallis formula for Elvis demonstrated one sure-fire way of doing so. Because of the success of the Wallis formula at Paramount, other companies – in particular MGM – borrowed strongly from it. There were to be no more Elvis 'social issues' films until the late 1960s.

The scenario whereby Parker negotiated contracts with Wallis and Paramount while at the same time negotiating outside contracts – principally with MGM but also with independents, like the Mirisch brothers' two picture deal that produced the interesting 'non-Wallis vision' films *Follow That Dream* and *Kid Galahad* in 1962 – continued fairly happily for the first half of the 1960s. However, although the pictures were always profitable, there was a very slow but steady decline in profit after *Blue Hawaii*. This was the main reason why Parker made a two-picture deal with producer Sam Katzman, the legendary king of exploitation cinema.[3] Katzman had made a career producing profitable films extremely quickly with minimal budgets. He was extremely careful to closely control on-set costs – for example, as opposed to the standard six to eight weeks, fifteen days was a standard Katzman shooting time. The Katzman short schedule approach was clearly at odds with some key aspects of the Wallis formula of utilizing exotic locations and decent production values, but it maintained the bright, fast-paced musical comedy aspect (Guralnick 1999: 155–60). However, it is clear that the principal reason for the cost-cutting was to maximize Presley's (and Parker's) profit margins. Even though the now Katzmanized-Wallis vision continued to frame Elvis film production during the 1965–67 period, several factors combined to dislodge it – to the extent that the Elvis films of the 1968–69 period bear remarkably little trace of it.

First, the flaws in the Katzman approach had become evident with the release of *Harem Scarum* in October 1965. Although Kay Dickinson (2008: 3–12) spends considerable time erroneously treating this film as somehow emblematic of Presley's Hollywood career,[4] she fails to acknowledge that its aesthetic failure – recognized even before its release – actually threw a scare into the Presley camp. Parker learnt from the film's failure and made some significant policy changes as a result – in particular, that the strategy of bare minimum production costs – itself, as mentioned earlier, a reaction to the blow-out that occurred during the production of *Viva Las Vegas* – was just as likely to bring about box office failure as it was to lead to aesthetic failure. Furthermore, the strategy of a very fast movie shoot with Elvis appearing in every scene was considered 'a recipe for disaster' (Guralnick 1999: 204–5). From this point on, even though the Presley films remained by and large exploitation films, neither the 'bare bones budget approach' nor the 'Elvis in every scene approach' was considered good practice.

Second, Paramount itself decided not to renew the contract. *Easy Come, Easy Go*, released on 22 March 1967, was to be the last Wallis/Paramount film. I have no evidence regarding the rationale for Paramount's decision; presumably it came from above Wallis' office, and it was a straight business response to what was a clear long-term decline in Paramount's Elvis movie grosses.

Third, in 1965 Parker had won a significant contract upgrade from the record company RCA. For the previous five years or so, Parker had basically run a synergistic formula between movies and soundtrack albums — 'the soundtrack album promoted the movie release, and the movie release guaranteed a certain level of sales and publicity for the album' (Guralnick 1999: 123). This formula meant that almost all Presley's recorded output during this time had been soundtrack music. The new contract upgrade came with an expectation from RCA that Presley would produce more recorded material. Although the effects of this contract weren't immediate, in the short term it meant a number of recording sessions of material were not used in the movies, but released on soundtrack albums. Over the longer term, it had the effect of facilitating a rekindling of Elvis' interest in singing, recording and ultimately performing live.

Fourth, by 1966 it had generally become clear that the days of youth-oriented, light-hearted musical comedy were numbered. For example, American International Pictures (AIP) released the last of its famous Beach Films — *The Ghost in the Invisible Bikini* — in April 1966, and from this point on AIP's youth-oriented film production concentrated on bikers and counter-culture. More generally, in the wake of The Beatles and the British invasion, and the subsequent rise of the counter-culture more generally, the musical and movie preferences of young people were clearly changing — something Hollywood clearly understood, particularly in the wake of the success of films such as *The Graduate* (1967) and *Easy Rider* (1969).

Fifth, despite the myth that Elvis regained control of his career — especially around the time of the famous *Comeback Special*, broadcast on NBC prior to Christmas 1968 — and that this facilitated Elvis going back on stage, this isn't really what happened. When Paramount made its last Elvis movie in early 1967, the MGM contract still had two films in pre-production and a further three to run. It quickly became clear that MGM wasn't interested in renewing its contract after this, although it did come back later to produce a couple of documentary/concert films in the 1970s. There was one film on the United Artists contract to run (*Clambake*), and aside from a single-picture contract with the smaller company National General for what eventually became *Charro!*, there was no interest from any film company in further Elvis film projects (Guralnick 1999: 272, 283). With no one wanting to fund a Presley film project, Parker went to NBC and negotiated the famous television special. As part of that deal involved a single movie project, it turned out that the final Elvis feature released was *Change of Habit* in 1969 (283). As a result of this combination of factors, in the final movies we can note a significant change in the kinds of films being produced and the kinds of roles played by Elvis. In the last three films, Elvis is playing authority figures – a sheriff in *Charro!*, a boss in *The Trouble With Girls* and a doctor in *Change of Habit*.

The Southerner as Rebel

I suggest that the mainstream or orthodox romantic rock discourse betrays a tendency to identify with and invest heavily in its object of inquiry. It wants to be able to 'rock' itself. As a result, uncritical assumptions around issues such as 'selling out', 'complacency' and 'inauthenticity' can all too easily enter into the critical analysis of such issues. As a result, such analysis can have trouble recognizing the 'banal' but complex industrial reality of popular music in relation to film history precisely because of its reliance upon an overriding romantically derived ethical research framework.

However, even though greater attention to the industrial context of the Elvis films helps us avoid romantic distortions, we still have to account for the fact that there is clearly a significant change in Elvis movies from 1960 onwards. In order to consider this shift, we need to take very seriously indeed those arguments suggesting that in the 1960s, Elvis' rebelliousness – understood explicitly in terms of his outsider status as a working-class Southerner – *disappears* in the act of making Elvis available to a general audience, an argument that has been developed most forcefully by Susan Doll (1998; see also Bertrand 2005; Graham 2001; Dickinson 2008).

Discussing Hollywood rebel characters – and in particular focusing upon the 1956–58 press comparisons between Presley, James Dean and Marlon Brando – Doll (1998: 120) makes a distinction between anomie and alienation. She suggests that anomie occurs:

> when people do not fit in with the norms of society because they feel those norms are pointless. Anomie is very closely related to angst – it does not challenge the existing power relations in society. Alienation occurs when the goals and norms of society belong to groups *outside* those of the person in question.

For Doll, Hollywood rebels – like the middle-class James Dean in *Rebel Without a Cause* – are *anomic* rather than alienated. Rebellion here is understood as nothing more than an ordinary part of being a teenager, and will inevitably pass as the teenager matures. Elvis, by contrast, represents 'true alienation' in Doll's terms. Because of his upbringing and identification as a member of the poor, rural, white, Southern working-class or hillbilly 'subculture', he was by definition alienated from the mainstream of American society (121), which condescendingly regards Southern working-class culture as tasteless, backward . . . and overtly racist (Bertrand 2005: 118).

Doll draws two conclusions from this. First, once Elvis becomes a Hollywood film star in the 1950s, he is grouped with Dean and Brando and becomes *anomic* rather than *alienated* – and thus deemed acceptable to mainstream audiences (Doll 1998: 120–2). This argument is elegant, but it is not entirely accurate. All four of the 1950s Elvis movies are set in the deep South, and flag Elvis as an explicitly Southern, alienated rebel – a confederate still fighting the Civil War after it is over in *Love Me Tender*; an orphaned Southern working-class boy who develops a career in an exploitative music industry in *Loving You*; a Southern ex-prisoner who is represented explicitly as a Hollywood outsider in *Jailhouse Rock*; and a working-class boy navigating a corrupt New Orleans club and entertainment industry in *King Creole*. Furthermore, it is not at all clear that the Dean of *Giant* rather than *Rebel Without a Cause* and the Brando of, for example, *A Streetcar Named Desire, On the Waterfront* or *The Wild One* can easily be considered anomic rather than alienated figures. In these cases, the individuals Dean and Brando perform stand outside the goals and norms of mainstream society.

Doll's second conclusion is also elegant but problematic. In constructing a new 'everyman' Elvis to replace 'Elvis the pelvis', Doll (1998: 122–3) suggests that Elvis' Southern background – and thus potential for rebellion – was simply eliminated from his image. Bertrand (2005: 88) puts forward a very similar argument. To make this case, Doll's analysis of 1960s Elvis rests on two assumptions. The first, and most explicit, is that 'this set of vehicles drew upon Presley's character in *G.I. Blues* to form a specific iconography, visual style and narrative structure that was consistent from vehicle to vehicle' (135). The second is that, in order to arrive at her conclusion, Doll doesn't believe she needs to analyze all of the movies. Assuming they're pretty much all one of a kind, she engages in close analysis of only *G.I. Blues* (Paramount), *Girl Happy* (MGM) and *Viva Las Vegas* (MGM). This suggests that the three are representative of the set, 'making it redundant as well as impractical to discuss all of them' (136–7).

Doll's decision here has the effect of seriously distorting her understanding of the movies. It is true the Wallis 'vision' conforms fairly neatly with that outlined by Doll. However, it is simply not correct to suggest that Wallis' vision of Elvis represents the entirety of Presley's filmed output during this period. While the vision is undeniably extremely influential – particularly on at least half of MGM's eleven 1960s Elvis movies – Doll is unable to account for those films that clearly stand outside the Paramount/MGM 'musical' tradition – for example, the earlier 'social problem' films and those produced by the Mirisch brothers. Further, by invoking a kind of static account of the commonalities, Doll is unable to consider the ways in which, in the later films, the Presley persona wrestles, in circumscribed but interesting ways, with complex social issues: race in *Stay Away Joe* and *Change of Habit*, and gender in *Live a Little, Love a Little* and *The Trouble with Girls*.

The Southerner in the 1960s Elvis Films

In opposition to the argument that Southernness disappears from the 1960s movies, I suggest that Elvis Presley's Southernness is writ large across the films of this period. I want very briefly to signal just two key aspects of this.

First, let's look at the Western Elvis. Writing for *Harper's Magazine* in 1958, James and Annette Baxter suggest the following:

> The sum of Presley's qualities matches the national image of the Southland. For *the South today popularly represents what the West once did*: the self-sufficient, the inaccessible, the fiercely independent soul of the nation. With the taming of the West completed, only the deep South retains a comparable aura of mystery, of romantic removal from the concerns of the steadily urbanized and cosmopolized America.
>
> *(Baxter and Baxter 1992: 33)*

To this I add that the South today popularly represents what the Western *still* does: providing fantasies of self-sufficiency, the inaccessible and the fiercely independent soul of the nation. In my view, the Western is the *obvious* place to find Presley's Southernness. In the Elvis oeuvre, there are three 'genuine' Westerns: *Love Me Tender* (1956), *Flaming Star* (1960) and the quasi-spaghetti *Charro!* (1969). Along with the 'genuine Westerns' there are at least 14 Elvis films that present a clear relationship with rural culture. Almost all feature contemporary settings, and variably but routinely allude to the Western either through aspects of *mise-en-scène*, narrative or direct reference.[5]

The most significant feature of Elvis as a Western hero is that he is always caught in a state betwixt and between. In *Love Me Tender*, he is caught in a romantic triangle with his brother and his brother's true love, to whom he happens to be married. In the aftermath of the Civil War, he's caught between the ghost of a South that no longer exists and a Union that doesn't provide a new sense of belonging. As a 'half-caste' in *Flaming Star*, he's caught up in the middle of a war between whites and Indians, both sides of which seek to enlist him. In *Charro!* he hovers betwixt and between outlaw and law. Jess Wade is a wanted man at the same time as he is a sheriff. In general, the Western Elvis is a dislocated social figure eking out a marginal economic existence with no guarantee of social improvement – *Love Me Tender* and *Flaming Star* both conclude with the death of an Elvis hero who literally has nowhere to run.

A second way in which Southernness is inscribed in the films concerns the issue of work. Michael Bertrand (2005: 31) argues that poor white Southerners have traditionally been alienated from mainstream America by not being fully integrated into the 'culture of work, discipline, efficiency, saving, and capitalist social relations associated with Yankees and Europeans'. Both social advancement and the American dream itself were considered largely out of reach for poor white

Southerners. Elvis' very particular status as a 'poor white' Southerner made good has a few important effects on the movies. One of the key mainstream Yankee Protestant virtues is, of course, working really hard. For rural working-class Southerners, the incentive or even the means to work diligently in the hope of acquiring capital was virtually non-existent. A significant form of oppositionality available to the poor Southerner was thus 'taking it easy'. Being leisurely in his work and working hard at his leisure is a defining feature of many Elvis characters. For most of *G.I. Blues*, for example, Elvis and his pals are goofing off from the army. The few times he is working, Elvis spends his time working on his tank in the way a teenager might work on his car. Basically, the army is represented as a steady income while Elvis pursues other interests.

A good – if extreme – example of the fusion of leisure and work occurs in *Viva Las Vegas*. Elvis – Lucky Jackson – uses his work as a hotel waiter as an opportunity to crash a 'private' date between his love interest, Rusty Martin (Ann-Margaret), and his rival, Count Elmo Mancini, effectively ruining the date by providing dreadful service. This is not just ordinary goofing off; by prioritizing his romantic interests when he is supposed to be working, Elvis is actively utilizing his paid work-time as an opportunity to advance his non-market leisure interests.

Conclusion

In this chapter, I have signalled my discomfort with the ethical approach dominating cultural studies discussions of Elvis movies on the grounds that this approach both fails to interrogate its own guiding assumptions *and* produces distortions in the actual object of analysis. Cultural studies, due to its entirely legitimate concern to foster a progressive politics, has had enormous trouble with 'Southern' culture, which is both marginal and manifests retrogressive political tendencies. A more promising approach is to take time to understand the precise industrial context of the films and, rather than view 1960s Elvis as a kind of everyman, to consider the 1960s movies in terms of their continuing and complex relationship to working-class Southernness. To this end, I have sketched out several aspects of this relationship. On one hand, Elvis remains an under-analyzed and extraordinarily complex figure in relation to discussions of mainstream or orthodox culture and its discontents or margins. On the other, he remains an absolutely central figure of mainstream popular culture, while at the same time the specifically 'Southern' or 'redneck' aspects of his masculinity work to marginalize him. Certain aspects of his career – in particular the early years and arguably his 'comeback' in the late 1960s and 1970s – are seen as central, while the 'Hollywood years' of the 1960s tend to be seen as marginal epiphenomena. Although an extremely successful Hollywood actor, Elvis always remained a marginal figure in Hollywood. Only by recognizing this complexity can we develop a thorough-going analysis of both Presley's career and his impact.

Notes

1 Simon Frith has, if not explicitly defended the movies, made a thorough critique of the way in which musicological, sociological and cultural studies scholarship has failed to account for or even come to grips with Elvis Presley. Frith (1996: 102) discusses a misleading academic orthodoxy: 'On the one hand, Presley is heard as the boy who first and most powerfully put together black and white sounds to "recode" mass music; on the other hand, he is recognised as the star who first and most powerfully caught the post-war mood of American (and then European) youth, who recoded the teenager. His phenomenal success was an effect of his integration of these musical and social forces but, from an academic point of view, what really matters is what Presley led to, and his own subsequent career is of no interest whatsoever.' Guralnick (1999), Bertrand (2005) and Brode (2006) have all been published subsequent to Frith's essay, and have helped to shift the story somewhat, but Presley remains a marginal figure in relation to the academic orthodoxy.

2 The following discussion is entirely dependent upon Guralnick (1994, 1999). Although I do not always agree with Guralnick's arguments and opinions, I am thoroughly indebted to his research into the Elvis industrial archive. For a complementary account to this one, see Messenger (2005).

3 A second important reason for the drafting of Katzman was the way in which MGM's *Viva Las Vegas* – although very successful – had gone way over budget because, as Guralnick (1999: 153) puts it, of 'all the unnecessary frills and fancy production numbers that would not add a penny to the box office'.

4 In my view, the central weakness of Dickinson's account of *Harem Scarum* is her principled and single-minded insistence that Presley was an artist exploited by MGM.

5 These films include: *Loving You* (Paramount, 1956); *Jailhouse Rock* (MGM, 1957); *Wild in the Country* (Twentieth Century Fox, 1962); *Kid Galahad* (Mirisch/UA, 1962); *Follow that Dream* (Mirisch/UA,1962); *It Happened at the World's Fair* (MGM, 1963); *Kissin' Cousins* (MGM, 1964); *Viva Las Vegas* (MGM, 1964); *Roustabout* (Paramount, 1964); *Tickle Me* (Allied Artists,1965); *Frankie and Johnnie* (UA, 1966); *Spinout* (MGM, 1966); *Stay Away Joe* (MGM, 1968); and *The Trouble with Girls* (MGM, 1969).

References

Baxter, J. and Baxter, A. (1992) 'The man in the blue suede shoes', in K. Quain (ed.), *The Elvis Reader*, New York: St Martin's Press.

Bertrand, M. (2005) *Race, Rock and Elvis*, Urbana, IL: Illinois University Press.

Bordwell, D. and Thompson, K. (2010) *Film History: an introduction*, New York: McGraw Hill.

Brode, D. (2006) *Elvis Cinema and Popular Culture*, London: McFarland and Co.

Dickinson, K. (2008) *Off Key: when film and music won't work together*, Oxford: Oxford University Press.

Doherty, T. (2002) *Teenagers and Teenpics: the juvenilization of American movies in the 1950s*, Philadelphia: Temple University Press.

Doll, S. (1998) *Understanding Elvis: Southern roots vs. star image*, New York: Garland.

Doss, E. (1999) *Elvis Culture: fans, faith and image*, Kansas City, KA: University Press of Kansas.

Feeney, M. (2001) 'Elvis movies', *American Scholar*, 70(1): 53–60.

Frith, S. (1996) 'The academic Elvis', in R.H. King and H. Taylor (eds), *Dixie Debates: perspectives on Southern culture*, London: Pluto Press.

Gomery, D. and Pafort-Overduin, C. (2011) *Movie History: a survey*, New York: Routledge.

Graham, A. (2001) *Framing the South: Hollywood, television, and race during the civil rights struggle*, Baltimore, MD: Johns Hopkins University Press.

Guralnick, P. (1994) *Last Train to Memphis: the rise of Elvis Presley*, London: Abacus.

—— (1999) *Careless Love: the unmaking of Elvis Presley*, London: Abacus.

Inglis, I. (2003) 'The act you've known for all these years: telling the tale of The Beatles', in I. Inglis (ed.), *Popular Music and Film*, London: Wallflower.

Marcus, G. (2000) *Double Trouble: Bill Clinton and Elvis Presley in a land of no alternatives*, New York: Picador.

Messenger, C. (2005) 'Act naturally: Elvis Presley, The Beatles, and "rocksploitation"', *Screening the Past*, 18, www.latrobe.edu.au/screeningthepast/firstrelease/fr_18/CMfr18a.html (accessed 20 March 2012).

Wallis, H. and Higham, C. (1980) *Starmaker: the autobiography of Hal Wallis*, New York: Macmillan.

9

WALKING IN MEMPHIS?

Elvis Heritage Between Fan Fantasy and Built Environment

Mark Duffett

> Haunting is increasingly a reminder that forces of history and economy create restless spaces whose uses and meanings are constantly being repurposed, each time displacing and marginalizing disturbed spirits.
>
> *(Curtis 2008: 14)*

Elvis Presley has always been interesting in relation to the idea of a specifically mainstream popular music. The much-debated term has variously denoted the mediocre centre ground of commercial culture in the eyes of those looking for a more hip and underground alternative (Thornton 1995); been challenged as theoretically irrelevant in an era when 'selling out' no longer holds an affective charge (Grossberg 1992); become envisaged as a temporally continuous, historically specific and substantively unifying field of culture (Toynbee 2002); and been reconsidered as a *process* – mainstreaming – caused by political and economic mechanisms (Huber 2007). If those definitions reflect the different theoretical perspectives and empirical findings of their researchers, what they share is attention to commercially dominant forms of music. Elvis Presley first conquered, then embodied, the populist realm of popular music. In the 1950s, as the 'Hillbilly Cat', he united the regional glamour of country music with the national youth market. His mainstreaming and ascent into the world of light entertainment were about 'buying in' rather than 'selling out', and remain interesting precisely because they symbolized the social groups who were previously left outside: Southern working-class folk, African Americans, teenagers. His spectacular national fame allowed him many of the rewards that came from being a star: mass adulation, recognition and affluence. Elvis fulfilled the American dream. As a 1960s matinee icon, though, he came to embody the blandness and potential compromise of mass culture (see Chapter 8 in this book). By the time he reached Vegas, his act drew together diverse vernacular musical roots and covered them in a veneer of a showbusiness spectacle. In some ways, by incorporating those on the outside, Elvis Presley came to represent the heart of the pop mainstream – by which I mean the broadest field of 'mass, popular, and massively popular cultural forms' (Huber 2007: 1). Yet, in turn, mass popularity has its own fringes and margins. Definitions of the mainstream have been a way to locate texts in the immediate social and cultural field rather than talk about audiences or temporal processes like nostalgia (see Grossberg 1997: 221). As an iconic star, Elvis came to embody the historical continuity of mainstream music (see Toynbee 2002: 156). Yet his most dedicated fans are now a visible minority, and their concerns can be at odds with those of the contemporary public sphere. In that sense, the loyal support for a star who once dominated the charts and now lingers in popular memory should cause us to reconsider the notion of the mainstream and address its contradictory formulation. Elvis' mainstream popularity and longevity are not reflected in the relative marginalization of his most ardent fans.

In February 1967, Elvis acquired a 163-acre ranch about ten miles south of Graceland. He named it the Circle G in homage to Graceland and the Circle Z ranch, an imaginary location from his 1965 film *Tickle Me* (dir. Norman Taurog 1965). According to Adam Victor, who wrote *The Elvis Encyclopedia*:

> To begin with the place was a cross between a commune and a dude ranch, with fun and communal living the order of the day. Elvis and the whole gang would spend up to two weeks at a time leading the frontier life.
>
> *(2008: 82)*

Most accounts suggest that the singer was disappointed by scripts he was offered at that point, and delayed working on his next film, *Clambake* (dir. Arthur Nadal 1967), to stay at the ranch. The Circle G gave Elvis a place to relax where he could enjoy his honeymoon, ride his horses and fool around with his entourage. By the summer of 1967, he had returned to his old life and the ranch lay dormant, but it was not finally sold on by the Presleys until 1973. Developers have proposed various plans since then, aiming to turn the ranch into a residential resort or perhaps an Elvis theme park, but the place has remained in a state of disrepair. In August 2010, a British Elvis fan named Lesley Pilling began a 'Friends of Elvis – Save the Circle G Campaign' on Facebook 'to rescue, restore and preserve the property formally known as The Circle G Ranch. To open meaningful dialogue between all interested parties and in doing so, secure the future of the Circle G in Elvis' memory.'[1] The 'pressure group' had over 3000 supporters. It attracted endorsements from a representative of the county tourism office and various members of Elvis' entourage. Pilling's idea was to raise sufficient funds – perhaps by selling shares – to purchase the property outright and turn it into an animal sanctuary or haven for fans.

While the campaign to save the Circle G was unusually prominent, the issues around it are typical of the complexities of Elvis heritage sites. At the same time as creating many of the places that are now being remembered as history, the modernist imperative to restructure the built environment has prompted romantic notions of a disappearing or preserved Memphis. While academic and popular discussions tend to talk about fan pilgrimages to Graceland (see Rodman 1996; Alderman 2002; Leaver and Schmidt 2010; Drummond 2011), the successful renovation of the mansion *as a heritage business* has maintained it as a focus of popular interest when other Elvis sites have decayed. A minority of devoted fans understand and conceptualize Memphis in a broader way than Graceland or Sun Studio. My argument in this chapter is that their desires often contradict the rhythms of a built environment, and will only preserve the landscape if they can translate into a feasible marketplace.

Walking in Memphis: The Place of Music Fan Fantasies

> I suppose I've been talking about Elvis since the day I met him as an eighth grader at North Memphis's Humes High School in 1948. I was amazed that this new kid in town had the talent and confidence to bring a guitar to school and sing 'Old Shep' for our music class.
>
> *(Klein 2010: ix)*

The fans who visit Memphis are already familiar with it long before they get there. Hundreds of books offer stories about Elvis' life and invite readers to imagine what it was like to be there. Some are written by biographers such as Peter Guralnick (1995, 1999). Members of Elvis' entourage, like George Klein, have also recounted tales of Elvis' life (e.g. see Fortas 1992; Esposito 1994). Such true stories invite us to fabricate imagined experiences, which I have called 'imagined memories' (see Duffett 2003, 2010). Often depicting a musical performance from a time before the artist was famous, the memories are imagined by readers who were not there to experience them *back then*. Narratives of history make such memories matter, helping to valorize and commodify them as foundations for various lines of media production. Imagined memories are encapsulated in a specific time period and geographic setting. Mikhail Bakhtin's notion of the chronotope (literally 'time-space') might help to conceptualize their spatial and temporal fixity. Although Bakhtin used the term for literature, it can usefully be applied to other cultural fields:

> In the literary-artistic chronotope, spatial and temporal indicators are fused into one carefully thought-out, concrete whole. Time, as it were, thickens, takes on flesh, becomes artistically visible; likewise, space becomes charged and responsive to the movements of time, plot and history.

This intersection of axes and fusion of indicators characterizes the artistic chronotope.

(Bakhtin 2002: 15)

This notion of the chronotope highlights an intrinsic connectedness between spatial and temporal relationships defined by a concrete, bounded specificity. Even though fans may have been fascinated by their star's musical performances, they also desire to explore his or her biographic world, and use the chronotope to immerse themselves in a realm of meaning and imagination. Its geographic dimension can therefore indicate ways in which place can encapsulate celebrity aura – at least as after-image – as well as accrete myths and authenticate cultural memories.

Referencing the period between when Elvis Presley came to Memphis and when he died, Sharon Urquhart (1993: 40) locates the boundaries of the Elvis-in-Memphis chronotope as 'Memphis: September, 1948 through August 16, 1977'. While he did not spend all his time in the city during this period, Memphis remains crucial to Elvis' mythology as the place he *claimed* as his own territory. Many older Memphians still have memories of some sort connected with him. His residency represented a decision to stay Southern and provincial when he could have lived elsewhere, so it also implied a certain claiming of identity.

Elvis has often been theorized in relation to his rootedness in the South (e.g. see Pratt 1992; Shelton Reed 1997; Doll 1998; Cox 2009). However, his image makes less sense in relation to the Gothic sensibility expressed by writers like William Faulkner than to the shape and fate of a humble region that by the 1940s was enthusiastically embracing modern life in the midst of a nation which was arguably biased against it. As some readings of titles such as Elvis' 1969 album *From Memphis to Vegas/From Vegas to Memphis (Back in Memphis)* (RCA LSP6020) might imply, his life and career spanned the period of American history from the Great Depression to high modernity. In the 1950s, he embraced many of the delights of modernity, such as flash clothes, fast food and faster cars. Yet even while Elvis continued to acquire symbols of material comfort, his move from a detached bungalow on Audobon Drive to the 'plantation' grandeur of a mansion in Whitehaven can be read in part as a veiled rejection of the class-based cultural value system shared by more dominant 'modern' Northern states (see Nickson 2005: 189).

Historically, American perceptions of the South have taken on a very specific character. Some commentators have suggested that Edward Said's notion of Orientalism is relevant here (see Said 2003; Jansson 2003). The concept suggests that particular social groups (in this case, Americans from Northern states) use geography as a pretext to project imagined 'otherness' on to territories beyond their immediate domain. These places then become seen through a filter of fear and desire. Local residents must then negotiate an image attributed to them and develop a kind of double consciousness. In the specific context of the American South, part of this image relates to the idea that the region is lagging behind –

a position that claims a unidirectional, ethnocentric, progressivist conception of American modernity:

> The reality that, over a century and a half of fading away, the South has staged what George B. Tindall called 'one of the most prolonged disappearing acts since the fall of Rome' is less a commentary on the stubbornness of its identity than on the way we have defined and perceived that identity in the first place.
>
> *(Cobb 2005: 7)*

Cobb adds that the South has been engaged not so much in a disappearance than an adaption: 'The history of southern identity is not a story of continuity *versus* change, but continuity within it' (2005: 7). Nevertheless, there is a sense in which the view of Southern identity as disappearing lends itself to conceptions of Memphis in general, and Elvis in particular, as representing a past that is slipping away. This perception is not just temporal (nostalgia) but spatial: it defines the 'rootsy' Memphis music scene through its perceived geographic marginality.

Scholars in popular music studies have conceptualized scenes as communities based upon the face-to-face meetings of practising musicians (see Straw 1991; Cohen 1991; Shank 1994; Bennett and Peterson 2004). Such accounts tend to emphasize the actuality and uniqueness of place in the construction and operation of music-making communities. However, when scenes are examined after the fact, they are inevitably subject to a process of mythologization. In relation to Memphis, Orientalist perceptions of Southern culture have located the city's music scene in a way that references the city's 'otherness'. The Memphis music scene has been understood, first, as emerging eccentrically in relation to the central thrust of modernity and, second, as tragically disappearing in the face of further change. Discussing a meeting with Sun producer Sam Phillips, who he affectionately framed as having 'the look of an Old Testament prophet in sneakers', music critic Peter Guralnick (2002: 326, 337) says, 'Memphis, always a haven for eccentrics and individualists, is the only locale I know that actually boasts of its craziness.' Another, more subtle, example comes from Robert Gordon (1996: 1) who explains, 'The blues musicians were giving me a geographical and historical grounding in Memphis. Their lives were the product of this particular place.' While Guralnick's description contrasts Memphis with the professional conformity of other places (perhaps New York, or more locally Nashville), Gordon's simply perceives the city as grounding and productive – a cradle, a crucible; a 'particular place' that implicitly contrasts with the anonymous and unmagical *spaces* manufactured by high modernity. Talking about soul music, Guralnick again plays on this notion of disappearance: 'Southern soul music developed out of a time and a set of social circumstances that are unlikely to be repeated' (2002: 1). Such statements align a sense of the South slipping away with concerns of musical uniqueness, heritage and preservation.

Memphis as a Space of (Heritage) Modernity

As the historic home of a melting pot of vernacular American music genres (blues, country, gospel, soul), Memphis has long held a special attraction for music fans. The racial segregation that fostered Beale Street as a regional hub of black entertainment has in turn enabled an ongoing social fusion that has helped to give rise to a magnificent series of musical innovations. W.C. Handy's famous 'Memphis Blues' had phenomenal sales after its publication as sheet music in 1912. Sam Phillips first arrived in Memphis to visit Beale Street in 1939. Because he was raised in the same town as Handy, Phillips felt an affinity with the composer (see Crouch and Crouch 2009: viii). Nine years earlier, Handy had been commemorated as part of Beale Street when a park named after him was opened in the lot of a demolished food market (Raichelson 1999: 46). Due to Beale Street's reputation, Memphis was already a place of legend and commemoration. Equally, once Elvis found inspiration on Beale Street and reached a level of international fame, he too became commemorated.[2] Beale Street remains open between Second and Fourth Street, but it is now a pedestrian tourist beat, with its cafes and blues halls. Ordinances against pan-handling and firearms allow tourists to be shielded from any potential inconvenience and danger while they enjoy local food and a high standard of musicianship. A new shopping and dining area is being created at the Mississippi end called the Beale Street Landing. Such spaces of urban regeneration and civic boosterism are primarily for mainstream tourists and locals, not just Elvis fans. Tourism is not the city's main employer (the honour goes to logistics), and Elvis fans make up a tiny fraction of the ten million annual visitors. Present-day music heritage visitors to Memphis discover a diverse series of sites. Graceland remains the jewel in the crown of the Elvis heritage industry, having opened its gates to the public 30 years ago after Priscilla Presley raised capital and consulted with Disney and the National Park Service (see O'Neal 1997: 105–23). A free shuttle bus provided by Sun Studio takes visitors between Graceland, Union Avenue and the Rock 'n' Soul museum near Beale Street.

A minority of dedicated fans explore localities beyond the pre-packaged route. Their aim is not so much to develop or display cultural capital (though that may be a by-product) as it is to experience concrete reference points to help them to understand Elvis' world. They draw on niche guidebooks such as Cindy Hazen and Mike Freeman's *Memphis, Elvis-Style* (1997), William Yenne's *The Field Guide to Elvis Shrines* (2004) and Andrew Ahearn's *Follow Me to Tennessee* (2007). The last of these was written by an English fan who has visited Memphis over 20 times and lists over a hundred places in the city, including at least eight of the singer's homes (not counting Graceland), three places where his father lived, various restaurants, schools, studios, movie theatres and even a roller skating rink. With this assistance, fans can explore particular places that once formed part of the chronotope, but they may find the urban fabric in a variety of states.

Modernity is characterized by processes of geographically uneven development (see Harvey 1991:294) in which some places thrive and others languish, and many alternate periodically between the two. Most locations are subject to cycles of modernization that operate at variety of rates. Even though Memphis did not receive the same investment during the industrial revolution that changed the Northern cities, it was not untouched by modernity. The places that fascinate Elvis fans are therefore in various phases of departure from their participation in his chronotope: some are preserved, some renovated, but many are decaying or lost.

Preserved locations serve to maintain Elvis' legacy by carefully being kept as they once were. Graceland is a preserved location, maintained in effect as a heritage business by Elvis Presley Enterprises. Elvis' home at 1034 Audubon Drive – the one he owned before Graceland – is also a preserved location. For seven years it was owned by the Elvis author Mike Hazen, who sold it in 2007 to Mike Curb, an ex-musician and head of MGM Records who was elected Governor of California in the late 1970s. The Mike Curb Foundation completed restoration of the house and donated it to Rhodes College. It is recognized as part of the National Register of Historic Places. Since Audubon Drive is still located in a secluded, middle-class neighbourhood, local residents do not encourage mass tourism. Instead, Freeman operates a private tour that takes fans on an individual or small-group basis to see the outside of the house. Audubon Drive is part of Elvis' legacy, but it is not at the centre of his heritage business. The house is preserved in the sense that it is kept as a historic site, but not inhabited by ordinary residents. Such sites are unusual in that sometimes they can remain static in contradiction to the rhythm of the built environment. They each require special recognition as a historic place and a business model or other source of finance.

Unlike preserved places, renovated ones are those that have either been continuously used or restored to a good state of repair with the same function that made them famous.[3] Sun Studio, the hallowed place that gave birth to some of the city's finest blues and rockabilly music, is now operational as both a tourist locale by day and a working studio by night. In a sense, its moment in the Elvis chronotope between July 1953 and December 1956 belies its regenerative journey as part of the built environment of Memphis. The popular attention to Sun's origins in 1950 ignores the various incarnations of its building on Union Avenue. John Schorr, the president of Sun Studio, explained how the location was developed well before Sam Phillips ever set foot in his studio:

> Our building was first built in 1908 as the Schneider Bakery and operated as a single address, 708 Union Avenue, until the Great Depression put it out of business in the 1930s. At that time, the building was subdivided up into three separate addresses, 706 Union (studio), 708 Union (upstairs) and 710 Union (downstairs cafe) for the purpose of renting out the spaces to different businesses. The year before Sam Phillips took over the lease on 706

Union (1949), the Memphis business directory has 'Sherry's Slip Covers' listed as the occupant of the address. At that time, Union Avenue was home to all the car dealerships in Memphis. There was a Buick dealership located to the right of our building with Walker Radiator shop on the left. The Cadillac dealership that Johnny Cash's brother worked at was right down the street on Union Avenue . . . Miss Taylor's Restaurant was located in 710 Union and 708 Union was a boarding house in 1950 when Sam moved in.

(personal comment)

After the studio stopped recording and releasing new music in the late 1960s, its building was sold to a plumbing company and eventually became an auto-parts store. It was reopened as a studio space a decade after Elvis died.

Another Memphian institution that has survived by moving location is the Lansky Brothers' clothing store. Lansky's is important to Elvis' story as the Beale Street clothier that helped him find his visual style (see Lansky 2010). In 1981, however, the store moved to the lobby of the Peabody Hotel, itself a Memphis landmark with a considerable reputation.[4] As Hal Lansky explained, referencing both the chronotopic imaginary of the fans and the necessity of adaption within tradition:

> We started out on Beale Street selling to, mostly, African-Americans. We supplied tuxedos to the Mid-South area. At one time we outfitted big and tall men. Every ten years we changed because the business changed. So if we hadn't changed, we wouldn't have been in business 65 years. Being clothier to Elvis sometimes – although we eat, sleep and breathe Elvis – it's a double edged sword; sometimes it's awesome, sometimes it's a turn off. If we had to depend on all Elvis fans, our business would be very limited. They're great fans, but we also appeal to business travelers, conventioners. We shop the market. We bring in product that is happening now, because if we were just one segment we'd get cornered. When these people come in from Europe they are expecting to walk into a time tunnel like it was 50 years ago with all retro stuff; a lot of times they are disappointed. If we were all that, I don't think we'd be in business.

(personal comment)

While the Lansky Brothers' business survived by capitalizing on its reputation and physically consolidating with another historic site, other historic spaces have fared less well. Recycled places are those that have departed from their role in the chronotope because they have been forced to change function to stay prosperous. Poplar Tunes was perhaps Memphis' earliest record shop, and was frequented by Elvis when he lived in relative poverty at Lauderdale Courts. Once he became a Sun artist, Elvis would visit to check for interest in his latest releases. Other Sun artists also held signings in the store. By the 1990s, Poplar had become a regular stop for coach-loads of fans who visited Memphis. Periodic visitors and the handful of locals buying music sold there could not maintain the store's profit-ability. Facing competition from the internet, Poplar closed its doors in 2009, only to be reopened as the Happy Tummy diner. While the site's participation in the chronotope sustained its function for many decades, economic pressures eventu-ally forced it to change roles. Ironically, the shop's famous neon sign is now on display as a cherished addition to the Rock 'n' Soul Museum.

The less prosperous geographic locations are not those that were preserved, renovated or even recycled, however. Instead, some remain in a state of disuse and decay. If recycled locations still participate in the cyclic of the development of the urban fabric, decaying places have become marginal to the process of capital accu-mulation. In that sense, they are precariously preserved by their own marginality as places in a gradual state of decline from their glorious past. These stagnant loca-tions only retain an aura through their inclusion in the chronotope, but they cannot translate it into heritage prosperity. Perhaps the greatest tragedy on the Memphian landscape is the Hotel Chisca. Positioned a few blocks from Beale Street, the Chisca was where DJ Dewey Phillips first broadcast Elvis' initial Sun record, 'That's All Right' (the word 'Mama' was omitted from the original title) on WHBQ in July 1954. The hulk of this vast building now lies in a state of abandon-ment. In 2006 it was announced that the property – which owed $190,000 in back taxes – was to be demolished by a developer who planned to create a new Hilton Hotel. Mike McCarthy, who worked at Sun, explained, 'Tearing down the Chisca would be an affront to Memphis' music history, to the memory of Dewey Phillips and to Elvis Presley' (Meek 2006). Yet the possibility of renovating the Chisca is prohibitively expensive, and local tourist and foot traffic is still minimal. Outside of a dedicated handful of location-spotters who visit during Elvis Week, this important building receives too little attention to make it viable. Its participa-tion in the chronotope positions it as a historic place, but it has not made the transition into a heritage centre.

A final category of places that have departed from their function in the chro-notope consists of those that have absolutely disappeared. The American Sound Studio at 827 Thomas Street in North Memphis was famous not just for Elvis' recording sessions with producer Chips Moman in 1969, but as the birthplace of some of the finest rock and soul music of its era. Opened in 1967 and closed in 1971, it played host to Dusty Springfield, Neil Diamond and Aretha Franklin. Yet American Sound was only located on Thomas Street because of the low ground rent in such a dilapidated part of town. Since studio businesses usually start out as risky, low-profit ventures, they tend to prefer areas with low overheads. While they can play a spectacular role in the chronotope, recording studios are often part of the early regeneration of the urban fabric. Just as the profits of those businesses that fostered the vanguard of Memphis music financially fluctuated, so did the price of the built environment that supported them. In that sense, the marginality of American Sound's location facilitated both its emergence and disappearance. Its story shows that relatively ephemeral sites can still be important to fans.

The idea of the popular music mainstream reflects commercial processes and cultural debates that do not map neatly on to the sociology of fans as an audience. As tourists, Elvis' most dedicated followers have persistent concerns that can be tangential to those of other people. While their hero's *music* both redefined and remains within the mainstream, at least in Toynbee's (2002) substantive sense, as time goes by elements of his spatial legacy are inevitably fading from view. Consequently, what began as fannish interest in a mainstream(ed) artist is now taking its adherents well off the beaten track. With their attachment to the Elvis chronotope, the Memphis visitors are perhaps utopian in their hope that the built environment will progressively become enshrined in the face of urban change. Their fear that Elvis' memory will disappear as the places where he lived gradually slip away raises the question of whether his monumental legacy merits the fossilization of the landscape. In some senses, Elvis was always bigger than Memphis, but in others it is now bigger than him. The same rhythms that gave rise to the locales he frequented from 1948 to 1977 are now reconstructing the landscape once again. As fans use their agency to preserve urban locations that participated in his chronotope, the fabric of the city will become a measure of their efforts, not his alone. The irony of such widespread fascination with Elvis' chronotope is that it leaves non-Memphians attempting to preserve a place and era that they never quite experienced. This disconnect is not just an element of nostalgic fandom, however; it is something characteristic of all modern experience. Discussing modernity, Marshall Berman (1988: 17) argues that 'we find ourselves today in the midst of a modern age that has lost touch with the roots of its own modernity'. Popular music heritage therefore represents modernity attempting to compensate for its own shortcomings.

Notes

1 Pilling's Facebook page, www.facebook.com/notes/friends-of-elvis-save-the-circle-g-campaign/press-release-september-2011/269740309715002 (accessed 20 March 2012).
2 Before he died, Elvis was already beginning to live in an environment dedicated to his own heritage: Highway 51 adjoining Graceland was renamed Elvis Presley Boulevard.
3 Other renovated places in Memphis connected to Elvis' life and legend include Stax Studio, Humes High School, the Memphian Theatre and Overton Park Shell.
4 The Lansky site lists them as having 'four different concept shops' in that location: www.lanskybros.com/king_en/lansky-bros-clothier-to-the-king-book-pre-order-may-2010.html (accessed 20 March 2012).

References

Ahearn, A. (2007) *Follow Me to Tennessee: an Englishman's guide to the Elvis hangouts*, Worthing: Essential Elvis.
Alderman, D. (2002) 'Writing on the Graceland wall: on the importance of authorship in pilgrimage landscapes', *Tourism Recreation Research*, 27 (2): 27–33.

Bakhtin, M. (2002) 'Forms of time and of the chronotope in the novel: notes towards a historic poetics', in B. Richardson (ed.), *Narrative Dynamics: essays on time, plot, closure, and frames*, Chicago: Ohio State University Press.

Bennett, A. and Peterson, R. (2004) *Music Scenes: local, translocal and virtual*, Nashville, TN: Vanderbilt University Press.

Berman, M. (1988) *All That is Solid Melts into Air: the experience of modernity*, New York: Penguin.

Cobb, J.C. (2005) *Away Down South: a history of Southern identity*, Oxford: Oxford University Press.

Cohen, S. (1991) *Rock Culture in Liverpool: popular music in the making*, Oxford: Clarendon Press.

Cox, K. (2009) 'The South and mass culture', *Journal of Southern History*, 75(3): 677–90.

Crouch, K. and Crouch, T. (2009) *The Sun King: the life and times of Sam Phillips, the man behind Sun Records*, London: Piatkus Books.

Curtis, B. (2008) *Dark Places: the haunted house in film*, London: Reaktion Books.

Doll, S. (1998) *Understanding Elvis: Southern roots vs star image*, New York: Garland.

Duffett, M. (2003) 'Imagined memories: Webcasting as a "live" technology and the case of little big gig', *Information, Communication and Society* 6(3): 307–25.

—— (2010) 'Sworn in: *Today*, Bill Grundy and the Sex Pistols', in I. Inglis (ed.), *Popular Music and British Television*, Farnham: Ashgate.

Drummond, K. (2011) 'Shame, consumption, redemption: reflections on a tour of Graceland', *Consumptions, Markets and Culture* 14(2): 203–13.

Esposito, J. (1994) *Good Rockin' Tonight*, New York: Simon & Schuster.

Fortas, A. (1992) *Elvis from Memphis to Hollywood: memories from my twelve years with Elvis Presley*, Ann Arbor, MI: Popular Culture Ink.

Gordon, R. (1996) *It Came from Memphis*, New York: Faber & Faber.

Grossberg, L. (1992) *We Gotta Get Outta This Place: popular conservativism and postmodern culture*, New York: Routledge.

—— (1997) 'Re-placing popular culture', in S. Redhead, D. Wynne and J. O'Connor (eds), *The Clubcultures Reader: readings in popular cultural studies*, Oxford: Blackwell.

Guralnick, P. (1995) *Last Train to Memphis: the rise of Elvis Presley*, London: Abacus.

—— (1999) *Careless Love: the unmaking of Elvis Presley*, London: Abacus.

—— (2002) *Lost Highway: journeys and arrivals of American musicians*. Edinburgh: Cannongate.

Harvey, D. (1991) *The Condition of Postmodernity*, Oxford: Blackwell.

Hazen, C. and Freeman, M. (1997) *Memphis, Elvis-Style*, Winston-Salem, NC: John F. Blair.

Huber, A. (2007) 'What's in a mainstream? Critical possibilities', *Altitude*, 8: 1–12, www.api-network.com/altitude/pdf/8/2_Huber_final_completeEP.pdf (accessed 10 June 2012).

Jansson, D. (2003) 'Internal Orientalism in America: WJ Cash's *The Mind of the South* and the spatial construction of national identity', *Political Geography*, 22(3): 293–316.

Klein, G. (2010) *Elvis My Best Man: Radio Days, Rock 'n' Roll Nights and My Lifelong Friendship with Elvis Presley*, New York: Crown.

Lansky, B. (2010) *Lansky Brothers: clothier to the King*, Nashville: Beacon Books.

Leaver, D. and Schmidt, R. (2010) 'Together through life: an exploration of popular music heritage and the quest for re-enchantment', *Creative Industries Journal*, 3(2): 107–24.

Meek, A. (2006) 'Hotel Chisca faces possible demolition', *Memphis Daily News*, 9 June, www.memphisdailynews.com/editorial/Article.aspx?id=30414 (accessed 20 March 2012).

Nickson, C. (2005) 'Graceland', in P. Kennedy (ed.), *Warman's Elvis Field Guide: values and identification*, Iowa City, IO: KP Books.

O'Neal, S. (1997) *Elvis Inc.: the fall and rise of the Presley empire*, New York: Prima Lifestyles.

Pratt, L.R. (1992) 'Elvis, or the ironies of a Southern identity', in K. Quain (ed.), *The Elvis Reader: texts and sources on the King of rock 'n' roll*, New York: St Martin's Press.

Raichelson, R. (1999) *Beale Street Talks: a walking tour down the home of the blues*, Memphis: Arcadia Records.

Rodman, G. (1996) 'Elvis space', in G. Rodman (ed.), *Elvis After Elvis: the posthumous career of a living legend*, London: Routledge.

Said, Edward (2003) *Orientalism*, London: Penguin.

Shank, B. (1994) *Dissonant Identities: Rock 'n' roll scene in Austin, Texas*. Middletown, TX: Wesleyan University Press.

Shelton Reed, J. (1997) 'Elvis as Southerner', in V. Chadwick (ed.), *In Search of Elvis: music, art, race, religion*, Boulder, CO: Westview Press.

Straw, W. (1991) 'Systems of articulation, logics of change: communities and scenes in popular music', *Cultural Studies* 5(3): 368–81.

Thornton, S. (1995) *Club Cultures: music, media and subcultural capital*, Oxford: Polity Press.

Toynbee, J. (2002) 'Mainstreaming, from hegemonic centre to global networks', in D. Hesmondhalgh and K. Negus (eds), *Popular Music Studies*, London: Arnold.

Urquhart, S. (1993) *Placing Elvis: a tour guide to the kingdom*, New Orleans: Paper Chase.

Victor, A. (2008) *The Elvis Encyclopedia*, London: Overlook Duckworth.

Yenne, William (2004) *The Field Guide to Elvis Shrines*, San Francisco: Last Gasp.

10

'FOLLOWING IN MOTHER'S SILENT FOOTSTEPS'

Revisiting the Construction of Femininities in 1960s Popular Music

Sheila Whiteley

My 13-year-old grand-daughter is in love with Justin Bieber. So is her best friend. He is an important element in their friendship: they can sing all his songs; they know his likes and dislikes, and what he looks for in a potential girlfriend. They contribute regularly to updates on his fan club, chatting about his latest concerts, rhapsodizing about his looks. They are also academically bright and articulate about their views on life. I think back to my own imaginary 'love affairs' with 1960s rock stars Mick Jagger and Jim Morrison and realize I remember most of their repertoire. But then, I also know that I would be able to sing along to most of the hits from the 1960s and that I have not only internalized lyrics by The Beatles and other iconic figures, but also (let's face it) the dolly-bird pop of Lulu and Cilla, albeit seemingly balanced by Sandie Shaw and Dusty Springfield. I like to think I was a rebel, influenced by French Existentialism. I still have my 1967 copy of Mikhail Bulgakov's *The Master and Margarita,* a book given to Mick Jagger by Marianne Faithfull, which fed the satanic fantasy associated with the Rolling Stones' hit 'Sympathy for the Devil' (1968). My trek to San Francisco in 1968 surely evidenced counter-cultural ideals, albeit fed by my love of The Doors. I was a feminist, immersed in women's lib (as it was called at the time) – and yet, as Sandi Toksvig (2001: 24) writes:

> It's when you go to the supermarket that you see the true triumph of women's liberation ...These are the women who have achieved the serenity of motherhood, the satisfaction of a creative career and the ability to achieve orgasm during the spin cycle of their many efficient household appliances. Women who know how to fondle a melon into ripeness, a child into slumber and a man into ecstasy. Is it true? Wander down any aisle and find out ...

Slightly overweight, slightly unfit, slightly distracted. Minimal makeup, maximum perma-press. These are the women who aren't supposed to exist any more. They were supposed to have woken to the clarion call of liberation given in the 1960s and 1970s and reached out to fulfill themselves. Instead these women had stolidly followed in their mother's silent footsteps.

Toksvig's observation relates to my investigation into the 1960s, more specifically what it is that influenced seemingly articulate women, motivated by the writings of Germaine Greer and other feminists of the time, to capitulate and follow 'in their mother's silent footsteps'. If rock was truly the voice of the counter-culture, how and why did it undermine the ideology that defined women's liberation, and to what extent did the seemingly rebellious voice of these cultural revolutionaries perpetuate mainstream sensibilities in their musical narratives? Surely it was mainstream pop that was responsible for reproducing conventional femininities, not rock. Why, then, with all the hype of the so-called sexual revolution, did mainstream pop *and* rock continue to perpetuate the normative gender discourse that dominated the 1960s and beyond?

The Paradox Surrounding Wayward Girls and Wicked Women[1]

As Eric Hobsbawm (1994: 6) suggests, the 1960s fell within 'a sort of Golden Age', which began with Western Europe's recovery from World War II in the early 1950s and ended with the onset of global recession two decades later. It was a period that 'changed human society more profoundly than any other period of comparable brevity' (6). The British parliament confronted outmoded laws with the abolition of capital punishment (1965), the *Homosexual Reform Act* (1967) and the *Abortion Act* (1967), and changes in legislation by the Labour Party led to a relaxation in divorce laws, aimed at providing a legal framework that would allow for greater self-determination in social life and relationships – the so-termed 'no blame' divorce.

Meanwhile, the Kinsey Reports discussed previously taboo subjects, including masturbation and the female orgasm; the contraceptive pill promised no more unwanted pregnancies, and for those who 'fell', Dr Spock provided advice on how to bring up your baby. With the 1960s challenging the grey-tinged norms of our parents' generation by embracing new sexual freedoms, the question is why so many women conformed to the myths of heterosexual adulthood perpetuated by a morally conservative mainstream. Why, given media reports on increasing promiscuity and an upswing in premarital sexual behaviour (so implying that the stranglehold of traditional gendered roles might be weakening), did the young remain mostly 'conformist, conservative and respectable', with 'three-fifths of women married by 1966' (UKTV History, *The Sixties: The Beatles Decade,* Program 5)? This, in turn, raises questions concerning influence and identity – not least whether the media and the gendered soundscape of popular music continued to normalize sex-role socialization while obscuring the various forms that sexism could take. In other words, were mainstream pop and the more rebellious vocabulary of rock really so different in their framing of gendered femininity?

Initially, there was little to distinguish pop from the emerging vocabulary of rock,[2] with both appearing on the same musical menu: the British singles charts.[3] For example, 1963 included The Beatles' no. 1 hits 'She Loves You' and 'I Want to Hold Your Hand', with other top singles across the year including tracks by Cliff Richard and The Shadows and Elvis Presley. The rock style of The Rolling Stones broke into the charts in 1964 with 'It's All Over Now' and 'Little Red Rooster'; the same year saw no. 1 hits by, among others, The Animals, Manfred Mann, Herman's Hermits and The Beatles, so heralding the start of the so-termed 'British invasion', which in 1965 also included no. 1 hits by Georgie Fame and the Blue Flames, The Moody Blues, The Kinks and The Hollies. Five years on – and following the impact of the so-called Summer of Love (1967) and the plenitude of tracks celebrating flower power – mainstream audiences had largely returned to a more conservative diet.[4] It would seem, as Jeff Nuttall (1970: 211) earlier observed, that the 1967 alternative scene was largely a matter of fashion, a copycat response fostered by the media's attention to 'Swinging London':

> The national press were quick to move in: the *People* and the *News of the World* . . . bandying around the Castalia Foundation's term 'psychedelic' like any popularized psychoanalytic phrase, talking about flower-power and drug-crazed youths with that menopausal tone of total scandal that is guaranteed to bring the English clustering like flies to the subject as participants or sight-seers. Nine months after the first gathering at Haight Ashbury, mill-girls and office workers were wandering down the Brighton and Blackpool seafronts, jangling their souvenir prayer-belts, trailing their paisley bedspreads; brandishing daffodils and trying to look tripped out.

As Nuttall points out, The Beatles had 'gone flower power' (211) with their 1967 LP, *Sgt. Pepper's Lonely Hearts Club Band*. The Stones had followed suit with *Their Satanic Majesties Request* (1967) and for the 1960s generation, who had grown up with the two bands, their example suggested both new directions (The Beatles) and opportunism (The Stones) – albeit that the former band was already disintegrating,[5] while the latter returned to the norm following the devastation of their 1969 concert at Altamont, with *Sticky Fingers* (1971) and the aptly titled *Exile on Main Street* (1972). The pathway their fans should follow was a matter of choice and influence, and my identification of The Beatles and The Stones as iconic representatives of pop and rock respectively conceals more than it initially suggests in their framing of femininity.

As discussed in my earlier work, 'Repressive Representations' (Whiteley 2000: 32–41), it would seem that for The Stones, the identity of a woman resided in her sex, in her mouth, in her ability to give pleasure. Songs such as 'Backstreet Girl',

'Under My Thumb', 'Parachute Woman' and 'Brown Sugar' conflate 'femininity with femaleness, femaleness with female sexuality and female sexuality with a particular part of the female anatomy' and, like pornography, place the feminine as the object of inquiry (Kuhn, 1985: 40). Identified by Frith and McRobbie as cock rock, 'an explicit, crude and often aggressive expression of male sexuality' (1990: 375), The Stones' dismissive attitude towards women is summed up in the Jagger/Richards song 'Yesterday's Papers'. Written about model Chrissie Shrimpton, Jagger's girlfriend who he dropped for Marianne Faithfull in 1966, the callous lyrics – 'Who wants yesterday's papers, who wants yesterday's girl' – were arguably a contributory factor in her attempted suicide. In turn, '[T]he specter of "fallen Marianne", constructed as the pop-singing beauty destroyed by trying to fly too close to the sun . . . evidenced her descent into drugs, addiction, and homelessness after she left their orbit' (Coates 2010: 184–5). This provides a graphic example of a 'wayward girl' damaged by the iconic rebels of the 'white, heterosexual male imaginary' (Auslander 2006: 72) of 1960s rock culture. It is somewhat paradoxical that The Stones' first song for Faithfull, 'As Tears Go By', was not simply a marketable portrait of the 17-year-old singer ('My riches can't buy everything'), it was also a prescriptive commercial fantasy, 'a song with brick walls all around it, and high windows, and no sex' (Oldham, cited in Faithfull with Dalton 1994: 23). The message couldn't have been more clear: morality for women at the time continued to mean sexual morality:

> [T]o be a wayward girl usually has something to do with pre-marital sex; to be a wicked woman has something to do with adultery. This means it is far easier for a woman to lead a blameless life than it is for a man: all she has to do is to avoid sexual intercourse like the plague. What hypocrisy!
>
> *(Carter 1986: x)*

'So what should a woman do to be *good* and could [the Sixties'] woman ever be *really* right and so evade the role of victim?' (x). While The Beatles' repertoire suggests a gentler framing of women, the lyric mode of address is nevertheless largely conservative, albeit framed by groundbreaking arrangements and an increasingly experimental musical soundscape. As a mainstream band, The Beatles' ability to popularize even the most esoteric trends in British and American rock, and the extent to which their music achieved worldwide dissemination, are strong indicators of why their music/lyrics/image could exert such a formative influence on their legion of young, female fans. From the sentiments expressed in The Beatles' first album, *Please, Please Me* (1963), and on tracks such as 'Love Me Do' and 'I Want to Hold Your Hand', relationships are demonstrably in the flirtatious, courting mode of address – an indication that the 'romantic code' – carrying 'the girl over the limbo of adolescence' and delivering 'her safely from the family of origin to the family of destiny' (McRobbie 1991: 135) – remained a powerful moral influence. Virginity mattered, and the consequences of sex before marriage were considered a serious matter. It is, then, relevant to note that John Lennon set an appropriate example to his fans by marrying Cynthia Powell (on 23 August 1962), whom he had been dating since 1958, because she was pregnant – even though the marriage ended in an acrimonious divorce in 1968 on the grounds of his adultery with Yoko Ono.

The release of *Revolver* (1966) was an indication that the teenage girl of The Beatles' earlier Beat days had matured to become in turn the provider, the forgiver and the healer portrayed in their song 'Here, There and Everywhere'. She is a symbol of what could be, and is always there for the masculine ego to inhabit when he wants to escape from the realities of life. Two years later, 'Lady Madonna' (1968), 'children at [her] feet', continues to convey some of the understanding necessary for the contemporary woman, as her lover 'Friday night arrives without a suitcase, Sunday morning creeping like a nun', while 'Hey Jude' (1968), which was written by McCartney for Lennon's son Julian (the Jules of the original title, 'Hey Jules') to comfort him during his parents' divorce, portrays the woman as mother, comforter and support ('let her into your heart . . . then you can make it better'). Arguably, such songs draw on traditional definitions of femininity, where such associations as 'gentleness, modesty, humility, supportiveness, empathy, compassion, tenderness, nurturance, intuitiveness, sensitivity, unselfishness' (Tong 1998: 3) provide a commonplace yet fiercely patriarchal basis for constructing appropriate codes for behaviour and identity. 'Running my hand through her hair' ('Here, There and Everywhere') – one of the key signifiers of femininity – contrasts with the stark passivity of 'wearing the face she keeps in a jar by the door' of the unloved spinster in 'Eleanor Rigby'. The former has no need to be named – 'she is everywhere'; the latter is singled out, the bleakness of her existence marking her as an unfulfilled woman. One has succeeded and her life is magically transformed as she fulfils her feminine destiny; the other has failed to meet these culturally defined norms and 'was buried along with her name'. As Elvis Presley had sung some ten years earlier, to succeed as a woman, she should 'Love Me Tender, Love Me True' (1956).

Betty Friedan's insights thus provide an astute observation of the sex ideology of the early 1960s and beyond as she reflects on the 'strange discrepancy between the reality of our lives as women, and the image to which we were trying to conform, the image I came to call the feminine mystique' (1963: 77). As such, it is considered relevant, at this stage of my investigation, to briefly explore the role of British female artists during the 1960s, and to look at the extent to which their hit songs implied conformity or a challenge to the established status quo.

Brit Girls and the Construction of Femininity

A survey of the 1960s shows remarkably few no. 1 hits by female artists. Helen Shapiro had pole position with 'You Don't Know Me' and 'Walkin' Back to

Happiness' (1961), but it was not until 1964 that the next no. 1 appeared, this time 'You're My World' by Cilla Black. Sandie Shaw also had no. 1 hits with 'There's Always Something There to Remind Me' and 'Long Live Love' (1964); Dusty Springfield with 'You Don't Have to Say You Love Me' (1965); and Petula Clark with 'This is My Song' (1967). Shaw's Eurovision no. 1, 'Puppet on a String', also entered the 1967 charts on 27 April, staying in pole position for three weeks. Mary Hopkin's 'Those Were the Days' was six weeks in the charts (1968), and Jane Birkin and Serge Gainsbourg came in at no. 1 in October 1969 with 'Je T'aime, Moi No Plus'. The only female to achieve a no. 1 position in 1970 was Freda Payne, with 'Band of Gold'.

As Judith Butler (1999: 174) explains:

> [G]enders can be neither true nor false ... [T]hey require the repetition of a set of acts and the reiteration of signifiers, and while masculinity is commonly situated as the norm – as natural, original and absolute – femininity is understood as both performative and constructed.

As such, 'all gender formations are the results of careful and sustained practice and are thus not simply *formations* but *per*-formations' (Biddle and Jarman-Ivens 2007: 5). The identification of femininity as both performative and constructed provides an effective starting point for teasing out the ways in which 'hegemonic gender formations enforce especially effectively the criteria to which the subject must conform if s/he desires the attendant privileges of a hegemonic gender identity' (5), and a cursory glance at the hit titles shows that all are, in some way or another, related to relationships. Happiness, it seems, depends on requited love – more specifically, that loaded signifier, 'the band of gold'. As such, it is interesting to see how these songs support Friedan's observations concerning 'the feminine mystique', and the extent to which their narratives continue to situate women as simply *following* '[the] battle-scarred champion(s) of the counterculture' (Roszak, 1971: 65), rather than *becoming* equal partners in the bid for social and political change. In other words, how did the 'Brit Girls' negotiate gender in their performance of femininity, and to what extent did these and similar songs from the 1960s provide a commonsense guide to normative femininity, which in hindsight was both conservative and repressive?

While Helen Shapiro was younger than many of the emerging bands on the Beat scene, her legacy as a 1950s novelty star performer arguably undermined her credibility, not least when her manager, Norrie Paramour, vetoed the opportunity to record 'Misery', written for her by John Lennon. Nevertheless, within the context of early 1960s pop, her teenage angst lyrics clearly resonated with many, as her no. 1 position indicated. Not least, the lyrics 'Just because I'm in my teens, and I still go to school', from the song 'Don't Treat Me Like a Child' (1961), echoed the arguments many teenagers were having with their parents, while the impassioned 'Don't mother me ... gotta have my fun' anticipated a theme later explored by The Beatles in 'She's Leaving Home' (1967), where the bewildered voice of the protagonist's parents creates a telling commentary on a daughter who has upped and left for 'a man from the motor car trade'. As such, while there is little doubt that her hits across the 1950s and early 1960s (often written by songwriting partners Goffin and King) were tailored to her youthful image, there is nevertheless an underlying feel of teen-authenticity. Even so, her carefully backcombed hair and dresses, evoking the big band era of Alma Cogan, undoubtedly situated her as belonging to an earlier epoch – one that contrasted sharply with the wit and down-to-earth performing style of Cilla Black, whose friendship with The Beatles and no. 1 hit, 'You're My World' (1964) confirmed her status as the fun-loving Scouser[6] of the Beat generation.

As Patricia Juliana Smith (2010: 41) writes, Cilla Black 'charmed audiences through a cheerful candidness based largely on an absence of sophistication', singing whatever material she was given, including cover versions of American pop hits, Broadway show tunes and the occasional song written by The Beatles. Nevertheless, hits such as 'Love's Just a Broken Heart' ('They told me love was not what I dreamed it would be'), 'Step Inside Love' ('You look tired, love . . . rest your head on my shoulder . . .') and the title track to the 1966 film 'Alfie' ('I believe in love, Alfie, Without true love we just exist'), combined with the 'ordinary' and often brash vocal delivery, created the necessary feel for a girl from the provinces whose personality was the driving force behind her hits. She was, for many young women, 'just like us', and as such her words, combined with her mod image and outspoken views on life and love, rang true.

In contrast, Sandie Shaw embodied more the 'nonchalance typical of the new freedom of women in Swinging London, and, simultaneously, the bewilderment and melancholia of innocence giving way to experience' (Smith 2010: 150–1) – a quality that was embedded in her vocal delivery, which could switch between a maturity of tone and a vocal coloration that expressed romantic anxiety and adolescent angst. Her string of fifteen hits between 1964 and 1968 often expressed proto-feminist subject-matter by reversing traditional gender roles, and included 'You Can't Blame Him', where the girl laughs off her boyfriend's infidelity 'in a spirit of sexual equality ("You see, I'm the same")', and 'Nothing Comes Easy', 'where she dumps a boyfriend who, once she has had him, becomes clinging and no longer interesting ("I had a hard time getting him/and I'm regretting it now")' (153). Her 1967 Eurovision chart-topping single, 'Puppet on a String', therefore reads as a regressive move on the part of her management. The woman is relegated to a passive role, stripped of will and autonomy, a living doll, an automaton that is markedly at odds with her earlier independent image. This sense of being out of control is curiously reflected in Shaw's feeling of helplessness when, in February 1967, she was relentlessly pursued by the tabloid press when named as co-respondent in a divorce scandal ('I wasn't a hooker and I wasn't even putting it about; I was simply engaged to the wrong person' (quoted in Smith 2010, 153). Five years later, Dusty Springfield left the United Kingdom for Los Angeles. As she stated at the time, she was distressed by the constant attention of the media who persisted in probing into her private life and her possible bisexuality. It is arguably the case that their treatment was markedly different from that given to male stars with active sex lives, whose notoriety as cock rockers served only to enhance their performing credentials. Mick Jagger's omnivorous sexuality, for example, was both obscured and boosted by his relationship with Marianne Faithfull, despite the fact that it sullied her own reputation, relegating her to the status of a 'wayward girl' – a fate shared by Shaw and Springfield.

Dusty Springfield, the white Queen of Soul, famous for her blonde beehive wigs, heavy mascara and beaded gowns, was in retrospect one of the most influential singers of the 1960s, her vocal quality and admiration for blues, R&B and jazz setting her apart from the Brit girls discussed earlier. While her first albums were dominated by cover versions of songs originally recorded by African American singers, her pop arias – the three-minute musical miniatures that drew on Italian operatic devices – provide a graphic example of the ways in which such hits as 'Anyone Who Had a Heart' (1964), 'All I See is You' (1966) and 'You Don't Have to Say You Love Me' (1966) constituted 'both an invitation and a warning ... speed[ing] the listener to a specific emotional location far removed from the equally specific one that started the song' by 'taking a route filled with emotional and musical upheaval' (Randall 2009: 77). While musically unusual relative to other love songs of the era, they nevertheless reinforced the image of a single woman looking for, but rarely finding, love. 'I Just Don't Know What to Do With Myself', for example, suggests both a spontaneous and grudging acceptance of a harsh reality while reinforcing the message that to be happy and fulfilled a woman needs her man – despite the fact that Springfield's hyperfeminine, camp performance style was read by more intuitive fans as 'queering the popular pitch' of heterosexual conformity.

It is also evident that Springfield's performance style and record releases were more sophisticated than those of the other Brit girls, and that by 1964 she was already a seasoned professional. Petula Clark was even more atypical, with a singing career dating back to the mid-1950s. Her 1967 no. 1 hit 'This is My Song' was written by Charlie Chaplin for the Marlon Brando/Sophie Lauren epic, *A Countess from Hong Kong*, and exemplifies how, in the midst of acid-tinged hits of 1967, mainstream pop and film music continued to exert a strong presence. In contrast, the high, sweet register of Mary Hopkin's 1968 no. 1 'Those Were the Days' situated her as an innocent ingénue, reflecting on the heady days of the summer of love at a time when student uprisings, racial conflict, the assassination of Martin Luther King Jnr and the continuing war in Vietnam dominated the media. When it is discovered that Hopkin's image of youthful innocence was successfully managed and promoted by Paul McCartney, the question nevertheless arises of whose version of femininity we are looking at. My feeling at the time was that McCartney's management of Hopkin was another example of 'repressive representations', and it is a strange coincidence that Sandie Shaw (whose experience of Swinging London would have appeared more authentic) also released her version of the song at exactly the same time as Hopkin, but only achieved 37th position on the charts. By 1969, London was no longer eulogized as 'the swinging city', with Paris scooping the No. 1 spot in Jane Birkin and Serge Gainsbourg's erotic fantasy, 'Je T'aime, Moi Non Plus', while Freda Payne's 'Band of Gold' (1970) was a composition by the former Motown songwriting team Holland–Dozier–Holland.

Conclusion

It is a salutary fact that the 1960s Brit Girls were given short shrift or dismissed as 'dolly birds' and 'pop tarts' by otherwise pioneering feminist critics – although, as my research indicates, there is little to suggest that, with the possible exception of Sandie Shaw, their hits songs challenged the status quo of normative femininity. It is also evident that the espousal of freedom – highlighted by both the counterculture and media reports surrounding 'Swinging London' – was underpinned by sexual stereotyping and an often overt sexism that was further inflamed by the increasing attention given to the women's liberation movement. Constructed by the press as 'bra-burning radicals', proto-feminist suggestions that, to be liberated, women must escape the confines of heterosexuality and be given the freedom to follow the lead of their own desires provided scope for increasingly misogynistic reporting. Paradoxically, this fed the dubious accolade of 'pussy power' in *Play Power* and its sensational reporting of groupies as the 'sexological phenomenon of the sixties' (Neville 1971: 70). It is also evident that reports associated with what was perceived at the time as a rising and more promiscuous sexuality brought their own pressures and contradictions for women, as evidenced in the media's attitude towards Faithfull, Springfield and Shaw. Meanwhile, songs by the Rolling Stones continued to situate women as sexual objects, while The Beatles demonstrated that the only solution was to look to the past and aim for fulfilment in matrimony – an example they also followed in their personal lives.

It would thus appear that the contest between an emerging feminist ideology, the continuing subordination of women within the counter-culture, and the warnings and advice contained in contemporary pop and rock was far from equal. Whatever challenge there was to sex ideology, this challenge was undermined by the power of mainstream sensibilities that informed both contemporary rock and pop. Consequently, it was not until the shock politics of punk that a more complex relationship between popular music and the social discourses surrounding gender and sexuality would finally emerge (Reddington 2007; Whiteley 2010).

Notes

1 I have borrowed the title of Angela Carter's 1986 edited anthology of stories about women who refused to be limited by society's expectations or culture's taboos.
2 My focus on The Beatles and The Rolling Stones is intended to provide a point of comparison between pop and rock.
3 All information from *The Guinness British Hit Singles* (Rice et al. 1985).
4 In 1967, The Beatles ('All You Need is Love') and Procol Harum ('A Whiter Shade of Pale') shared pole position. By 1970, top hits included tracks by the England Cup Squad; 1971 opened with 'Grandad', a no. 1 hit by Clive Dunn, 'Chirpy, Chirpy, Cheep Cheep', by Middle of the Road, and 'Ernie, The Fastest Milkman in the West' by Benny Hill. There was a marked absence of both The Beatles and The Stones.
5 The so-called *White Album* (The Beatles, 1968) seemed an ironic take on their earlier successes, with little to suggest either literary or musical unity. By 1969, The Beatles were splitting up and there was an increasing involvement in their solo careers.
6 Colloquialism for Liverpool-born.

References

Auslander, P. (2006) *Performing Glam Rock: gender and theatricality in popular music*, Ann Arbor, MI: University of Michigan Press.

Biddle, I. and Jarman-Ivens, F. (eds) (2007) *Oh Boy! Masculinities and popular music*, New York: Routledge.

Bulgakov, M. (1967) *The Master and Margarita*, London: Harvill Press.

Butler, J. (1999 [1990]) *Gender Trouble: feminism and the subversion of identity*, London: Routledge.

Carter, A. (ed.) (1986) *Wayward Girls and Wicked Women*, London: Virago.

Coates, N. (2010) 'Whose tears go by? Marianne Faithfull at the dawn and twilight of rock culture', in L. Stras (ed.), *She's So Fine: reflections on whiteness, femininity, adolescence and class in 1960s music*, Farnham: Ashgate.

Faithfull, M. with Dalton, D. (1994) *Faithfull: an autobiography*, Boston: Little, Brown and Co.

Friedan, B. (1963) *The Feminine Mystique*, New York: W.W. Norton and Co.

Frith, S. and McRobbie, A. (1990) 'Rock and sexuality', in S. Frith and A. Goodwin (eds), *On Record: rock, pop and the written word*, London: Routledge.

Hobsbawm, E. (1994) *Age of Extremes: the short twentieth century, 1914–1991*, London: Michael Joseph.

Kuhn, A. (1985) *The Power and the Image: essays on representation and sexuality*, London: Routledge.

McRobbie, A. (1991) '*Jackie* magazine: romantic individualism and the teenage girl', in A. McRobbie (ed.), *Feminism and Youth Culture*, London: Macmillan.

Neville, J. (1971) *Play Power*, London: Paladin.

Nuttall, J. (1970) *Bomb Culture*, London: Paladin.

Randall, A.J. (2009) *Dusty: queen of the postmods*, New York: Oxford University Press.

Reddington, H. (2007) *The Lost Women of Rock Music: female musicians of the punk era*, Hampshire: Ashgate.

Rice, T., Rice, J., Gambaccini, P. and Read, M. (1985) *The Guinness British Hit Singles*, 5th edn, London: Guinness Superlatives.

Roszak, T. (1971) *The Making of a Counter Culture: reflections on the technocratic society and its youthful opposition*, New York: Faber and Faber.

Smith, P.J. (2010) 'Brit girls: Sandie Shaw and the women of the British invasion', in L. Stras (ed.), *She's So Fine: reflections on whiteness, femininity, adolescence and class in 1960s music*, Farnham: Ashgate.

Toksvig, S. (2001) *Flying Under Bridges*, London: Time Warner.

Tong, R. (1998) *Feminist Thought: a comprehensive introduction*, 2nd edn, London: Routledge.

Whiteley, S. (2000) 'Repressive representations', in *Women and Popular Music: sexuality, identity and subjectivity*, London: Routledge, 2000.

—— (2010) 'Trainspotting: a gendered history of Britpop', in A. Bennett and J. Stratton (eds), *Britpop and the English Music Tradition*, Farnham: Ashgate.

11

MUSIC FROM ABROAD

The Internationalization of the US Mainstream Music Market, 1940–90

Timothy J. Dowd

'Mainstream' is a useful term for describing various domains of social life – including those associated with popular music. The 'main' portion of this word connotes the centre of a particular domain. Hence fans, critics and others often use the term to signify music that is produced for and consumed by a large section of the population. Of course, some may rail against such a centre – as do certain punk fans who look negatively upon the mainstream while celebrating alternative music and lifestyles (e.g. Císař and Koubek 2012). The 'stream' portion of the word signifies that the centre is not fixed and permanent, but rather marked by ebb and flow, sometimes altering course over time. For example, Ennis (1992) shows that the mid-twentieth century mainstream of US popular music (i.e. rock 'n' roll) flowed from the confluence of other streams of music, such as the blues, folk and gospel – with each of these earlier streams changing the mainstream.

Like Ennis, I have researched the evolution of the mainstream of popular music in the United States, focusing on the commercial market in which it is produced and disseminated (e.g. Dowd 2003, 2004, 2011). Among other things, I found that the US market for mainstream music grew deeper during much of the twentieth century – with the sheer number of musicians and firms active within the market rising considerably. It also grew broader by way of an increasing diversity among its musicians – with African American, female and international performers all making greater waves in terms of success. Finally, the mainstream market has not been limited to either a single genre or musicians of a single nation.

This chapter delves further into the 'internationalization' of the US mainstream market during the mid- to late twentieth century. Elsewhere I have offered both a theoretical framework and statistical analyses to make sense of this internationalization (Dowd 2011). In this chapter, I provide an overview of internationalization's extent and then explain how the actions of three types of 'gatekeepers' account for the burgeoning success of international performers from the 1960s onwards. While some writers focus on how popular music of the United States has spread around the world (e.g. Hitters and van de Kamp 2010; Regev 2011), this chapter is concerned with the reverse flow, whereby music from abroad finds its way into the US mainstream (see also Achterberg et al. 2011).

Mapping the Mainstream of the Past

Scholars who study popular music of the present confront a veritable wealth of information. In the internet era, a host of online materials have afforded much data on the *current* practices and dispositions of media firms (e.g. Rossman, Chiu and Mol 2008), critics and marketers (e.g. Donze 2010) and audiences (e.g. Salganik and Watts 2008). However, those surveying mainstream music of the pre-internet era face a different situation – one in which data for a century's worth of business are not always so readily available.

In the face of such challenges, researchers such as myself have resorted to a data source that, while not perfect, provides a systematic way to map what has occurred in the mainstream market in decades past – the popularity charts compiled by *Billboard* (e.g. Dowd 2004; Lopes 1992; Peterson and Berger 1975). *Billboard* has been offering journalistic and business coverage of US entertainment industries since the 1890s (Anand 2005). In the 1940s, it began offering 'charts' – such as the 'Hot 100' charts – that ranked on a weekly basis which recorded songs ('singles') were most successful in terms of such things as radio airplay and retail sales.

Originally, these *Billboard* charts addressed popular music in general – the 'mainstream' (Dowd 2004). However, from 1942 onwards, *Billboard* also gradually expanded its coverage beyond the mainstream: it offered additional charts that weekly ranked recorded songs in supposedly 'specialized' markets of popular music – such as rhythm & blues (R&B) (beginning in 1942 as 'Harlem Hit Parade'), country (beginning in 1944 as 'Folk Records'), easy listening (1948), jazz (1967) and rap (1989) (Anand 2005; Dowd 2004, 2005). Sometimes, songs and performers from these specialized markets had so much success that they 'crossed over' to the mainstream – enjoying hits, say, in both the R&B and mainstream markets (Dowd 2011; Ennis 1992).

By making use of the 'mainstream' charts, researchers can track *all* songs, musicians and recording firms that have at least a modicum of success in a musical market that targets the broadest group of listeners, as opposed to those markets targeting particular segments of the population (such as country music). Moreover, researchers can map this weekly inflow as it occurs over decades. *Billboard* charts also provide an important means by which business and musical personnel try to make sense of their marketplace, including what sells and what does not (Anand 2005; Negus 1999).

Broadening the Mainstream Market: International Performers

By inspecting *Billboard* charts, I identified 22,560 hit songs occurring in the US mainstream market from 1940 to 1990 – with 4,928 performing acts and 640 recording firms accounting for these hits. Of these 4,928 performers – some 20 per cent (1,019) – were from beyond the United States. However, the range of success enjoyed by all these performers could vary considerably. For instance, slightly more than 45 per cent of all performers (2,243 of 4,928) secured only *one* hit song and then exited the US mainstream market. Forty-eight per cent of international performers were such 'one-timers' (492 of 1,019), while 45 per cent of the US performers appeared once. At the other end of the spectrum, Bing Crosby led all US performers during this period by way of his 149 hit songs, and The Beatles led all international performers with 67 hits. Of course, most performers fell somewhere in between – having more than one mainstream hit song but far fewer than either Crosby or The Beatles.

Table 11.1 provides details of those performers who garnered the most hit singles in the mid- to late twentieth century. Four points bear mentioning. First, the table captures the evolving genres of the mainstream market (Ennis 1992; Garofalo 1997). The hit-leaders listed there include representatives of (1) big bands of the 1940s and early 1950s (such as Glenn Miller, Sammy Kaye and Guy Lombardo); (2) vocalists of the 1940s and 1950s who championed smooth renditions of standards, love songs and novelties (such as 'How Much is That Doggie in the Window?'), some of whom began as front-singers in big bands (for example, Perry Como, Dinah Shore); (3) rock 'n' roll performers who sprang on to the

TABLE 11.1 Performers from the United States and abroad with the most hit singles in the US mainstream recording market, 1940–90

US performers	Performers from abroad
Bing Crosby (1940–62): 149	The Beatles (1964–82, UK): 67
Elvis Presley (1956–77): 147	Guy Lombardo (1940–52, Canada): 65
Frank Sinatra (1942–80): 142	Paul Anka (1957–83, Canada): 53
Perry Como (1943–74): 131	The Rolling Stones (1964–90,UK): 52
Nat 'King' Cole (1943–60): 100	Elton John (1970–90, UK): 48
James Brown (1958–86): 93	The Bee Gees (1967–89, UK): 40
Patti Page (1948–68): 79	Rod Stewart (1971–90, UK): 40
Jo Stafford (1944–57): 76	Olivia Newton–John (1971–88, Australia): 33
Ray Charles (1957–75): 74	Tom Jones (1966–77, UK): 29
Glenn Miller (1940–48): 72	Anne Murray (1970–86, Canada): 27
Aretha Franklin (1961–89): 71	The Who (1965–82, UK): 26
Tommy Dorsey (1940–58): 69	The Dave Clark Five (1964–67, UK): 24
Dinah Shore (1940–57): 68	The Four Lads (1952–59, Canada): 23
Fats Domino (1955–68): 66	The Kinks (1963–84, UK): 23
Sammy Kaye (1940–64): 65	Queen (1975–89, UK): 23

scene in the mid-1950s (for example, Fats Domino); (4) R&B and soul performers who 'crossed over' to the mainstream market from the 1960s onwards (such as James Brown, Ray Charles and Aretha Franklin); (5) rock bands of the 1960s and beyond (like The Beatles and The Rolling Stones); and (6) vocalists of the mid- to late twentieth century who combined elements from such genres as country and pop (such as Anne Murray and Olivia Newton-John). Second, all but three of the acts secured hit singles for more than a decade – with The Beatles even earning hits after disbanding and Glenn Miller benefiting from a hit after his death in World War II. Third, the table shows the relatively prominent position of performers from the 1940s and 1950s (for example, Bing Crosby), which I explain in the next section. Finally, the table shows that the most successful of the international performers (in terms of hit singles) come from three nations (Australia, Canada and the United Kingdom).

However, when we consider *all* the international performers who had at least one hit in the US market, we see that these performers hail from more than 35 nations (see Table 11.2). While performers from English-speaking nations did fairly well in the US mainstream market (Australia, Canada and the United Kingdom), this was not the case for all such nations (e.g. New Zealand). Likewise, geographical proximity to the United States may have helped performers from Canada, but it did not do so for those from Mexico.

Now consider Figure 11.1. It takes the weekly number of hit songs by international performers, and groups them into three-month blocks (i.e. 'quarters'),

TABLE 11.2 Nationality of performing acts with hit songs in the US mainstream recording market, 1940–90

Argentina (2)	Japan (5)
Australia (193)	Mexico (1)
Bahamas (5)	Montu Island (1)
Belgium (7)	Multinational (315)
Brazil (23)	Netherlands (34)
Cameroon (1)	New Zealand (6)
Canada (568)	Norway (5)
Cuba (17)	Philippines (2)
Czechoslovakia (1)	South Africa (14)
Denmark (9)	Soviet Union (3)
France (40)	Spain (27)
Germany (56)	Sweden (41)
Greece (2)	Switzerland (5)
India (2)	United Kingdom (2,260)
Ireland (37)	United States (18,822)
Israel (1)	Venezuela (2)
Italy (28)	West Indies (1)
Jamaica (17)	Yugoslavia (2)

Note: Numbers in parentheses are the number of hit songs per nation.

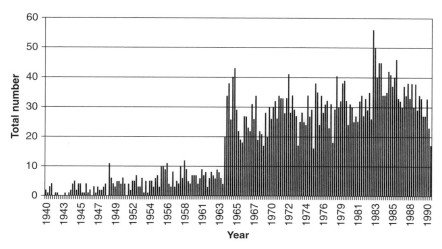

FIGURE 11.1 Quarterly number of hit songs by international performers in the US mainstream market, 1940–90

and then it graphs the quarterly number from 1940 to 1990. This figure shows a remarkable rise in music from abroad, particularly from 1964 onward. In fact, prior to 1964, *no* international act had compiled more than 20 hit songs in the US mainstream market, with the exception being three Canadian performing acts – Paul Anka (33 hits by then, with 20 more to follow), the Four Lads (23) and Guy Lombardo (65).

At first glance, the information in Figure 11.1 appears to contradict the findings of Achterberg et al. (2011). Likewise, using popularity charts to assess the internationalization of music in the United States from 1965 to 2006 (as well as in France, Germany and the Netherlands), they find a *declining* share of hit songs from abroad in the US mainstream – dropping from around 25 per cent annually in the mid-1960s to less than 5 per cent in the 2000s. This apparent contradiction can be reconciled as follows. On the one hand, Achterberg et al. (2011) focus only on the ten highest-ranked mainstream hits per year rather than all mainstream hits. Thus, whereas I consider nearly 13,500 hit songs from 1965 to 1990, they consider 310 hits on the *Billboard* charts (ten hits per 31 years). They do so because they are interested in what they describe as the 'head' rather than the 'long tail' of success – such as the few superstars rather than, say, the many one-timers – and they acknowledge that perhaps there is more diversity and variety when moving below the Top 10 hits per year. Figure 11.1 clearly reveals that this is the case – with internationalization on a mostly upward trajectory across the time period. On the other hand, the time period that Achterberg et al. investigate (1965–2006) commences right when internationalization explodes in the US mainstream market (1964). Consequently, their study lacks the baseline of what came before – whereby the 1940s and 1950s were marked by substantially less music from abroad than later decades.

Two of my findings, however, very much resonate with those of Achterberg et al. (2011). Foreign-language songs were nearly non-existent in the US mainstream market of the mid- to late twentieth century. Only a mere 66 hit songs (out of 22,560) were sung in another language – with 33 of those sung by US performers and 33 by performers from abroad. Furthermore, hit songs that were instrumentals only (that is, no lyrics) were relatively few in the mainstream market – with 1,271 in total, 1,095 of these by US performers and 176 by non-US performers. Thus the internationalization of the US mainstream market mostly involved performers from abroad singing in English – as was the case with ABBA of Sweden, with 20 hit songs in the US mainstream.

One other temporal pattern is not apparent in Figure 11.1. Scholars often speak of the global dominance of popular music from the United States *and* the United Kingdom – although some find that, after the 1980s, Anglo-American music began losing some of its commercial sway in European nations like the Netherlands and France (Achterberg et al. 2011; Hitters and van de Kamp 2010). Yet – as Regev (2011) reminds us – this pairing of musical giants has not always existed. As Table 11.3 reveals, British performers accounted for virtually no mainstream hits in the 1940s and 1950s (in contrast to the aforementioned success of certain Canadian performers). Yet in 1964 British performers suddenly became a sizable presence in the US mainstream, accounting for more than 13 per cent of hit songs. The sudden influx and remarkable success of The Beatles, The Rolling Stones, The Kinks, The Dave Clark Five, The Who and others inspired the description of a 'British invasion' (Garofalo 1997). From that point onwards, British musicians remained fixtures in the American mainstream. In 1983, they experienced another notable bump upwards – accounting for some 26 per cent of all hit songs – with this bump mostly continuing throughout the 1980s (the age of MTV and music videos). Part of this 1980s influx involved British acts who were new to the US mainstream market – led by such visually compelling individuals and groups as Billy Idol (16 hits in the 1980s), Culture Club (10), Duran Duran (16), the Eurythmics (15), Human League (7) and the Thompson Twins (11). Not surprisingly, this inspired the label 'second British invasion' (Garofalo 1997).

Whereas Canadians were the prominent performers from abroad in the US mainstream market of the 1940s and 1950s, British performers dominated from the 1960s onwards. From that time, the diversity of nations represented in Table 11.2 mostly accounted annually for some 10 per cent of all mainstream hit songs. This non-UK churn occurring on the margins of the US mainstream shows the limits to its internationalization. Non-US performers from places other than the United Kingdom have often faced sporadic, if not fleeting, success in the US mainstream – such as Deodato (Brazil, with four hits from 1973–82), Manu Dibango (Cameroon, one hit in 1973), Nena (Germany, one hit in 1983), Vangelis (Greece, one hit in 1981), Domenico Modugno (Italy, two hits from 1958–59), Jimmy Cliff (Jamaica, two hits from 1969–70), Yellow Magic Orchestra (Japan, one hit in 1980), Golden Earring (Netherlands, five hits from 1974–84) and Miriam

TABLE 11.3 The evolving share of hits by US performers, UK performers and performers of other nationalities in the US mainstream recording market, 1940–90 (%)

Year	US	UK	Other	Year	US	UK	Other
1940	94.2	0.6	5.1	1965	81.0	16.5	2.2
1941	95.9	0.0	4.1	1966	87.8	9.8	2.4
1942	98.7	0.6	0.6	1967	86.2	11.2	2.6
1943	97.9	0.0	2.1	1968	85.9	8.8	5.2
1944	94.7	0.4	4.8	1969	85.8	7.7	6.2
1945	96.0	0.4	3.6	1970	82.6	11.3	6.2
1946	97.2	0.4	2.4	1971	79.9	11.3	8.9
1947	95.3	1.6	3.1	1972	77.1	14.5	8.5
1948	96.0	2.7	1.2	1973	81.2	10.0	8.9
1949	92.4	3.5	4.1	1974	77.9	10.1	11.9
1950	93.9	0.0	6.1	1975	80.7	13.2	6.2
1951	96.8	0.0	3.2	1976	77.4	12.7	9.9
1952	92.4	1.9	5.7	1977	75.3	14.1	10.5
1953	91.2	1.8	7.0	1978	73.3	15.2	11.3
1954	91.3	3.1	5.6	1979	70.8	16.4	12.9
1955	91.0	1.0	8.0	1980	75.8	15.2	8.9
1956	93.3	1.6	5.1	1981	71.4	14.5	14.1
1957	96.1	1.0	2.9	1982	71.2	14.9	14.0
1958	94.2	1.1	4.8	1983	61.3	26.1	12.5
1959	95.6	1.0	3.4	1984	63.5	27.3	9.4
1960	96.1	0.7	3.3	1985	61.8	26.6	11.6
1961	96.0	1.3	2.6	1986	62.3	27.4	10.1
1962	96.0	1.9	2.1	1987	64.5	23.0	12.5
1963	95.9	1.8	2.3	1988	63.9	23.6	12.6
1964	83.6	13.8	2.6	1989	68.6	22.4	9.0
				1990	73.0	17.8	9.1

Note: Percentages do not always total 100% in a given year due to rounding.

Makeba (South Africa, two hits from 1967–68). Nonetheless, the collective impact of such performers has made the US mainstream market far less insular than it once was.

Changing the Course of the Mainstream Market

The patterns of internationalization found in the previous section can be explained by emphasizing three important types of 'gatekeepers' – those entities that respectively decide (1) which performers will be recorded, (2) which will be given airplay, and (3) which will be granted access to desirable performance venues. In the internet era, there are some ways of getting around these gatekeepers, especially with the possibility of musicians using various online resources for accessing audiences directly (such as YouTube and Facebook) or with the ease by which fans can discover music via online browsing (see Tepper and Hargittai 2009; Young and Collins 2010). Yet in the pre-internet era, it was much more difficult to circumvent such gatekeepers – particularly because recording technology was relatively expensive, the physical shipment of recordings required deep pockets, and radio was the primary means for introducing audiences to (new) music (Dowd 2005). In fact, statistical analysis reveals that the conservative approach of these gatekeepers accounted for the dearth of international performers in the 1940s and 1960s, and shifts away from that conservatism created the conditions in which music from abroad flowed into the mainstream (Dowd 2011). Let me explain those results by drawing upon my previous work (Dowd 2003, 2004, 2005, 2011).

In the mid- to late twentieth century, large recording corporations were well situated, given their expansive resources that allowed them to release numerous recordings and to ship those recordings across the nation, if not around the world. Consequently, their choices of which performers to sign and promote could have quite an impact on the mainstream market. Initially, the giants of the industry – such as CBS, Decca and RCA Victor – took a very conservative approach to such choices. In particular, they centralized their operations by having only a few divisions (one to three 'labels' – such as CBS' Columbia Records), with only a few people making all the key decisions. Those decision-makers, in turn, took the following approach: they emphasized the type of music that succeeded in the past (purposefully avoiding what they deemed to be musical 'fads' that would quickly die out); they focused efforts on the collection of performers currently under contract (rather than constantly looking to discover new talent); and they hoped to use the production and distribution might of the company to stave off competitors – flooding the marketplace with their recordings, so as to make it difficult for the recordings of competitors to get any attention.

This centralized approach made them very adept at producing recorded songs in a quick, assembly-line like fashion – hence the numerous hits for the pre-1955 performers in Table 11.1. But this approach also made them sluggish in responding to shifting tastes and trends. Thus, despite their considerable resources and their 'flooding' of the marketplace, the largest recording corporations of the 1940s and early 1950s lost ground to small recording firms that dealt in country, R&B and rock 'n' roll – the very genres that were growing increasingly prominent in the mainstream market.

Having learned that rock 'n' roll and other genres represented something more than short-lived fads, the large recording firms – which now included Capitol Records (acquired by EMI of the United Kingdom) and Mercury Records (later acquired by Philips of the Netherlands) – shifted from centralized to decentralized production, which began in the mid-1950s and grew more pronounced in the decades that followed. This decentralization involved overseeing an expanding number of labels at the firm – some of which they started from scratch, some that they acquired outright from small competitors, and others that they did not own but distributed for a share of the profit. Warner Bros Records (eventually owned by Time-Warner) became an industry giant while pursuing such decentralization – starting with one label in 1959 and presiding over more than 70 labels it either owned or distributed by the early 1990s. This decentralization also involved the following elements: numerous decision-makers at the various labels; an increased attention to up-and-coming performers and musical styles; and an attempt to benefit from small competitors by dealing quickly in the music that showed itself to be profitable (which included luring performers away from small competitors, as well as entering into contracts with these small firms). As this decentralization grew more pronounced – which it did in the 1970s and 1980s – it became easier for musicians of various types to gain both attention and investment from the largest recording corporations, including new performers as well as African American and female performers. In fact, this expanding decentralization is one factor responsible for the influx of international performers shown in Figure 11.1.[1]

If large recording corporations were conservative in the 1940s, then the dominant radio corporations of that time were especially so. At that time, two giant radio networks – CBS, which owned Columbia Records, and NBC, which owned RCA Victor – operated with an eye and ear towards the general audience. Seeking as wide a listenership as possible – so as to secure the best advertising dollars possible – both CBS and NBC emphasized music they deemed to have broad appeal across the entire nation. Hence, in this pre-civil rights period, supposedly peripheral music like hot jazz or R&B – as well as African American performers – was either ignored or relegated to late-night broadcasts. Moreover, the two networks tended to emphasize the performers found on the (musically conservative) record labels that they each owned. Things changed, however, when both networks turned their attention to television in the late 1940s, and especially the early 1950s, transferring much of their programming to that medium. Numerous radio stations emerged to fill the gap left by the old networks. They did so by targeting not the nation as a whole, but rather local tastes, as well as specialized tastes within those locales. As a result, there occurred an explosion in radio stations dealing in country music, R&B and rock 'n' roll – with the various types of specialized radio growing more numerous in the next three decades (for example, adult contemporary stations, album-oriented rock stations, Latin music stations). As the dominance of old network radio declined and then bottomed out, performers of various types found it easier to secure radio airplay, as well as audiences. Not only was this the case in the mainstream market for new performers and African American performers, it was also the case for international performers.

Performance venues mattered during these decades as well – particularly as they served as important sites at which musicians gained attention that could advance their careers. Here again, one actor was particularly conservative in the early to mid-twentieth century – the American Federation of Musicians (AFM). This union represented instrumentalists and was once among the largest labour unions in the United States. In order to play in certain venues, performers needed to be members of the AFM. However, not all members were treated equally. Since the early twentieth century, white union members had been granted the privilege of playing in the best venues, while African American members were relegated to other venues. As the civil rights movement ushered in changes – including legal ones such as equal employment policies – the AFM leadership decided to integrate its union. With the Los Angeles branch eliminating the white–black distinction in terms of venues as early as 1953, the other AMF locales would do so between 1965 and 1971. As this integration proceeded across the nation, it not only benefited the success of African American performers in the mainstream market, but also created an environment in which other types of performers would benefit – including international performers in the US mainstream.

Conclusion

Ennis (1992) compellingly makes the case for thinking of popular music in the United States as resulting from a confluence of various streams – with the blues, folk, gospel and so on serving as tributaries that fed into the ever-flowing mainstream. This chapter shows that we can also think of the internationalization of the US mainstream as resulting from the intersection of something else – the approaches and actions of key gatekeepers who initially limited the flow of the mainstream before unleashing it in later years. Major recording corporations, powerful radio networks and a centrally placed labour union all took a conservative approach to mainstream music in the 1940s and early 1950s. In stressing the familiar – which often meant music by and for white Americans – their actions combined to make a mainstream market where success for various types of performers was limited, including the success afforded to international performers. When each of these gatekeepers turned away from such a conservative approach – as traditional networks did when they mostly exited radio broadcasting in the early 1950s, as recording giants did with their expanding use of decentralized production from 1955 onward, as the American Federation of Musicians did by ending its racial segregation by 1971 – the floodgates were opened for musicians of various types, including those from abroad. Furthermore, the mainstream success of these international performers proved contagious: the more of them who enjoyed hit songs within a few months, the more would enjoy success in the months that immediately followed (Dowd 2011). Thus music from abroad was not even a trickle in the US mainstream of the 1940s and 1950s, but turned into a tributary of its own in the 1960s and especially in the 1970s and 1980s – when the intersection of these gatekeeper approaches reached their most favourable state (the high levels of decentralized production in the 1970s and 1980s).

While the growing extent of internationalization in the US mainstream is noteworthy, its limits in the latter decades bear consideration as well. Due to various mergers and acquisitions, the ownership of most of the recording giants moved overseas as the 1950s gave way to subsequent decades – with EMI of the United Kingdom owning Capitol Records, Philips of the Netherlands owning Mercury Records, Bertelsmann of Germany owning RCA Records, Sony of Japan owning Columbia Records and Matsushita of Japan owning MCA (formerly Decca) Records (Dowd 2004). Yet such shifting ownership did not result in an influx of performers from those respective nations. The EMI acquisition of Capitol happened in 1955 – nearly ten years before the first British Invasion commenced; meanwhile, as Table 11.2 reveals, performers from Germany, the Netherlands and especially Japan never became commonplace in the US mainstream in this time period (or later – see Achterberg et al. 2011; Negus 1999). In short, heeding both what promotes and what limits internationalization within the US mainstream market reminds us that the global flow of music and performers is shaped by the actions and decisions of particular gatekeepers.

Note

1 Decentralized production also entailed a move away from performers regularly issuing recordings in quick succession. Consequently, the time-lag between Michael Jackson's three albums *Off the Wall* (1979), *Thriller* (1982) and *Bad* (1987) – which collectively accounted for 18 mainstream hit singles – was not unusual in this environment.

References

Achterberg, P., Heilbron, J., Houtman, D. and Aupers, S. (2011) 'A cultural globalization of popular music? American, Dutch, French, and German popular music charts (1965 to 2006)', *American Behavioral Scientist*, 55: 589–608.

Anand, N. (2005) 'Charting the music business: *Billboard* magazine and the development of the commercial music field', in J. Lampel, J. Shamsie and T.K. Lant (eds), *The Business of Culture: emerging perspectives on entertainment, media, and other industries*, Mahwah, NJ: Lawrence Erlbaum.

Císař, O. and Koubek, M. (2012) 'Include 'em all? Culture, politics and a local hardcore/ punk scene in the Czech Republic', *Poetics*, 40: 1–21.

Donze, P. (2010) 'Popular music, identity, and sexualization: a latent class analysis of artist types', *Poetics*, 39: 44–63.

Dowd, T.J. (2003) 'Structural power and the construction of markets: the case of rhythm and blues', *Comparative Social Research*, 21: 147–201.

—— (2004) 'Concentration and diversity revisited: production logics and the US mainstream recording market, 1940 to 1990', *Social Forces*, 82: 1411–55.

—— (2005) 'From 78s to MP3s: The embeddedness of technology and the US market for prerecorded music', in J. Lampel, J. Shamsie and T.K. Lant (eds), *The Business of Culture: emerging perspectives on entertainment, media, and other industries*, Mahwah, NJ: Lawrence Erlbaum.

—— (2011) 'Production and producers of life styles: fields of classical and popular music in the United States', *Kölner Zeitschrift für Soziologie und Sozialpsychologie Sonderheft*, 51: 113–38.

Ennis, P.H. (1992) *The Emergence of Rock'n'roll in American Popular Music*, Hanover: Wesleyan University Press.

Garofalo, R. (1997) *Rockin' Out: popular music in the USA*, Boston: Allyn & Bacon.

Hitters, E. and van de Kamp, M. (2010) 'Tune in, fade out: music companies and the classification of domestic music products in the Netherlands', *Poetics*, 38: 461–80.

Lopes, P.D. 1992, 'Innovation and diversity in the popular music industry, 1969 to 1990', *American Sociological Review*, 57: 56–71.

Negus, K. (1999) *Music Genres and Corporate Cultures*, London: Routledge.

Peterson, R.A. and Berger, D.G. (1975) 'Cycles in symbol production: the case of popular music', *American Sociological Review*, 40(2): 158–73.

Regev, M. (2011) 'Pop-rock music as expressive isomorphism: blurring the national, the exotic, and the cosmopolitan in popular music', *American Behavioral Scientist*, 55: 558–73.

Rossman, G., Chiu, M.M. and Mol, J.M. (2008) 'Modeling diffusion of multiple innovations via multilevel diffusion curves: payola in pop music radio', *Sociological Methodology*, 38: 201–30.

Salganik, M.J. and Watts, D.J. (2008) 'Leading the herd astray: an experimental study of self-fulfilling prophecies in an artificial cultural market', *Social Psychology*, 71: 338–55.

Tepper, S.J. and Hargittai, E. (2009) 'Pathways to musical exploration in a digital age', *Poetics*, 37: 227–49.

Young, S. and Collins, S. (2010) 'A view from the trenches of music 2.0', *Popular Music and Society*, 33: 339–55.

PART IV

Production Aesthetics and the Mainstream

12

'SOUNDS LIKE AN OFFICIAL MIX'

The Mainstream Aesthetics of Mash-Up Production

Adrian Renzo

Are mash-ups scenes part of a popular music 'mainstream'? Some critics imply that the answer is 'no'. They point to the illicit aspects of mash-up scenes, such as the rampant use of unauthorized samples (Serazio 2008; McLeod 2005; Duckworth 2005; Rimmer 2005; Sinnreich 2010: 134–8). Since mash-ups involve a cappella versions of songs being placed over instrumental versions of others, copyright often prevents the music from circulating in mainstream spaces. At the same time, writers have emphasized how mash-ups rely on mainstream pop, as evidenced by the vast number of Eminem, Beyoncé and Britney Spears mash-ups (Ewing 2002; McLeod 2005). We can extend such arguments by looking not only at *what* producers sample, but also at *how* they sample it.

   In this chapter, I argue that amateur producers use *mainstream aesthetic criteria* to judge existing mash-ups, and to make new mash-ups. This occurs in several ways. First, online mash-up scenes sometimes replicate the gatekeeping mechanisms of the mainstream; they encourage producers to police their own (and others') work to fit mainstream songwriting conventions. We can see many examples of the trend on one of the more popular mash-up message boards, Get Your Bootleg On (GYBO) (at the time of writing, GYBO could be found at www.gybo5.com and was formerly located at www.gybo.org). Second, the implicit ideal for many mash-up producers is to make something that sounds 'official', or that sounds like it could have been a 'real' song. 'Real' songs in this context are those recorded and approved by the original performers, usually released by major record labels. I demonstrate how the ideal manifests itself by referring to producers' and listeners' comments about specific tracks on GYBO. I also draw on my own participant observation on GYBO between 2006 and 2011, which included making my own mash-ups and exploring the 'micro-decision-making' of the process. As I will demonstrate, even some of the smallest decisions in this non-mainstream space (where to place an instrument in the mix, whether to include a sample or not) are guided by mainstream aesthetics.

For the purposes of this chapter, the term 'mainstream' refers to Top 40 pop music. 'Mainstream' is a problematic term, because some popular music fans use it as an ideological term of derision (implying artificial, commercial or 'feminized' culture) rather than as a straightforward description of particular music (Thornton 1995). Furthermore, the Top 40 is heterogeneous: many genres may appear in it at any given time (Thornton 1995: 100; Brackett 2002a: 68). However, certain production standards and processes arguably dominate the Top 40 at various points (Toynbee 2002: 149; Brackett 2002b: 223). Musicians trying to breach the mainstream take deliberate steps to ensure that their music fits certain criteria, as demonstrated in Pauline Pantsdown's 'I Don't Like It' (Stratton 2000: 15–16; Huber 2004: 14). Therefore, I suggest it is reasonable to use Top 40 music as a manifestation of (one type of) 'mainstream'.

Mash-Ups as Non-Mainstream

Given that many mash-ups sample Top 40 music, why do so many writers distinguish mash-ups from mainstream pop music? One reason is that mash-ups are 'unofficial': producers often sample music without seeking permission from the copyright-holders. This places them outside the mainstream realm of televised music programs, chart placings and so on. For any song to reach the Top 40, its constituent samples need to be approved by the relevant copyright-holders. Disputes over the authorship of a song must be resolved before the song can circulate in mainstream settings. For example, when Swedish DJ Avicii claimed that a forthcoming Leona Lewis song ('Collide') drew heavily on one of his own tracks, the two parties came to an arrangement before releasing the song – an arrangement that resulted in a co-performing credit ('Leona Lewis/Avicii') (Halliday 2011). When Loleatta Holloway learned that Black Box had (extensively) sampled her voice for the 1989 hit 'Ride on Time', she demanded a percentage of royalties from the single (Harley 1993: 214–15). In short, to have a chance of making the Top 40 (and profiting from the exposure), musicians who work with samples must use *approved* samples.

Almost by default, mash-ups do not fit in this arena (exceptions include Loo and Placido's 'Horny as a Dandy' and Mylo's 'Doctor Pressure'). The most common modes of distribution for mash-ups are (still) blogs, internet message forums and streaming video sites such as YouTube. Users typically upload material without the permission of the copyright holders. Scholars do not always use the term 'mainstream' here, but they often distinguish mash-ups from other types of pop music by foregrounding the 'illegitimate' aspect of mash-up scenes (Brøvig-Hanssen 2010: 170; Duckworth 2005: 148–55). McLeod refers to the internet as the 'Wild West of today, sort of like hip hop in the late 1980s before laws and bureaucracies limited its creative potential' (2005: 83). His statement implies that mash-ups are interesting precisely because they are *not* part of the mainstream – on the contrary, they are part of the 'Wild West', where musicians can sample anything with or without acknowledgement.

A second reason to distinguish mash-ups from the mainstream is that mash-up communities are more open to amateurs than the mainstream is. This claim needs to be qualified, as some would argue that the mainstream is more open to amateur producers today than it has been in previous decades. For instance, popular magazines such as *Future Music, Computer Music, Guitar Player, Keyboard* and *Sound on Sound* provide detailed suggestions on how to produce slick, 'official'-sounding music; many articles implicitly promise some form of mainstream success to the budding bedroom producer. For example, the front page of *Future Music* magazine has featured headlines such as 'How to make a HOUSE HIT!' (August 2010) and 'Get the skills, get the stems, get famous!' (August 2009). Interviews with musicians in broadsheet newspapers and television documentaries such as the *Classic Albums* series offer further windows into the production process (Williams 2010; Bennett and Baker 2010). For instance, in a video posted on *The Guardian*'s website, Frankmusik (Vincent Frank) guides journalist Paul Morley through the process of making a dance track (Morley and Soldal 2009). Much of the video seems to provide helpful hints to budding producers; at one point, Frank describes the importance of not 'quantizing' all the beats, and plays examples of what he means by 'quantizing'.

However, we can read all this commentary in a different way. These documents send a clear message to budding producers: they suggest that amateurs need to *professionalize* to break into the mainstream, by buying equipment, investing time in learning how to use the equipment, networking and so on. Typical footage from the *Classic Albums* television series has engineers and producers flanked by large mixing desks and studio monitors. The Frankmusik interview similarly highlights his investment in the field: two large computer monitors dominate the room. A glance at the US and UK Top 40 charts reveals a familiar story: 'professionals', variously defined, still produce many of the recordings in this mainstream setting. Initiatives such as the now defunct bandstocks.com, in which fans funded the production of albums, still assumed that 'professionals' needed to be hired to provide the required sheen. The Bandstocks-produced album *Dark Young Hearts* (2009), by Fryars, featured production work by Mark 'Spike' Stent, who has mixed records for the Pet Shop Boys, Lady Gaga and Oasis (Tingen 2010). Furthermore, a whole range of other (that is, non-musical) processes need to be in place if songs are to have a chance of breaking into the Top 40: one needs to choose the 'right' music video producer and the 'right' remixers, and arrange access to television and radio, to name just three measures (Huber 2004: 14). In short, despite significant changes over the past 30 years, the mainstream is still relatively inaccessible to amateurs.

Mash-up scenes differ from the mainstream because they are far more open to amateur producers. It is much easier to circulate a mash-up to interested listeners via a message board or a blog than it is to air a new piece of music on television or radio. The number of potential gatekeepers here is dramatically lower. Mash-ups may constitute a kind of 'non-mainstream' music in several ways, but in this chapter I argue that mash-up scenes mimic the mainstream. In particular, producers act as their own (or others') gatekeepers. Public and private judgements about 'good' mash-ups tend to nudge the production process closer to mainstream pop practices.

Establishing Gatekeepers

Mash-up scenes resemble the mainstream partly because they have their own gatekeepers. Some gatekeepers are conventional – for example, GYBO has several moderators who act in much the same way as moderators on any web-based message board. For example, on 17 April 2011, a moderator locked an 'advertisement' thread, preventing anyone else from continuing the discussion in this particular thread. The moderator justified locking the thread, noting that the advertisement occupied space on the site's 'front page', and that this space would be better used by other producers whose tunes were already available. This is very much in keeping with the standard gatekeeping role of moderators on other internet message boards and chat sites. At other times, GYBO's gatekeeping functions specifically as a *music* filter. For example, as of 20 March 2010, the 'GYBO Rules' thread includes the following advice: 'You may find your thread moved to the Tweak board if it's out of key or out of time … Don't take it personally – we're just trying to employ a little quality control on this board.' Such a gatekeeping mechanism is modest compared with the gatekeeping that characterizes the mainstream (Hirsch 1970; Negus 1996: 55–6; Wikström 2009: 53–7), but it is nevertheless a form of gatekeeping.

GYBO also fosters a more powerful form of gatekeeping: participants internalize a set of unspoken rules and monitor their *own* contributions. Many Web 2.0 sites encourage users to monitor themselves. Alexander Halavais, for example, analyzed the contributions of 6,468 participants on Digg.com (Halavais 2009). Digg.com allows users to recommend websites of interest, and allows other users to publicly rank recommendations. Halavais argues that such sites vastly expand the opportunities for people to publicly judge others, and that the 'mere existence of public metrics is likely to change the behavior of users' (447). Kylie Jarrett (2006: 116) makes a similar argument about eBay users. While eBay constantly foregrounds users' autonomy (stating, for example, that '*you* can choose to make your profile public'; '*you* can choose to leave feedback for other buyers'), it disciplines its users by encouraging them to monitor their own behaviour. For instance, according to eBay you may 'choose' to keep your profile private, but doing so may inhibit your chance of making a sale because many buyers avoid private profiles. You may 'choose' not to pay for your purchase, but doing so may affect your public rating. Rather than issuing direct instructions ('you *must* do this'), eBay encourages users to internalize its values and police themselves ('it is in your own best interests to do this').

Mash-up sites such as GYBO do not operate in the same way as Digg.com or eBay, but one thing connects these sites: they all facilitate public judgements about other users' contributions, encouraging users to become their own gatekeepers. Public judgements shape the kind of music that will make its way to the site. For example, consider the following exchange between several well-established producers and a newcomer on GYBO, regarding the latter's mash-up of David Bowie and Falco:

> have you stretched the music – the kick drums are not crisp enough for club play, which I presume was your intention. The David Bowie is a different key from the other track: they do not fit ... The trumpet solo made me cringe. I've had enough of putting up with bootlegs that are just below ... par:
>
> *(posted 9 November 2006 at www.gybo.org, accessed 4 August 2008)*

The producer of the track responded as follows:

> I do it for the FUN of it and not for any higher intellectual or artistic purpose and I'd rather make 20 boot[legs] a month having just a few good ones rather than work days or even weeks on a tune .... .
>
> *(posted 10 November 2006 at www.gybo.org, accessed 4 August 2008)*

At this point, one of the moderators entered the discussion:

> No no no no. that's totally the wrong attitude. You can still have fun making a bootleg, but there's no fun in releasing. All you're doing when you post it is a) looking for praise and b) opening yourself up to criticism, which IS a good thing, because it helps you improve.
>
> Making 20 boots a month, and having just a few good ones is NOT good for you ... You might not be bothered about your reputation as such, but if you want people (or even MORE people) to continue to download your tracks (and I assume you do or you wouldn't post em) then a little bit of quality control goes a long way.
>
> If you're aware that some of those 20 aren't up to scratch before you post it, don't bother. write them off as a failed experiment and move onto the next thing.
>
> *(posted 13 November 2006 on www.gybo.org, accessed 4 August 2008)*

As the above exchange demonstrates, public judgements about an ideal product are often 'revealed in negative evaluations, when [the product] fails to measure up to the ideal' (Paulsen and Staggs 2005: 146). In this particular discussion, the ideal mash-up was construed as one in key, mastered adequately (with 'crisp' drums), and following a recognizable song structure. In short, GYBO's users quickly learn that if they want to receive constructive feedback or praise, they need to internalize the norms of the online community. Those norms often use mainstream pop music as a model. Therefore, it is not surprising that even the smallest details of the production process – what to include, where to include it and so on – are guided by mainstream pop.

Reproducing the Mainstream

On GYBO, we can see many examples of mainstream aesthetics guiding the production process. For example, consider the case of 'Unexpected' (2006), an 'intensely layered mashup' featuring samples from 21 songs, posted by producer Anonymous Bosch (hereafter 'Bosch'). When asked why so many samples were necessary in this mash-up, Bosch responded: 'For me, it was more a matter of: can I do this? And can I make the arrangement as detailed as a "real" song might be?' Note the reference to 'real' songs here. Bosch made this mash-up keenly aware of the genre rules of psychedelia (Fabbri 1982), and made a conscious effort to include 'a dense soundscape . . . and lots of little details and nonsense thrown into the mix'. If the track had been modelled on Kraftwerk rather than psychedelia 'it would [have been] only a few samples thick'. To put this differently, the mash-up functions as a kind of ventriloquism, where the central aesthetic criterion is 'how convincing is this?' When pressed on why 21 (rather than, say, 12) samples had been used, Bosch defended 'Unexpected' in quasi-musicological terms, arguing that even deceptively simple songs have myriad details in their arrangements, which give the songs their power. For instance, Bananarama's 'I Want You Back' features several key changes even before the first chorus; Duran Duran's 'Hungry Like the Wolf' atypically moves *downward* for a key change at the start of the chorus; and ABBA's 'Dancing Queen' is as memorable for its decorative piano chords as for its actual melody.

These comments represent an interesting way to validate mash-ups: Bosch describes the music using a discourse usually preserved for mainstream popular music. His appreciation for well-constructed songs recalls the discourse of mainstream pop producers such as Max Martin, who declares: 'if it takes a month to mix one song, we do that' (Graham-Brown 2002). This puts considerable distance between mash-ups and other types of non-mainstream music, where listeners and musicians are much more likely to see themselves as working *apart from* the mainstream. For instance, during the 1970s, punk musicians disdained many features of more mainstream musics: the virtuosity of progressive rock, the demand for professionalism in pop and the cultural politics of disco (Laing 1985: 22; Frank 2007: 293). More recently, Borlagdan found that several members of the independent music community distinguished their preferred music from the mainstream:

> This underground thing, it's not for the majority. It is for these people who are willing to take a risk of something new. Whether they're in a band putting something original, their own sort of slant on something or whether they're going to a different kind of gig to experience a different form of music, a different style that they may end up appreciating, they may not but they're willing to take that risk.
>
> *(2010: 188)*

Such musicians and fans marked the distinction in aesthetic terms, referring to actual production techniques:

> To me, lo-fi seems less sterile than any sort of well-produced performance or well-produced piece of music or whatever. Like listening to lo-fi records and you can hear the people talking in the background and stuff like that and they haven't edited it all out when the lead singer's gone 'was that alright?' and stuff like that . . .
>
> *(2010: 190)*

This respondent does not mention the term 'mainstream', but certain phrases (for example, 'well-produced performance', 'well-produced piece of music', 'they haven't edited it all out') recall familiar descriptions of Top 40 pop music as heavily 'manufactured' (Negus 1996). It is also worth recalling descriptions of Madonna's music as 'polished' (Danielsen and Maasø 2009: 136), characterized by 'burnished state-of-art production' (Reynolds and Press 1995: 322). Borlagdan's musicians see the mainstream as *too constructed*. They establish an oppositional space where different genre rules can flourish (for example, 'going to a different kind of gig to experience a different form of music').

Bosch's comments differ from Borlagdan's 'DIY' musicians and fans. Rather than trying to establish a space for 'new' music, Bosch's main agenda was to emulate a whole series of details gleaned from mainstream pop. I do not make this claim to pass judgement on Bosch's work. The question here is not 'was "Unexpected" a good piece of music?' or 'was "Unexpected" sufficiently *underground*?' Rather, I am arguing that, unlike earlier forms of anti-mainstream discourse, mash-up producers often draw on mainstream understandings of music production. The aesthetics of the mainstream pervade each stage of making mash-ups, from deciding which records to sample to deciding how long particular sections should last.

We can detect mainstream influences in many mash-ups, beyond the simple act of using Top 40 material. For instance, on 29 July 2008, the producer Wax Audio posted a mash-up of the Bryan Adams song 'Run to You' with Metallica's 'Enter Sandman' on GYBO. The production process was slightly more complicated than usual because Wax Audio lacked a full instrumental version of 'Run to You'. Nevertheless, the producer saw fit to persevere with the mash-up, combining two different recordings to form an instrumental backing track: 'I use the original Run to You (basically all the bits where Bryan isn't singing – except for the outro) and cross fade it in and out with a "backing track" I found on-line (a sort of glorified karaoke version)' (posted 29 July 2008). This process was more labour-intensive than usual, involving fine adjustments to volume levels, carefully 'camouflaging' cross fades by using prominent vocals, and so on. The more labour-intensive process was designed to make the mash-up sound as 'convincing' as possible.

In addition, Wax Audio chose the a cappella track 'Enter Sandman' specifically because it sounded 'pristine'. Some homemade, reverse-engineered a cappella tracks sound amateurish because they include residues of the production process; one can hear faint snare drums and other instruments that have not been cleanly removed from the mix. The 'Enter Sandman' a cappella, in contrast, had no discernible residues or artefacts, and was consequently used by Wax Audio. In short, several aspects of 'Enter You' were shaped by mainstream aesthetic criteria. Just as Bosch chose many samples to try to make a 'real' song, Wax Audio chose samples that could pass as parts of a 'real' song. Responses to the track reinforced this sense of the mainstream-as-model. One respondent wrote that 'this is easily mainstream radio fodder', while another labelled it 'BRILLIANT . . . You would think that this was an original recording.'

As well as choosing 'pristine' source material for a mix, mash-up producers often betray an interest in mainstream aesthetics through their 'tweaks'. In 'tweaks' – those relatively small adjustments to a mix – producers incrementally nudge tracks closer to the conventions of Top 40 music. For example, consider the changes I made to a sample of JX's 'Son of a Gun' in order to make it fit with an existing mash-up. The JX riff (appearing at 0'00' of the song's radio version) consists of the chords D–C–G. I wished to superimpose this pattern on AC/DC's 'You Shook Me All Night Long', which plays the same chords but in reverse order (G–C–D). Therefore, I needed to cut and paste individual chords from JX so as to reorder them. The initial result sounded amateurish. Cutting and pasting JX had removed the delay effect from 'Son of a Gun'. Without the delay effect, my re-edited notes resembled the rhythm shown in Figure 12.1, where dead silence occupies the space between the notes. The silences between the notes made them sound 'fake' – they were obviously re-edited. In a clumsy effort to disguise this, I created an echo effect by inserting low-volume repetitions of the offending notes in the space *between* the notes. The result was similar to Figure 12.2, where manually added 'echo' notes are shown at half-size.

FIGURE 12.1 Re-edited notes with silence between each chord

FIGURE 12.2 Re-edited notes with manually added 'echo' notes

This process recalls Petersen's semi-fictionalized account of an academic at work:

> You are writing along when suddenly you come to a halt: 'Nah, that's too …' with a frown, perhaps, or a slight tension of the neck muscles. Without finishing the thought, your mind is already working on finding an alternative, something that would not be 'too …' Something that would be 'more …', something 'not so …' You catch your finger pressing down on the backspace key, deleting, mending the transgression, making space for the more appropriate enactment.
>
> *(Petersen 2008: 57)*

Like Petersen's academic, I pressed the equivalent of a backspace key every time I heard an 'inadequate' sample in my mash-ups: I eliminated any elements that were 'too …' . Significantly, the micro-edits nudged the mash-up closer to mainstream ideals: even the amount of echo *between* the notes became subject to monitoring. Like several of the producers cited above, my main criterion when it came to selecting, cutting and combining sounds was: 'Does this sound like a "real" song?' Such micro-edits may seem trivial, but they are important because they hint at the aesthetic ideals to which producers aspire. Amateur mash-up production is full of such trial-and-error moments, when things do not quite sound 'right', and producers make the necessary adjustments until they arrive at a satisfactory version. The adjustments – sensed intuitively – often coincide with mainstream understandings of the production process.

Conclusion

In this chapter, I have argued that the desire to sound 'real' (read: official or mainstream) is a significant part of amateur mash-up production. My findings demonstrate that distinctions between the mainstream and its 'others' are problematic even in strictly musical terms. This amplifies Thornton's (1995) sociological argument about how people devalue the mainstream. Thornton met many people who drew sharp distinctions between the mainstream and their own preferred club scene(s). In these clubbers' accounts, the mainstream was largely homogenous, exclusive and conformist, while their own scenes were heterogeneous, inclusive and non-conformist. Thornton rightly criticizes such distinctions. For example, she points out that the Top 40 charts often consist of several niche genres rather than being entirely homogenous (100). She also notes that she could not find any 'homogenous', 'mainstream' club crowds, even after attending over 200 British club events: every crowd was marked by local distinguishing features (107). In short, she could not easily dissociate the mainstream from its 'others', at least in terms of consumption practices.

I would argue that the same applies to production practices: it is difficult to dissociate the mainstream from its 'others' in terms of the music itself. Mash-ups may include 'unauthorized' samples, and may democratize music-making by opening access to amateur producers. Nonetheless, mash-up producers often begin with Top 40-inflected ideals of what sounds good. Those ideals are often reinforced by other producers' comments in Web 2.0 environments. The aesthetics of mash-ups, then, are shaped to a large extent by mainstream popular music.

References

Bennett, A. and Baker, S. (2010) '*Classic Albums*: the re-presentation of the rock album on British television', in I. Inglis (ed.), *Popular Music and Television in Britain*, Aldershot: Ashgate.

Borlagdan, J. (2010) 'The paradox of "do-it-yourself" in unpopular music', in E. De La Fuente and P. Murphy (eds), *Philosophical and Cultural Theories of Music*, Boston: Brill.

Brackett, D. (2002a) '(In search of) musical meaning: genres, categories and crossover', in D. Hesmondhalgh and K. Negus (eds), *Popular Music Studies*, London: Arnold.

—— (2002b) ' "Where's it at?" Postmodern theory and the contemporary musical field', in J. Lochhead and J. Auner (eds), *Postmodern Music/Postmodern Thought*, London: Routledge.

Brøvig-Hanssen, R. (2010) 'Opaque mediation: the cut-and-paste groove in DJ Food's "Break" ', in A. Danielsen (ed.), *Musical Rhythm in the Age of Digital Reproduction*, Aldershot: Ashgate.

Danielsen, A. and Maasø, A. (2009) 'Mediating music: materiality and silence in Madonna's "Don't Tell Me" ', *Popular Music*, 28(2): 127–42.

Duckworth, W. (2005) *Virtual Music: how the web got wired for sound*, London: Routledge.

Ewing, T. (2002) 'King of the boots', *Freaky Trigger*, 1 February, http://freakytrigger.co.uk/ ft/2002/02/bootlegs (accessed 8 September 2011).

Fabbri, F. (1982) 'A theory of musical genres: two applications', in D. Horn and P. Tagg (eds), *Popular Music Perspectives*, Göteborg: International Association for the Study of Popular Music.

Frank, G. (2007) 'Discophobia: antigay prejudice and the 1979 backlash against disco', *Journal of the History of Sexuality*, 15(2): 279–306.

Graham-Brown, A. (director) (2002) 'Pure pop', *Walk On By: the story of popular song*, ABC TV, 2 June.

Halavais, A. (2009) 'Do dugg diggers digg diligently? Feedback as motivation in collaborative moderation systems', *Information, Communication and Society* 12(3): 444–59.

Halliday, J. (2011) 'Leona Lewis resolves legal dispute with Swedish DJ over new single', *The Guardian*, 16 August, www.guardian.co.uk/music/2011/aug/16/leona-lewis-new-single-avicii-collide (accessed 10 September 2011).

Harley, R. (1993) 'Beat in the system', in T. Bennett, S. Frith, L. Grossberg, J. Shepherd and G. Turner (eds), *Rock and Popular Music: politics, policies, institutions*, London: Routledge.

Hirsch, P. (1970) *The Structure of the Music Industry: the filtering process by which records are preselected for public consumption*, Ann Arbor, MI: Institute for Social Research, University of Michigan.

Huber, A. (2004) 'How to get your juices going: The Starburst incident and mapping Top 40 culture', *Perfect Beat*, 7(1): 3–16.

Jarrett, K. (2006) 'The perfect community: disciplining the eBay user', In K. Hillis and M. Petit (eds), *Everyday eBay: culture, collecting, and desire*, London: Routledge.

Laing, D. (1985) *One Chord Wonders: power and meaning in punk rock*, Milton Keynes: Open University Press.

McLeod, K. (2005) 'Confessions of an intellectual (property): Danger Mouse, Mickey Mouse, Sonny Bono, and my long and winding path as a copyright activist-academic', *Popular Music and Society*, 28(1): 79–93.

Morley, P. and Soldal, H. (2009) 'Frankmusik's Vincent Frank helps Paul Morley go disco', *The Guardian*, 20 August, www.guardian.co.uk/music/video/2009/aug/20/frankmusik (accessed 13 September 2011).

Negus, K. (1996) *Popular Music in Theory: an introduction*, Cambridge: Polity Press.

Paulsen, K.E. and Staggs, K. (2005) 'Constraint and reproduction in an amateur craft institution: the conservative logic of the county fair', *Poetics*, 33: 134–55.

Petersen, E.B. (2008) 'Passionately attached: academic subjects of desire', in B. Davies (ed.), *Judith Butler in Conversation: analyzing the texts and talk of everyday life*, London: Routledge.

Reynolds, S. and Press, J. (1995) *The Sex Revolts: gender, rebellion and rock 'n' roll*, London: Serpent's Tail.

Rimmer, M. (2005) '*The Grey Album*: copyright law and digital sampling', *Media International Australia*, 114: 40–53.

Serazio, M. (2008) 'The apolitical irony of Generation Mash-up: a cultural case study of popular music', *Popular Music and Society*, 31(1): 79–94.

Sinnreich, A. (2010) *Mashed Up: music, technology, and the rise of configurable culture*, Amherst, MA: University of Massachusetts Press.

Stratton, J. (2000) 'I don't like it: Pauline Pantsdown and the politics of the inauthentic', *Perfect Beat*, 4(4): 3–28.

Thornton, S. (1995) *Club Cultures: music, media, and subcultural capital*, Cambridge: Polity Press.

Tingen, P. (2010) 'Secrets of the mix engineers: Mark "Spike" Stent', *Sound on Sound*, February, www.soundonsound.com/sos/feb10/articles/it_0210.htm (accessed 10 September 2011).

Toynbee, J. (2002) 'Mainstreaming: from hegemonic centre to global networks', in D. Hesmondhalgh and K. Negus, *Popular Music Studies*, London: Arnold.

Wikström, P. (2009) *The Music Industry: music in the cloud*. Cambridge: Polity Press.

Williams, A. (2010) ' "Pay some attention to the man behind the curtain": unsung heroes and the canonization of process in the *Classic Albums* documentary series', *Journal of Popular Music Studies*, 22(2): 166–79.

13

CHASING AN AESTHETIC TAIL

Latent Technological Imperialism in Mainstream Production

Denis Crowdy

Watching a dance floor clear as one track cross fades to another can be very revealing of mainstream musical taste. At a gathering of the Papua New Guinean (PNG) community in Sydney in 2006, a packed dance floor moved to a local PNG song by well-known musician Telek. As this faded to another Telek song – this time one produced in Australia in a 'world music' style – the dance floor emptied. The track was left to play for a while before a local song recorded in PNG started, this time by a different but equally popular local artist. A group of Papua New Guinean women of all ages led a surge to the dance floor and it filled again. When the PNG community wants to party in celebration of its nation's independence, the clear crowd favourites are local acts in a local, mainstream style, rather than the Australian-produced versions that might make it to a world music festival.

The producers and artists know this, of course, as it is their job to create for particular markets. The producer of the world-music-style track just described, David Bridie, has an acutely developed understanding of production aesthetics in both countries, and a long and engaged history and relationship with PNG music and musicians. Telek also actively pursues a dual recording career, with a carefully managed approach to the different markets.

In this chapter, rather than discuss perceptions of authenticity and the politics of representation in world music, I intend to explore mainstream music production from a cross-cultural perspective. I will specifically focus on links between the studio equipment used to produce music and related discussions about sound aesthetics. Such a perspective offers useful insights into cultural production, particularly when – at least in the Anglophone industries – aesthetic discussion by producers is often used as a proxy for other values. By this, I mean that discussion by audio engineers and producers about sound can become so nuanced that the differences being talked about are often no longer actually audible. In these cases, analysis of this discourse can expose a range of other values about music, from brand loyalty to justification of expense, exclusivity and professionalism, but all justified through apparent sonic difference. These values help expose how deeply entrenched the logic of capitalism is during processes of production, not just audience consumption. In addition, I argue that these values are used in the construction of aesthetic positions that resist change brought on by the supposed democratization of music production technology.

To frame this, consider the following statement from Simon Frith:

> One effect of the digital 'revolution' in recording (another aspect of the changing relationship between hard and software) has been to transform the grounds of 'local' production: what Paul Theberge has characterized as a 'universalization' of sound means that music can sound the same (share the global acoustic) wherever it comes from; what once were 'demos' are now to all intents and purposes 'finished' products.
>
> *(1991: 267)*

While this prediction might have been logical in 1991, the benefit of hindsight demonstrates that it under-estimated the resilience of Western capitalist modes of production through reification – in this case, by selling music and approaches to recording by generating a particular aesthetic of production that relies on expensive equipment associated with professional studios. This supports Hesmondhalgh's (1998) concerns about those aspects of the cultural imperialism debate that need to be considered and maintained despite criticisms about the term's supposed lack of relevance due to the complexities of globalization (166–8). He points out that it is important for us to remain aware of the fundamental ideas that exponents of the argument of cultural imperialism were trying to address:

> unequal access to the means of production, distribution, ownership, control and consumption; and its connections to a global system of consumer capitalism (181).

In this chapter, I describe experiences that exemplify different angles on the history and development of particular mainstream popular music sound aesthetics linked to equipment and issues of access to it. I then look at some important discourse surrounding similar connections between production choice and equipment, although with a necessarily more industrial focus – one relevant to the more capitalist and commercial context in which it is produced. I then explore how these mainstreams can usefully be compared using Turino's (2009) framework of music-making fields, and look at how this might be developed further in refining analysis of cultural production (Hesmondhalgh 2006; Bourdieu 1996) – particularly where, following Born (2010), aesthetics are included as part of that process.

This work has been influenced by studies from the fecund intersection of popular music studies and ethnomusicology, focusing on the production of recorded music, and is part of the gathering momentum of work surrounding the study of production in general. With its grounding in ethnography, ethnomusicologically focused studies in this area have been effective in examining and theorizing local processes and relationships to global media flows (Porcello 1998, 2004; Greene and Porcello 2005; Meintjes 2003). Material from popular music studies engaging with music production has been quite effective in refocusing musicological analysis to address the increasing importance of sound aesthetics resulting from the prominence of recordings and associated musical activity (Brown 2000; Camilleri 2010; Clarke 1983; Hodgson 2010; Horning 2004; Zak 2001).[1] Less evident in both areas has been how such analysis might be useful in understanding broader processes in the operation of music as part of cultural production.

The Sound of Equipment

People involved in producing recorded music regularly engage in discussions about the equipment used, describing the sonic effects with adjectives such as warm, round, full, thick, clear, transparent and focused. Sometimes the difference this equipment makes is clearly audible, but often it is not. While teaching classes in recording over the last few years, I have organized and overseen a number of informal double-blind 'ABX' listening tests[2] with students, exploring perceptions of sonic difference between use of equipment that many people say sounds distinctive, and the results are revealing. In one instance, for example, those in a student group that included experienced engineers with solid industry reputations were unable to reliably differentiate between high-resolution mp3 and CD-quality files. Prior to the test, the same group of people posited strong opinions on the differences between these formats. Other students of mine have tested outboard compressors versus their digitally modelled versions, A/D converters,[3] and again many people who say they can hear differences are unable to reliably demonstrate this under test conditions. Yet rarely, in my experience, do such experiences seem to change people's views.

Arguments about the consistency of the test process, listening environments or simply denial of the experience often follow. The implications of this are interesting. We have a situation where sound aesthetics with particular desired characteristics are the primary focus of such discussions, but it can be the case that the aural differences are so subtle that most people are unable to actually hear them. Here we have sound aesthetics effectively acting as a proxy for other areas of opinion and value. These may include appearance, usability, brand loyalty, peer pressure and justification of expense.

Production aesthetics rely very much on shared listening histories, shared approaches and systems, and industries of production. Here I want to use this peripheral position to explore production values and sound aesthetics towards improving our analytical position to place ourselves 'at the origins of a world whose functioning has become so familiar to us that the regularities and the rules it obeys escape our grasp' (Bourdieu 1996: 48).

An Aesthetic Perspective From Melanesia

In 2008, I was invited by the Solomon Islands Music Federation to present a workshop on recording techniques, and about 70 people attended, including many well-known local musicians and home studio recordists who create a good deal of the music that circulates via cassette, CD, flash drive and mobile phone throughout the Solomon Islands and other parts of Melanesia.[4] To demonstrate the various techniques discussed, we recorded our own version of a popular Solomon Islands classic song, *Wokabauti lon Saenataon* (Walk/wander around Chinatown). The song, originally written by Edwin Sitoro in the late 1950s, was popularized (and modified slightly) by Fred Maedola in the late 1960s. One participant built a drum track using the sequencing software Reason, then we overdubbed bass, electric and acoustic guitars, lead vocals and keyboard, then backup vocals sung by all of us as a makeshift 'We are the World'-style choir. Using the raw tracks, various participants then mixed the song and a selection of these were played to everyone. That evening, while relaxing with some of the workshop participants in a local hotel bar, one of the mixes was played on a popular FM radio station, and continued to be played for a week or so after the workshop.

In all of the mixes created by Solomon Islanders, particular keyboard sounds were deliberately chosen from a wide selection of softsynths,[5] and the parts were pushed forward in the mixes. Dating back to at least the early 1990s, there is a history of keyboard usage that would widely be regarded as 'consumer' grade in places like Australia to provide sequenced drum, bass and keyboard parts in Melanesian popular music. Pacific reggae skanks (the offbeat 'chops' played by guitar on more global reggae styles) are often played by keyboards in Melanesia, and various fills with a brass patch are common. I dare say most Western producers/ engineers and musicians would avoid those keyboard sounds, or at least push them way back in favour of the 'live' version.[6] Piracy has given these Solomon Islanders access to more softsynths, plugins and audio recording software than we have in our professionally equipped and expensive studio at Macquarie University, so the choices were not constrained by access.

The Solomon Islands' population is small, and the recording scene is increasingly dominated by the work of such project studio musicians using equipment to hand. On one level, the Melanesian mainstream scene lacks infrastructure, musicians earn little (if anything) and piracy is rife, but on another it is a very dynamic scene. Access to recording and subsequent airplay on radio and distribution via electronic means are relatively within reach. Although the recording scene/industry is larger in PNG, and has a more commercial focus with the dominant studio Chin H Meen essentially having a monopoly over distribution, Solomon Islands music has become very popular there. While industrially, commercially and in terms of infrastructure such as copyright, the Melanesian mainstream might be seen to be more ad hoc than the highly corporate, structured, influential industries of the West, it still creates music that resonates with its audience and it functions very effectively at a social level.

Turning back to the opening description of the dance floor experience, two clear aesthetic choices have been made here. For the Melanesian partygoers, a preference was shown for music that resonated with a Melanesia they knew, one of shared listening history and memories, and not the constructed authenticity of world music. In terms of production, the Honiara workshop participants deliberately chose keyboard sounds that formed part of a particular Melanesian pop aesthetic. While generational issues no doubt need further exploration, for a large number of Papua New Guineans, the keyboard sounds just described are the known sounds of shared listening histories, while the sounds of world music trying to construct a sense of Melanesian authenticity through the use of traditional instruments and other effects – particular keyboard washes and atmospheric patches – are from a largely foreign listening trajectory.

There are, of course, Papua New Guineans who want a pre-European contact traditional instrument and music-based authenticity to be returned to PNG music, and who argue from a philosophical and cultural perspective why it would be better for PNG than the existing commercial music scene, which is seen as formulaic, derivative and second rate (for discussion of this, see Crowdy 1998, 2005; Crowdy and Subam 2004). The difference in usage and popularity between styles developed and encouraged by the former (such as the music of Sanguma) in relation to commercial music, however, tends to make this position marginal, or one characterized by an art versus popular music debate.

One of the consequences of the way in which the tools of production have become available in Melanesia is that significant components contributing to a popular music sound aesthetic (for example, keyboard sounds) have developed through the use of consumer (rather than pro) equipment; as a result, in professional Australian working studios this can be regarded as 'cheap'-sounding. To explore this issue of cost and resultant sound further, a lively place exists around discussion about the music equipment manufacturing company Behringer. Although commercially successful, Behringer generally gets a bad rap in the professional banter about music gear. Consider comments made on a video blog by Chris Holder, one of the editors of *Audio Technology* magazine, who had visited Behringer's then-new Chinese factory:

> Making music is about passion, it's not just another job or another hobby and we kind of expect the people who make the gear we use to share that passion, I mean – it's gotta have soul, doesn't it?

... I've got to admit I'm old enough to have some lingering prejudices about Behringer. In the early days – back in the early to mid 90s – the name Behringer stood for everything that was wrong with the home studio explosion. Those in the know were concerned that the kids buying Behringer simply didn't know any better. They were getting throw away gear that was unreliable, noisy and had no place in a real studio and in the early days some of those claims were well founded.

(www.youtube.com/watch?v=NqUGLUJF7y4&
feature=youtube_gdata_player, accessed 3 February 2012)

First, Holder posits that people who make the gear should have the same passion about music as those who make music. This reinforces the tight links between modern music production and the equipment that enables it. Second, he suggests there are 'real' (professional) studios, and an explosion of under-skilled amateurs using inadequate equipment.

As the Melanesian music industry has drawn more and more on small, often home-based independent studios, equipment by companies like Behringer has become central to its success, due to its relatively low cost. This becomes charged with potentially imperial power relations when comparisons between national mainstream pop musics are made – or, more importantly, when Melanesians express interest in gaining access to an overseas market. It is all too common for those of us able to work in professional studios with costly gear to ignore the social context and construction of our own aesthetic positions, and start to wield that in more judgemental terms, so that 'cheesy' and 'plastic' or 'over-produced' are used in relation to a Melanesian aesthetic instead of more 'clearly defined', 'pure in tone' or even 'carefully sonically manipulated'.

When things obviously sound different, analysis is clearly based around relative sound aesthetics, and how they have developed and continue to change. Where analysis becomes more complicated, is when aesthetic judgements and values are discussed in terms of sound, but the differences are not obviously – if at all – audible.

Can You Really Hear It?

Electronic amplification has been central to developments in both live performance and studio recording. Early electronic components that carried out the main work of amplifying signals are known as 'valves' (largely UK) and 'vacuum tubes' or, more commonly in the music world, simply 'tubes'. These devices were also used in other electronic equipment, but were largely superseded by transistors from the 1960s onwards. One of the final areas in which tubes remain important, however, is music – from guitar amps to studio equipment. It is quite clear that tubes can impart a particular kind of distortion to sound that is often referred to in its milder forms as 'warmth' (Barbour 1998; Hamm 1973). In a magazine interview with Daniel Desiere, an 'audio designer', owner of Dex Audio and builder of handmade studio equipment and monitors in Melbourne, the interviewer asks about the pursuit of warmth. Desiere replies:

> DD: In the '50s and '60s everything was valve-based and had far too much character ... At the end of the day, a good deal of what you heard was the equipment. Then, with a massive technology shift in the '70s and '80s, we went completely the opposite way and music started sounding harsh and really cold.
>
> *(Clews 2000: 32–4)*

It makes historical sense that the associated (and clearly audible) sound of gear that helped shape the sound of recorded music would develop into a valued aesthetic. Why warmth, though? Why not another adjective like 'oily'[7] or 'rich' or 'red'? The set of adjectives used for timbre is complicated, and by no means universal across cultures (e.g. see Fales 2002). Is it warm because of the actual heat – the glow? Or is it warm because, for a now middle-aged generation of largely male engineers, it is known, comfortable and representative of a golden industrial age of production now threatened by the accessibility of digital alternatives?

I will now turn to something that is harder for most people to hear. In a magazine article about the production of Bjork's album *Vespertine*, written by Chris Holder, the chief engineer of Air Lyndhurst studio, Geoff Foster, states:

> GF: My preferred format is analogue SR at 15ips on Quantegy 456. It sounds lovely ... I still haven't heard any digital format that begins to come close to analogue. Even with your 24-bit/96k turbo-charged, overhead cam blah blah blah ...!
>
> CH: So you can smell a digital recording at 10 paces then?
>
> GF: I can. There's a hollowness that you get with digital. It's like there's something about the digital format which loses some of the essence, the humanity. I'm not saying analogue is perfect – you're not capturing exactly what's leaving the desk necessarily – but analogue preserves the humanity of the performance.
>
> CH: Although, the advocates of digital will be quick to point to their analyzer plot and tell you that you can't possibly be hearing what you're hearing.
>
> GF: Yes, and certainly you're not losing the obvious front-line stuff which you can measure with a 'measure-ometer', it's more the subliminal stuff ... For what it is worth I've got a degree in electronic engineering so I know the theory behind what I should and shouldn't be hearing, but from a real world, use-your-ears standpoint, with digital we're still not there yet.
>
> *(Holder 2000a: 47)*

While there is also widespread agreement that analogue tape sounds different from digital recording (it is noisier for a start), why should digital be hollow and lacking in humanity? Why should encoding something in numbers – a fundamentally human activity – be 'less human' than a continuous change in voltage? Is it perhaps because digital was not known as well by the same generation of engineers I describe, thus representing a technological and ultimately social and professional challenge? Also interesting here in relation to ABX testing is the final caveat about audibility. Arguing subliminality must surely be a last-ditch stand of the self-proclaimed golden eared, and suggests that engineers might have more in common with the audiophile world than they might like to admit.[8]

In an article by Rick O'Neil (2000), owner of and engineer at the mastering studio Turtlerock in Sydney, he describes comparing as many converters as he can before deciding what to purchase: 'I have bought the ones that sound the best – because that's my gig, to surround myself with the best equipment and get down to work' (114). That makes a great deal of sense for a professional audio engineer, but has the potential to venture into the world of the audiophile when dealing with devices specifically designed *not* to have a sound. Consider the response on this issue in an article talking about recording Sting when engineer Simon Osborne is asked about converters:

CH: What sort of differences were you hearing from converter to converter?
SO: Sonically, there weren't major differences. You could say that a couple of A/D converters sounded a bit soft, a bit wimpy, not really coming through.

(Holder 2000b: 38)

Filtering is an important stage in conversion, and the differences noticed in the year 2000 might well have been due to this, but the case is quite different today as conversion has improved significantly. Despite this, however, from my own experience, and in magazines and other forums, the discourse of the sound of conversion continues.[9] Here we have a lingering thread of talking about gear and the sound it imparts even with devices that are supposed to be as transparent as it is possible to be. It is extremely unlikely that anyone would reliably be able to tell the difference between modern A/D converters. There is more going on here when these arguments are still evident in realms that are almost certainly inaudible. Sound aesthetics act as a proxy for other areas where different cultural and creative values lurk. Why can't we simply admit that we prefer one piece of software over another because we are loyal to the brand, or that one compressor is preferred over another because of its look, feel and glowing lights? The answer, of course, is that there is a great deal more symbolic capital in wrapping the apparent banalities of materialist consumption in an aesthetic discourse. I say 'apparent' because ultimately music production is a creative process, and if a particular piece of equipment is preferred over another because its knobs feel better, and that contributes somehow to the creative endeavour, then that has some value in itself.

One interpretation of this is to draw on O'Connell's (1992) groundbreaking work by shifting his subject of audiophiles to audio engineers. My aim, however, is to take the links between technology and cultural meaning as exposed by O'Connell and see how they might be used in broader analyses of music as cultural production. To enable that, some means is required to better understand cultural meaning and value in relation to musical activity, and Turino (2009) is useful here – first by categorizing fields of musical activity, and second by establishing ideas about priorities of value to be ascribed to these categories. Two fields are most applicable to this: that of participatory music-making where social activity and engagement are prioritized over other elements; and that of high-fidelity activity, where sound aesthetics occupy a similar position of priority.

Conclusion

In Melanesia, there is a growing high-fidelity tradition emerging from a largely participatory background. In Australia, we have a growing participatory tradition emerging from a largely high-fidelity one, so the possibilities for comparison between the two are obvious. Bluntly expressed, Melanesians are likely to care more about the relevant social engagement aspects of the music – its Melanesianness and shared connection, experiences and histories – while Australians are more likely to prioritize sound aesthetics linked to particular trajectories of shared listening experience. For the purposes of this chapter, those most invested in sound aesthetics (audio engineers as music producers) will be most challenged in an environment where values of social engagement are on the rise, and those of sound aesthetics on the wane. Let me use this as a driving idea behind a particular interpretation of the history of mainstream production and associated aesthetics over the last couple of decades.

Digital gear was originally sold on the basis of convenience and clarity. It was very expensive. During its introduction, a generation or two of experienced people relearned parts of the trade with regard to the recording and manipulation of recorded music. As it rapidly became more accessible, project studios multiplied, large studios shut down, jobs were lost, and the recording industry contracted. It then became in the interest of studios and professionals to promote analogue gear, because that is what is now expensive and hard to access. The analogue aesthetic has developed with retro genres, and the idolization of tubes has grown. Professional positions have become reinscribed with purpose, authority and relevance because access to that equipment is something they have. At the same time, a market has opened for the plethora of new music engineers and producers, and the manufacturers of analogue gear and software have attended to this market through the digital emulation of analogue gear, further complicating the aesthetic discourse.

Ultimately, commerce is deeply tied in to music production, with a system of complicated – sometimes circular – relationships driven by an ultimately capitalist imperative to keep consuming. The fact that this is often obscured and sometimes driven by reasons focused on sound (the best sounding converters, for example) reinforces this. While there are clearly aesthetics to be found in the use and development of vacuum tubes and other tools of mainstream music production, aesthetics do not exist in a vacuum, and investigating that space offers lively material for analysis.

Acknowledgements

Thanks to Andrew Alter, Andy Bennett, John Crooks, Peter Doyle, Craig Herbert, Adrian McNeil and Patrick O'Grady.

Notes

1 The *Art of Record Production* journal, association and conferences are also important sources.
2 An ABX tests whether listeners can reliably distinguish between two different audio examples, A and B. Over a number of trials, A and B are played, followed by a random A or B (presented as X) and the listener has to decide whether X is A or B.
3 Devices that convert analogue signals to digital ones.
4 See Philpott (1995); Webb (1993); and Crowdy (2007) for more background on commercial recording in Melanesia.
5 Synthesizers implemented in software, often emulating classic hardware synthesizers.
6 Indeed, I was directly involved in such an incident while recording an album featuring US slide guitarist Bob Brozman and a variety of string bands from PNG. One of the bands, usually consisting of just guitars, ukuleles and voices, was keen to include a keyboard in its recording. Brozman was not so enthusiastic, and I understood why given the production and audience requirements of the end-product. It would be a CD and DVD documentary sold to a largely Western audience interested in 'acoustic authenticity'. On the DVD, supporting this, a good deal of Brozman's banter reinforced ideas about cultural purity and authenticity in the face of a Western media grey-out threat.
7 Thanks to Adrian McNeil for pointing out this term to me, and its use in India to describe a particular vocal timbre.
8 See O'Connell (1992) for an acute multi-layered analysis of the context and issues surrounding audiophile activity.
9 See this thread at the popular forum *Gearslutz* as an example: www.gearslutz.com/board/gear-shoot-outs-sound-file-comparisons-audio-tests/660499-ultimate-converter-da-ad-loopback-shootout-thread.html (accessed 20 March 2012).

References

Barbour, E. (1998) 'The cool sound of tubes [vacuum tube musical applications]', *Spectrum, IEEE*, 35(8): 24–35.
Born, G. (2010) 'The social and the aesthetic: for a post-Bourdieuian theory of cultural production', *Cultural Sociology*, 4(2): 171–208.

Bourdieu, P. (1996) *The Rules of Art: genesis and structure of the literary field*, Cambridge: Polity Press.

Brown, L. (2000) 'Phonography, repetition and spontaneity', *Philosophy and Literature*, 24(1): 111–25.

Camilleri, L. (2010) 'Shaping sounds, shaping spaces', *Popular Music*, 29(2): 199–211.

Clarke, P. (1983) ' "A magic science": rock music as a recording art', *Popular Music*, 3: 195–213.

Clews, R. (2000) 'Daniel Desiere, Dex Audio', *Audio Technology*, 14: 32.

Crowdy, D. (1998) 'Creativity and independence: Sanguma, music education and the development of the PNG contemporary style', *Perfect Beat*, 3(4): 13–25.

—— (2005) 'From black magic woman to black magic men: the music of Sanguma', PhD thesis, Macquarie University.

—— (2007) 'Studios at home in the Solomon Islands: a case study of Homesound Studios, Honiara', *The World of Music*, 49(1): 143–54.

Crowdy, D. and Subam, T. (2004) 'Sanguma and jazz in Papua New Guinea', in P. Hayward and G. Hodges (eds), *The History and Future of Jazz in the Asia-Pacific Region: refereed proceedings of the inaugural Asia-Pacific Jazz Conference (September 12th–14th 2003)*, Mackay: Central Queensland Conservatorium of Music.

Fales, C. (2002) 'The paradox of timbre', *Ethnomusicology*, 46(1): 56–95.

Frith, S. (1991) 'Anglo-America and its discontents', *Cultural Studies* 5(3): 263–9.

Greene, P.D. and Porcello, T. (eds) (2005) *Wired for Sound: engineering and technologies in sonic cultures*, Middletown, CT: Wesleyan University Press.

Hamm, R.O. (1973) 'Tubes versus transistors: is there an audible difference?' *Journal of the Audio Engineering Society*, 21(4): 267–73.

Hesmondhalgh, D. (1998) 'Globalisation and cultural imperialism: a case study of the music industry', in R. Kiely and P. Marfleet (eds), *Globalisation and the Third World*, London: Routledge.

—— (2006) 'Bourdieu, the media and cultural production', *Media, Culture and Society*, 28(2): 211–31.

Hodgson, J. (2010) 'A field guide to equalisation and dynamics processing on rock and electronica records', *Popular Music*, 29(2): 283–97.

Holder, C. (2000a) 'Recording Bjork', *Audio Technology*, 18: 40–7.

—— (2000b) 'Simon Osborne: recording Sting', *Audio Technology*, 14: 36–40.

Horning, S.S. (2004) 'Engineering the performance: recording engineers, tacit knowledge and the art of controlling sound', *Social Studies of Science*, 34(5): 703–31.

Meintjes, L. (2003) *Sound of Africa! Making music Zulu in a South African studio*, Durham, NC: Duke University Press.

O'Connell, J. (1992) 'The fine-tuning of a golden ear: high-end audio and the evolutionary model of technology', *Technology and Culture*, 33(1): 1–37.

O'Neil, R. (2000) 'Last word: it's the sum of all the parts', *Audio Technology*, 14: 114.

Philpott, M. (1995) 'Developments in Papua New Guinea's popular music industry', *Perfect Beat*, 2(3): 98–114.

Porcello, T. (1998) ' "Tails out": social phenomenology and the ethnographic representation of technology in music-making', *Ethnomusicology*, 42(3): 485–510.

—— (2004) 'Speaking of sound: language and the professionalization of sound-recording engineers', *Social Studies of Science*, 34(5): 733–58.

Turino, T. (2009) 'Four fields of music making and sustainable living', *The World of Music*, 51(1): 95–117.

Webb, M. (1993) *Lokal Musik: lingua franca song and identity in Papua New Guinea*, Apwitihire: Studies in Papua New Guinea Musics series, Port Moresby: National Research Institute, Cultural Studies Division.

Zak, A. (2001) *The Poetics of Rock: cutting tracks, making records*, Berkeley, CA: University of California Press.

Discography

Bjork, *Vespertine*, Elektra, 2001.

Bob Brozman, *Songs of the Volcano*, Riverboat, 2005.

Telek, George, *Telek,* ORiGiN (Australia), 1997.

—— *Vol 8 Em i Kam*, Chin H Meen, 2004.

14

THE HOBBYIST MAJORITY AND THE MAINSTREAM FRINGE

The Pathways of Independent Music-Making in Brisbane, Australia

Ian Rogers

On 10 October 2007, British rock band Radiohead self-released its *In Rainbows* album online using an optional pricing model that included zero payment. At the time, it was still a rather unconventional move, one that carried with it a perceived rejection of more established music distribution channels. For a brief moment, the distribution model itself became newsworthy, and delivered a significant cache of media coverage to the band. Additionally, there were two other similar success stories from the same period: American R&B artist Prince was a precursor, having distributed copies of his July 2007 album *Planet Earth* as a cover-mount on UK newspaper *The Mail on Sunday*; and industrial musician Trent Reznor of Nine Inch Nails gave away *The Slip* free of charge in 2008. What occurred within this very short period was a heightened awareness of how a select group of popular musicians acted independently. In return, they reaped considerable rewards in terms of audience building, product positioning and promotion.

In the same year as Radiohead's experiment, I began working on a doctoral thesis for the University of Queensland. As part of my research, I interviewed a sample of the Brisbane's independent rock musicians about their careers and aspirations. Over the course of 23 one-hour interviews with local Brisbane musicians, the moves made by Radiohead and Trent Reznor were cited as positives by respondents and the buoyant tone of music reportage during that period coloured much of what was discussed. There was a sense that perhaps mainstream music artists – those successful or aspirant artists aligned with the commercial music industries – were changing course. As one respondent put it, bands such as Nine Inch Nails and Radiohead were 'reacting to the way they see independent music less and less needing industry' (Adam King, personal communication, July 2008). Yet by the end of my project in 2011, very little had changed for the musicians with whom I spoke. For the most part, few of them had noticeably prospered from these still-emergent digital distribution technologies. Instead, a small group of local bands had aligned themselves with the broader commercial music industries of old and, having done so, risen to prominence, while the remainder attended to similar hobbyist music routines.

In this chapter, I aim to examine and contextualize this narrative, and provide an account of Australian independent music practice. The widespread uptake of digital music technologies, I argue, has affected the aspirations of hobbyist and career musicians but – as in the case study above – these developments have seldom altered the week-to-week experience of music-making. Instead, digital technologies (and a range of other factors) have engendered small but widespread shifts in practice that only very occasionally alter the conditions of popularity and the commercial success of local musicians.

Musicians and the Mainstream

Traditionally, the term 'mainstream' in colloquial and journalistic usage has tended towards the pejorative: the mainstream was the zone of arch homogeneity, one where popularity was seldom read as a collective hegemonic challenge but instead as a crass entertainment, something bought and heard by passive consumers. This type of usage can similarly be found in parts of the early scholarly work on popular music as well – particularly within the Birmingham School's[1] early subcultural studies – yet this usage has been in decline almost ever since. Sarah Thornton's (1995) influential work on rave culture revised such a take on the mainstream in particular, questioning its perceived binary strictures and repositioning it as ever-fluid and subjective. Meanwhile, Jason Toynbee (2000) complicated this further, acknowledging Thornton but also citing 'mainstream' music as a self-evident genre category – something produced by the music industries' utilization of 'musical texts and generic discourse which "fold difference in", and articulate distinct social groups together' (122–3). In recent years, after a decade of widespread music file-sharing and iPod use, both the mainstream and mainstream music are still with us, but both appear ever more fluid; the mainstream is now the amorphous presence Thornton described, yet it also still performs the articulation of which Toynbee speaks. Furthermore, it still – in the very short term – maintains a signature sound. In the present, the mainstream of music is articulated quickly, and is typically accompanied by incredibly complex and meta types of production, media promotion and listener-ship. Far from being considered a dominating cultural force in popular music, the mainstream now appears to increasingly jut in and out of the lives of music listeners.

Within my research data, there exists a clear distinction between the mainstream as a genre or commercial allocation and the vast widespread audience that is seen to compose it at any given time. As a listener, entering the mainstream or belonging momentarily to the mainstream was considered by the musicians interviewed to be a relatively straightforward and immediate process – one needed only to become a consumer of ordained mainstream popular music and represent this consumption to others. While none of the musicians with whom I spoke considered themselves mainstream artists, almost all could be included in its audience in some way; at interview, all of them alluded to mainstream music, or artists they clearly considered part of the broader, global commercial media sphere. While their own mainstream consumption was often sidelined or undermined or relegated to the past, few openly derided contemporary mainstream music, and fewer still disagreed with it as a concept. What was demonstrably different was how musicians viewed the mainstream when considering it as a potential audience for their own work. Here, the mainstream became incredibly remote and difficult to navigate. The perceived mass of listeners that could rapidly be drawn together by the mainstream was always distant; they were spread across the globe and sat behind significant barriers to entry, chief of which were the dictates of the commercial music industries.

When considering this divide between the mainstream as music and the mainstream as an assembled audience, an interesting paradox reveals itself, especially when considering the perspective of the musician. What exists is a divide between mainstream music as a part of ordinary life and mainstream music as a viable career – something considered so improbable as to become a type of fantasy or dream. This paradox is well illustrated by a conversation I had with Benjamin Thompson of Brisbane 'avant-pop' band The Rational Academy. I asked him about a professional career with a major recording label, and he replied:

> I don't really think about them at all any more. I think I realized maybe … maybe I realized that four years ago that they'll probably never be anything to do with my musical existence … I've spent more time thinking about … how small labels and independents are distributing themselves and making themselves known through the internet and … I actually never think about big labels. Every now and then when I'm walking home I think how cool it would be if Geffen called and said, 'Here's a couple of million, do you want to make a record?' but that's like the dream I have where I win the lottery and buy things.
>
> *(Benjamin Thompson, personal communication, May 2008)*

While mainstream music may be a popular, accessible consumer item, producing music that draws together a mainstream audience does not constitute the ordinary working lives of the majority of musicians. Part of mainstream music's appeal is the scarcity of its performers. As an ideological institution and product category, it may interact with the lives of musicians – it may shape their aspirations and the sound of their work and their identities – but it is very seldom a part of their day-to-day work. For the vast majority of musicians, it is perceived as a sphere of engagement that is remote because, as a practice, it is rarely experienced at first hand.

This is not a new concept for academia. In *Sound Effects*, Simon Frith (1983) mentions a spectrum of career engagement for musicians, starting at one extreme and finishing at another, from the superstar 'moving leisurely, luxuriously, excessively between studio and stadium, cocooned (and cocained) by an entourage of servants and sycophants – to ... a local bar band ... moving desperately and sporadically between welfare and squalid gig, sustained by dreams' (64). Almost every time the academy has paused to consider the musician or musician communities or scenes, we have discovered and reported on emergent or fringe music, hobbyist music and music made in spite of market failure. Significant ethnographies made around practitioner communities, such as the work of Holly Kruse (2003), Sara Cohen (1991) and Ruth Finnegan (1989), as well as broader research into music scenes utilizing Will Straw's (1991) scene theory (see Kahn-Harris 2007; Bennett and Peterson 2004; Shank 1994), have all provided accounts of unpopular or unsuccessful music practice. There is also a smaller body of work that specifically addresses the beliefs and values of musicians with regard to career (and failure), to which Mike Jones (2003) and Jason Toynbee (2000) have made noteworthy contributions. In fact, Jason Toynbee's work in *Making Popular Music* goes a long way towards filling the gap between Frith's disparate poles: he describes a variety of aspirations held by musicians, mapping out what he calls 'proto-markets' (hobbyist scenes or groups of scenes), within which he describes musicians driven by the 'love of it, sometimes for the esteem and sometimes because they expect in the future to enter the music industry proper' (27). From my own research, I have concluded that most of the aspirations listed by Brisbane musicians fit these drivers Toynbee describes. While I would also add revenge, micro-celebrity, cultural capital and friendship to that list, I'll concentrate here on Toynbee's drivers (love, esteem and career aspiration), as I too feel they are key to understanding why most musicians persist in isolation from mainstream careers.

Despite the prevalence of these diminished goals and aspirations, the mainstream remains influential here. In fact, it was when considering aspiration and career trajectory more formally that I found that all of my respondents had self-reflexively realized a connection – however slight – to the mainstream and its imagined audience. It is a complex interaction, but still a potent one. Contrary to the archetypal myths of musicians striving for the mainstream's audience for its rewards (wealth and celebrity), the narrative of these localized aspirations and beliefs is a dramatic inversion of how music practice traditionally is understood. It is a schematic of music engagement that completely acknowledges the divide between mainstream as a momentarily specific product category or sound or career pathway, and the mainstream as a collected audience of people listening. This hobbyist engagement aims to rationally push the mainstream further and further from everyday consideration. In its place, this new narrative positions hobbyism and independent autonomy at the very centre of popular music production.

Trajectories of Music-Making

In *The Hidden Musicians*, Ruth Finnegan (1989) describes a schematic of music scene engagement that is discursive in nature. From her research in Milton Keynes (UK), she found that musicians tended to follow familiar trajectories – that the way they moved through a music scene was not only determined by the available infrastructure (what was there, who was there), but also by time and how it was felt and understood by participants. Finnegan writes:

> In their regular music making local musicians and their associates are dominated not by mathematically rational principles but by socially recognized and recurrent practices: the weekly, seasonal or yearly cycles set by and in the habitual musical pathways they jointly share with others . . .
>
> One way of looking at people's musical activities is therefore to see them as taking place along a series of pathways which provide familiar directions for both personal choices and collective actions. Such pathways form one important – often unstated – framework for people's participation in urban life, something overlapping with, but more permanent and structured than, the personal networks in which individuals also participate. They form broad routes set out, as it were, across and through the city. They tend to be invisible to others, but for those who follow them they constitute a clearly laid thoroughfare both for their activities and relationships and for the meaningful structuring of their actions in space and time.
>
> *(1989: 323)*

Finnegan's music pathways can be seen as an early precursor to scenes. Here she interrogates the trajectories along which musicians traverse music scenes, finding – much as I did – that the routines of musicians fell along particular pathways. When I spoke to musicians in Brisbane, I stumbled across a great deal of procedural information, both formal and informal. The local music community adhered to particular tenets, pools of common sense, and the guidance and taste of particular groups and individuals, and all of these things were powerful because of how they were situated in a particular space and time.

As I collated my interview data, I found that a master pathway began to emerge within Brisbane music. It should not be read as wholly accepted or denied by all respondents, but it represents a schematic of aspiration and practice that covers aspects of most, if not all, of the individual pathways described by the musicians. It is my best attempt at providing an account of what David Muggleton (2000) calls the 'indigenous meanings' of participants. It is offered here in the same spirit with which Muggleton tackled punk in *Inside Subculture*; I too hope to avoid speaking 'quite so excessively about reality' (7) when interpreting the often heartfelt opinions of the people with whom I spoke. As such, what follows is a reflection of what I was told, not what can be objectively judged as absolutely correct.

The Pathways of Brisbane Musicians

Simon Frith (1996: 156) remarks in *Performing Rites* that music 'works as a commentary on – an experiment with – our everyday experiences of time'. In Brisbane, the respondents described their early, naïve aspirations and dreams in terms similar to this: in youth, music was primarily seen as a small, daily escape into the fantastic, intangible and boundless. These are the very same attributes of music to which more experienced musicians later return, having tried and failed to professionalize their practice. Instead of dreaming of a life spent working on big stages, they cherish moments on smaller stages with their friends. Instead of being transfixed by the mysterious allure of a song, they learn to explore and play within their own song craft. Instead of looking to music as a career, they look to it as a means of escape from their daily work. Their logic dictates that if the subjective, small pleasures of music practice are honoured, nurtured and protected, even the most meagre hobbyist engagement becomes time spent outside of mundanity. As ARIA[2] award-winning songwriter Heinz Rielger said during our interview, 'I think as soon as you remove the objective to make it, that's when it becomes great. I've experienced that every time' (personal communication, September 2008).

When this reprioritization is considered in the schema of Finnegan's pathways, this process of reappraisal becomes a very important and meaningful ideological turn. It can happen late within a musician's practice, after much deliberation and experience, or earlier, in light of the dictates of an external career, the beginning of a family or any other major intrusion from everyday life that forfeits the dream of a professional career in music. This revised idea of the music engagement focuses on immediate pleasures (the 'love of it'), as mapped out in Figure 14.1.

The two contingent dimensions of pleasure discussed by respondents form the axes of this schematic:

1. Speed/ease of practice.
2. Creative/market limitations.

Within these two dimensions, hobbyist practice sits at the centre. It is a type of practice that tends to be faster to accomplish and 'easier' or more readily integrated within everyday life. This is charted by the first dimension: speed/ease of practice. This axis is not static in a temporal sense as it encompasses the varied range of processes from which the musicians take pleasure: most had some form of frequency at their core; some bands wrote, recorded and released music quickly and frequently while others took years to record but gigged weekly and at short notice. This dimension also represents the degree to which respondents tended to find themselves in practice tailored to their individual skills and interests. They often played in bands that did not require rigorous technical development, time-consuming practice or finesse – for instance, local two-piece The Ambitious Lovers did not rehearse in any serious way and singer-songwriter Cam Smith often assembled Mt Augustus from whoever was available the week of the show, or failing that he played solo.

The second dimension (creative/market limitations) is slightly more ideological in nature, as it deals far more with perception than experience. Note that the

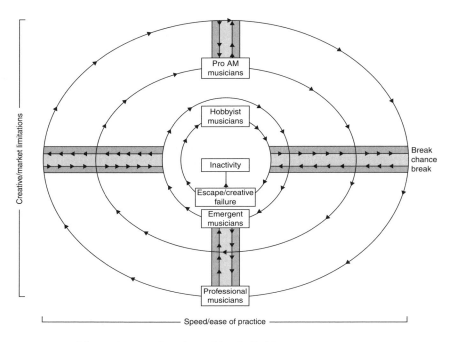

FIGURE 14.1 The pathways of music-making in Brisbane

outer pathways are larger (and thus slower) and that they map out a field of practice far more restricted in nature. In the centre, practice is small, fast and free, and the pleasures provided there can be similarly short in duration but also frequent and far more reliable. This core mode of dependable, pleasurable operation is what is risked when a musician moves on to the outer pathways towards the mainstream. In the centre, musicians meet any opportunity to 'break' from hobbyist-styled practice as the potential forfeiture of these short-term and available pleasures. Experience teaches them this.

Accounting for Chance

What the musicians learned through this continued practice was how to account for chance (marked in grey in Figure 14.1). I use the term 'chance' as it implies possibility and opportunity rather than luck, which infers an outcome completely outside a subject's own control. Over time, Brisbane musicians came to understand chance; they rarely attributed success or failure to luck. For most musicians, chance is something that takes place on their own pathways infrequently, yet on parallel interrelated pathways (the outer paths mapped above) the odds are better. The sense they make of chance is complex, involving self-reflexive accounts of Finnegan's pathways as they exist in the local and translocal environments around them. Via their belief in chance, they qualify and subjectively account for much broader aspects of music-making, such as talent, creativity and innovation. During interviews, they often provided nuanced accounts of the commercial music marketplace around them; hobbyists in particular are commonly mistaken for ideologues, but within my sample their decisions could be seen to be dictated far more by aesthetics, their own technical and business abilities and market realities than by essentialist and political beliefs and values concerning creativity. These traits are revealed in how they view movement between the pathways, from inner to outer, hobbyist activity to mainstream activity, and vice versa. For example:

> Interviewer: How do bands become successful?
> Adam Dodd (of Del Toro): Some are just so damn amazing that it's inevitable. But most are just doing the right thing, and looking the right way, at the right time to coalesce the multiple market forces that need to cooperate in order to make a band 'successful'.
>
> *(personal communication, June 2009)*

Dodd does not talk about luck here. There is the plausible inevitability of supreme talent calling attention to itself, Toynbee's (2000) holistic music product making a well-timed entry into the market and an account of multiple forces within the music industries that need to 'cooperate' (the alignment of 'breaks' in the pathway) in order to route oneself from the centre to the mainstream outer. Dodd's responses were emailed in after a failed recording, so the inverted commas around 'successful' are his own doing and dryly acknowledge that what he is referring to is commercial success, not otherwise. Later in the same interview, he describes the Australian music industry as 'cultural conservatism masquerading as decadent liberation from the norm' (personal communication, June 2009). He is not apolitical, but when asked about success, a structural account of the music industries do not spring directly to mind (that came after some prodding). Instead he cedes that talent, chance and market forces are at the root of commercial success.

Elsewhere, even when respondents used the term 'luck' they typically made accounts of chance, always including some element of self-determination and know-how into their stories of how opportunities arose:

> Adam King (of Turnpike): It's not unreasonable for us to get a decent support – and it does happen, we're probably luckier than lots of people – but it doesn't feel like there's ever anyone really pushing for us at any time, [then again] we're not pushing for ourselves either.
>
> *(personal communication, June 2008)*

> Jo Nilson (of Butcher Birds): You really need to be lucky for the right person to see you. You can try as much as you want to try and get an A&R person to come to your show but they won't, they're lazy. They just want

something to be hyped and planted in front of them basically. It's a weird question. It's just luck really, you don't have to be good. You really don't.

(personal communication, November 2007)

Pat Elliot (of Little Scout): I've always been really lucky. I've always been involved with someone that one way or another knows what they're doing. In terms of what makes a band successful, I pretty much agree with Cam [Smith] but my experience with Rooftop Nightwatch was – and it was only around for a couple of months – I'd never been in a band before where we had the whole image thing worked out perfectly right. And we had this incredible hype for a little while. The name was out there, we had people in the band that people in Brisbane knew about. But then it was really funny, we started to rise in popularity but we quickly realized that we didn't have the musical talent to match at that point, you know what I mean. I think what Cam said before, you can have a spark or you can have an image, but if you don't have (a) the hard work or (b) the musical talent to back it up, I reckon Brisbane will chew you up.

(personal communication, June 2008)

Even Jo Nilson's more pessimistic outlook is tempered by its specificity: she dismisses talent but in direct comparison to the power of a frequently disinterested industry. For her, to ever find herself playing in front of an industry talent scout is unforeseeable on the inner pathway, but she also admits that market and scene-related forces (hype, promotion) play a role elsewhere. Alternatively, Pat Elliot's take on chance is surer as he uses it to describe personal circumstances; he was lucky enough to find a band mate in Melissa Tickle, someone who could better navigate the local music scene. Elliot would probably dispute that his meeting Tickle was anything more than luck, but he has continued to work with her ever since – no doubt because of the possibilities their partnership has afforded each of them.

The uptake of this ideology – the belief in hobbyism's central place in the scene and its relationship with other types of professional practice and chance – was a key moment of self-awareness for the individual respondents when it arrived. It was also a change in outlook that was made all the more potent by virtue of the value attributed to honesty and authenticity in hobbyist rock music communities (see Bennett 2001). At this point of departure, musicians make adjustments to practice instead of foregoing it, mainly because pleasure remains, much as everyday mundanity remains. This is not misunderstanding or cynicism; this is supremely rational within the context of the community I studied.

From a more objective standpoint, it also appears supremely rational to gain a greater understanding of the national and global commercial music sectors – their slim chances of profit-return and their personally disruptive working environments – and to steer practice away from mainstream professionalism to local hobbyism. Information concerning the pitfalls of practising music in the Australian commercial music industries abounds in the media – especially online – and potent and relevant alternatives now exist via the same technologies. It is far easier and more appropriate to keep one's day job, as all but a few of my respondents have. Turning away from a music career no longer demands a defeatist attitude, as it can be – in its own way – a rich and inspiring path of alternatives; it even has its own growing mythology of quiet, slow-burning independent success, the promise of new digital distribution models, media democratization and niche audiences. For musicians located in Brisbane, the desire to serve pleasure rather than career can improve everyday life and coexist within a diminished yet satisfying fantasy of escape from it. It is a mindset that does not have to entirely preclude mainstream success, only openly and readily admit that it is very unlikely, and in doing so it is a mindset that also promotes music's more immediate pleasures.

Implications for the Study of Popular Music

There are a range of reasons why the pathways of music engagement described here are important. Within the academy, there is a tendency to teach contemporary music practice as a vocational pursuit, to gauge its outputs against commercial benchmarks, techniques and values. This is a focus on the outer pathway that misreads and misunderstands the hobbyist's central role in the work of many musicians (rock musicians in particular). Despite the fact that most Australian popular music successes stem from the social circles and practice of this inner pathway, it is seldom discussed as a fully integrated driver of the mainstream music industries. It is, at best, seen as the research and development arm of commercial industries/success, when instead it is the primary site of practice for the vast majority of Australian musicians playing today. It is where most graduates will spend most of their time making music, and thus requires serious consideration.

Also important is the way in which the neglect of hobbyism's centrality has misdirected much of the analysis surrounding online digital music technologies. Too often, we consider the revolutionary potentials of digital distribution systems, online media promotion/reportage, e-commerce and home-recording primarily as competitive gains for the independent musician. Yet these technologies are also opening up vast new arenas of resolutely hobbyist music interaction at the local and translocal levels. One of the primary drivers of this influx in hobbyist activity is the tendency of digital music technologies to diminish the personal risk of music engagements. What once demanded extraordinary commitment, time, capital, social forfeiture and technical skill can now be achieved – if desired – as an almost routine part of everyday life. Digital music technology presents the emergence of semi-professional music-making as a convenience and as a leisure pursuit almost akin to listening. To my mind, this is rich ground for further academic inquiry.

Conclusion

In my introduction, I discussed examples of popular mainstream musicians utilizing distribution techniques that were perceived as borrowed from the inner pathway.

It was a moment in music history that revealed some of the interrelation between the hobbyist and professional pathways. This moment in music history excited and encouraged my respondents, but it did not seem to significantly alter their engagements. It was not a harbinger of significant institutional change. Most of the musicians with whom I spoke still remain within hobbyism's inner pathway today; a very small minority have travelled beyond, and most of them have failed and are in the process of returning to hobbyism. As the dreams of a sustainable career began to wane, the musicians focused on other things, but they seldom ceased production. Nor did they did completely disconnect from the mainstream pathways on the fringes of their work. This was reiterated by Adam King of Turnpike during an interview. As I spoke with the guitarist and vocalist, he sat in the print shop where he worked and discussed his new role as a parent and the band's almost 20-year history in Brisbane. When I asked him his opinion of the Australian mainstream, he said, 'I don't understand the music that they're making or the motivations for the artists they're putting out [but] I guess that it scales down analogously, it kind of laps at the shore' (personal communication, July 2008).

Notes

1 The University of Birmingham's Centre for Contemporary Cultural Studies (CCCS) operated from 1964 until its closure in 2002. The Birmingham Centre aimed to generate dialogue concerning post-war 'youth culture', specifically reintroducing class as a major topic of inquiry. Stuart Hall and Tony Jefferson's (1976) edited collection *Resistance Through Rituals: youth subcultures in post-war Britain* and Dick Hebdige's (1979) analysis of punk in *Subculture: the meaning of style* introduced subculture as a means to read youth culture of the period. These studies and other post-CCCS works (Mungham and Pearson 1976; Willis 1978) drew largely on the Marxist notions of class-based power.
2 Australian Recording Industry Association (ARIA). The annual televised ceremony for the award presentations is a popular media event in Australia, akin to the Grammies in the United States and the Brit Awards in the United Kingdom.

References

Bennett, A. (2001) ' "Plug in and play!" UK "indie-guitar" culture', in A. Bennett and K. Dawe (eds), *Guitar Cultures*, Oxford: Berg.

Bennett, A. and Peterson, R. (2004) *Music Scenes: local, translocal and virtual*, Nashville, TN: Vanderbilt University Press.

Cohen, S. (1991) *Rock Culture in Liverpool*, Oxford: Clarendon Press.

Finnegan, R. (1989) *The Hidden Musicians: music-making in an English town*, Cambridge: Cambridge University Press.

Frith, S. (1983) *Sound Effects: youth, leisure and the politics of rock*, New York: Pantheon.

—— (1996) *Performing Rites: evaluating popular music*, Oxford: Oxford University Press.

Hall, S. and Jefferson, T. (1976) *Resistance Through Rituals: youth subculture in post-war Britain*, London: Harper Collins.

Hebdige, D. (1979) *Subculture: the meaning of style*, London: Methuen.

Jones, M. (2003) 'The music industry as a workplace', in A. Beck (ed.), *Cultural Work: understanding the cultural industries*, London: Routledge.

Kahn-Harris, K. (2007) *Extreme Metal: music and culture on the edge*, New York: Berg.

Kruse, H. (2003) *Site and Sound: understanding independent music scenes*, New York: Peter Lang.

Muggleton, D. (2000) *Inside Subculture: the post-modern meaning of style*, Oxford: Berg.

Mungham, G. and Pearson, G. (eds) (1976) *Working Class Youth Culture*, London: Routledge.

Shank, B. (1994) *Dissonant Identities: the rock 'n' roll scene in Austin, Texas*, Austin, TX: Wesleyan University Press.

Straw, W. (1991) 'Systems of articulation, logics of change: communities and scenes', *Cultural Studies*, 5(3): 368–88.

Thornton, S. (1995) *Club Cultures: music, media and subcultural capital*, London: Routledge.

Toynbee, J. (2000) *Making Popular Music: musicians, creativity and institutions*, London: Arnold.

Willis, P. (1978) *Profane Culture*, London: Routledge.

PART V

The Mainstream and Vernacular Culture

15

OFF THE BEATEN TRACK

The Vernacular and the Mainstream in New Zealand Tramping Club Singsongs

Michael Brown

> If you stand on Lambton Quay,
> On Friday night then you will see,
> In rain and snow the trampers go,
> To the Tararua Ranges.
>
> Away, away, with billy and pack,
> A rollicking down the mountain track,
> We'll all get lost and never come back,
> In the Tararua Ranges.
>> *(Anon. 1971: 4)*

From the 1940s to the 1970s, informal music-making was a significant feature of club tramping in New Zealand – 'tramping' being the local term for recreational walking in wilderness areas.[1] Singsongs were especially popular, occurring en route to the hills, in bush huts, around campfires and at parties back in town. Encompassing an eclectic repertoire of evergreens, popular hits, bawdy songs and tramping parodies – like 'The Tararua Ranges' quoted above – this was a form of self-entertainment influenced by both 'the mainstream' musical culture of New Zealand and 'the vernacular': a homemade approach that saw trampers informally customizing their music. This chapter aims to locate the vernacular and the mainstream in selected aspects of the tramping singsong culture in the context of two Wellington clubs: the Tararua Tramping Club (TTC), founded in 1919, an organization with a broad and long-standing membership of around 600; and the Victoria University College Tramping Club (VUCTC), founded in 1921, with a transient student membership of around 100. It utilizes original research by the writer conducted in 2004–08, including oral history interviews conducted with trampers contacted via family connections or personal introductions, investigation of published and archival material and experiential insights gained through being a TTC member and long-term tramper myself.[2] The chapter argues that however much trampers vernacularized their music – venturing off the beaten track, as it were – the mainstream remained a crucial reference point.

Tramping in New Zealand

Tramping is a recreational pursuit akin to 'hiking' in America or 'rambling' in Great Britain, where people savour an experience of nature on foot (Solnit 2000). Tramping trips are usually undertaken by small groups following a route through wilderness areas. The means of survival – food, stormproof clothing, sleeping bag, maps, first aid, and so on – are carried by backpack, with shelter provided by rudimentary huts, tents or natural bivouacs. The dense bush, mountainous terrain and dynamic weather of the New Zealand wilderness are exhilarating, but physically demanding and potentially treacherous, and trampers have long insisted that the term 'tramping' captures the recreation's adventurous flavour far better than 'feeble' alternatives like 'hiking' (Mason 1958: 29). This self-identification hints at the sense of pride and exclusivity engendered by tramping's rigors.

Tramping, as a recreational pursuit where people seek realities, roles and identities alternative to those of everyday life in a modern society, also fits anthropologist Victor Turner's conception of 'liminoid' activity (1982: 54–5). Certainly, one of tramping's fundamental aims is to trade the formalities of urban living for the rough freedoms of the hills, where one enters into a self-contained mode of existence, undertaking the basic acts of walking, fire-lighting, cooking, eating, washing and sleeping on an equal basis with one's companions. 'Tramping is a great leveller' is a popular adage. People lose a sense of relative status and wealth out in the bush. They become 'trampers'.

The origins of tramping can be dated to the 1919 founding of the Tararua Tramping Club in the New Zealand capital, Wellington, which is situated conveniently close to two mountain ranges: the Rimutaka Range and the Tararua Range (Ross 2008: 52). Clubs have been associated with tramping ever since – around a dozen have been formed just in Wellington over the years (Maclean 1994) – helping to foster safety, share resources and maintain back-country facilities. Socially, they operate as small interest communities bound together by friendships and sense of shared identity. Both the TTC and VUCTC – although each has its own demographic profile and special interests – have been typical in catering mostly to Pākehā New Zealanders (those of European descent) and, prior to the late 1950s, having a higher proportion of male than female members.

Music was part of TTC and VUCTC socializing from the clubs' earliest years. In the 1920s and 1930s, the TTC held clubroom dances and concerts, while community singing featured at interclub gatherings. By the 1940s, however, singsongs had become the main music-making format, a trend reinforced after World War II with the return of ex-servicemen and the 1946 roll-out of the

40-hour working week (which afforded most people an entire weekend's freedom). These developments energized club activities – inspiring a spate of new hut-building projects, for instance – and informal group singing was well suited to the lively spirit of the era. Singing, veteran tramper Don Boswell told me, 'was part of the whole scene, you couldn't escape from it' (interview, February 2008). The heyday of the tramping singsong culture lasted until the 1970s, by which time hundreds of parodies had been created, dozens of club songbooks compiled, and even a commercial recording released: *Bush Singalong* (Cleveland et al. 1963).[3]

The tramping singsong culture, however, has received relatively little attention in New Zealand music studies. As the informal music of communities constituted around another activity – rather than being a professional, recordings-based or standalone musical practice – it has seemingly lain outside the scope of sub-disciplines like popular music studies and ethnomusicology. The only group to have shown much interest has comprised local folksong collectors, who have included the occasional 'tramping song' in their anthologies (e.g. see Bailey and Roth 1967; Cleveland 1991; cf. Ross 1998); some preliminary song cataloguing has also been undertaken (Harding 1992: 89–91). Such coverage is limited, however. Most folksong collectors have apparently found it difficult to incorporate tramping material within their appreciably romantic-nationalist conception of 'traditional New Zealand folksong' (see Brown 2007).

In retrospect, this minimal treatment may seem just: of what wider importance is the casual singing of city dwellers off in the bush at weekends? Yet in retrospect, tramping singsongs can be regarded as a significant variant of a much wider – and also largely overlooked – pattern of informal singing in mid-twentieth century New Zealand. In this regard, they can usefully be considered under the rubric of 'vernacular music'.

'Vernacular' and 'Mainstream'

The term 'vernacular' is most commonly used to denote everyday speech or local dialects, but has also come to be applied metaphorically or analogically to a range of other activities. Perhaps the first influential usage in music studies was by H. Wiley Hitchcock (1969), who proposed that there was an American 'vernacular tradition' of music, which was 'plebeian, native, not approached self-consciously but simply grown into as one grows into one's vernacular tongue' (43–4). Other writers have since used 'vernacular' as a kind of meta-category encompassing popular, community and traditional genres; as a synonym for 'folk'; or as a way to consider music (like the tramping singsongs) that falls between other classifications. Aside from an article concentrating on early usages (Green 1993) and a short encyclopedia entry (Bohlman 2001), however, no critical survey of 'vernacular music' concepts has emerged to date.

A useful clarification of vernacular's central meanings is offered by Pickering and Green (1987), who conceptualize the vernacular as a 'distinctive cultural mode' in the symbolic construction of community. Wherever people bring together and adapt musical resources to suit their shared experience of community – 'vernacularizing' them, as it were – we can perceive this mode being accessed. Pickering and Green highlight 'the process of localization ... the process of "making our own" ' embodied by the vernacular (12), also noting the distinctively 'hotch-potch' appearance of vernacular cultures, arising from material being culled and assembled from diverse sources (12). More contentious is Pickering and Green's conception of the vernacular as primarily a means for 'subordinate groups and classes' – what they call 'vernacular social groups' – to define themselves within an oppressive class structure (2, 24). This class-based conceptualization seems to contradict the commonsense and sociolinguistic understanding of vernacular speech, to take the most obvious analogue, as a facility shared by all people. As William Labov (1972: 112) notes, 'most of the speakers of *any* social group have a vernacular style' in their overall speech inventory (italics added). Other music writers similarly have valued the concept of vernacular for its implication of a universal capacity for musical participation (e.g. Small 1987: 7). This more open-ended premise is preferable to Pickering and Green's, I believe, if only in acknowledging that musical communities cannot always be neatly divided along class lines, and that the vernacular's motive force will not always be social resistance.

In further characterizing the 'distinctive cultural mode' of the vernacular in music-making, we can also turn to the idea of vernacular speech as 'casual ... and least self-conscious varieties' (Niedzielski 2005: 415). In this sense, the vernacular is defined more by *the informal mode* that imparts casual dominion over such activity than any underlying symbolic process (like 'localization'). Moreover, such informality – the result of feeling 'at home' – speaks to the Latin root meanings of 'vernacular' as denoting the 'homemade' or 'homeborn' (Illich 1981: 24). Music writers have themselves observed that the vernacular seems to collapse distinctions between musical consumption and production (e.g. Pickering and Green 1987: 2–3), with making-our-own music becoming the realization – however humble and partial – of an autarky unmediated by market exchange or state-organized redistribution. Ivan Illich's term for the entire field of such autarkic possibilities, 'the vernacular domain', reminds us of the empowerment the vernacular confers upon individuals and groups (of whatever social class), whether this occurs via the backyard vegetable garden or the informal singsong (1981: 24–6).

The tramping singsong culture can also be considered using the very different idea of 'mainstream'. This term generally is used to denote music shared by or marketed to a majority of people in a given society, sometimes in terms of a single normative culture: 'the mainstream'. At times, 'mainstream' is also deployed more pejoratively to promote 'alternative' popular music, seen as less commercially driven and more artistic (Shuker 2005: 8–9). As we will see, the grassroots vantage point of the tramping singsongs furnishes its own special perspective on 'mainstream' music in mid-twentieth century New Zealand, and how it variously enabled, animated and was inflected by the vernacular.

Singsongs

The interplay between vernacular and mainstream can first be considered in terms of the main format trampers adopted for their music-making: the singsong. The sheer popularity of singing among trampers highlights a key feature of 'main-stream' music of the early to mid-twentieth century period: a backdrop of musical practices in which most New Zealanders participated, including singing at school assemblies, church and community concerts, around a piano at home and at parties. While few trampers would have counted themselves as fully fledged 'singers', singing was a form of self-entertainment with which most were already 'at home'.

A 'singsong', however, is a musical vernacular domain that can be shaped informally in various ways – for example, whether there is a supervisory role, an accompanist, or more group versus solo items. Indeed, different tramping scenarios – hut parties, campfires or Christmas gatherings – created their own practical parameters. Some general characteristics can be gauged, however, from considering the sessions most frequently mentioned by interviewees: truck singsongs. From the 1940s until the 1970s, when private car ownership had become more or less ubiquitous, Wellington clubs chartered small carrier or furniture trucks to transport parties between the city and the hills, with each vehicle accommodating 10 to 25 people. Here is a medley of memories of these journeys:

> 'Charlie Free ran a carrier business and . . . on Friday nights he used to sweep all the coal off the back of his truck-tray, put . . . a canvas canopy over the top. Pick you up at the Wellington Railway Station . . . about half past six . . .'; '. . . you've been getting excited, packing your pack . . . there's a pretty electric atmosphere in the back of a vehicle like that . . .' ; 'If you were going into Otaki Forks . . . that was probably a couple of hours . . . it was probably too noisy to talk . . . but singing was something that could unite the whole group . . .'; 'It helped people to relax. There was no discrimination or stigma to get involved . . .'; 'There'd always be people on the trips who knew the words and . . . you'd gradually learn them.'; 'We'd have some wonderful singsongs and . . . a lot of other shenanigans . . .'; '. . . singsongs seemed to be the natural way to occupy the time . . . a totally informal, impromptu thing.'[4]

Infused with a spirit of Friday-night liberation, these singsongs became unpredictable brews of melodious leading, lusty chorusing, banter and laughter. Although there were some solo songs or recitations, group singing predominated, perhaps accompanied by a light portable instrument like a ukulele. At times, the singing might attain a rich blend; at others, a straggling texture of half-remembered lyrics and melodic 'accidents'. Either way, self-entertainment, not technical finesse, was the main goal.

In many respects, these outward-bound truck journeys represented a special liminal interlude within the overall liminoid framework of the tramping trip – an

FIGURE 15.1 TTC members departing for a weekend tramp, May 1946

(*Source: The Evening Post* files; copyright *The Dominion Post*).

in-between phase during which people shrugged off their workplace responsibilities and everyday selves, but were not 'trampers' just yet. Liminality, Victor Turner notes, often involves a loosening of normal rules of conduct and a heightened sense of *communitas* (1982: 44–51). The truck singsongs in effect became a kind of rehearsal for the social dynamics of the tramp ahead, an interpretation supported by four basic singsong characteristics: first, they were valued for their spontaneity – for 'just sort of happening' and proceeding without any plan; second, group consensus decided whether they 'caught on' and the ensuing repertoire choices; third, people with good voices and memories for songs served a special enabling role, but actual leadership was minimal; and fourth, individual participation was discretionary – people could join in, suggest songs, give solos or just sit back and listen. Tramping singsongs thus embodied a similar social ideal to tramping itself: a makeshift balance of comradeship, individual autonomy and low-key leadership.

Club Repertoires

The repertoires of TTC and VUCTC singsongs during their heyday in the 1940s to the 1970s were huge. 'It became a point of honor not to repeat yourself,' Andy Andersen told me. 'I've been on trucks coming back from Ruapehu – seven hours and no repetitions' (interview, May 2008). Although challenging to ascertain some 50 years after the fact, large portions of these repertoires have been recovered from songbooks and ephemera, club periodicals, recordings, manuscripts and through interviews: some 573 songs have been linked to the TTC (in the 1942–71 period) and 342 with the VUCTC (in the 1946–68 period). While these collations do not give precise or all-inclusive pictures of the thousands of unique singsong combinations performed over several decades, they reveal some further vernacular/mainstream relationships.

A basic attribute of both club repertoires was their heterogeneity. Each can be divided into three broad groups of material, which will be described here with some representative titles. First, there were widely known songs of various sorts, such as:

- evergreens ('Tavern in the Town', 'Loch Lomond')
- sea shanties ('Blow the Man Down', 'Shenandoah')
- English folksongs ('Green Grow the Rushes Ho', 'Greensleeves')
- American folksongs ('Home on the Range', 'On Top of Old Smoky')
- classical music ('La Donna è Mobile', 'Die Forelle')
- popular hits ('Harbour Lights', 'Mockin' Bird Hill')
- religious songs ('Swing Low, Sweet Chariot', 'Wide, Wide as the Ocean')
- folksong revivals ('If I Had a Hammer', 'The Unicorn').

Second, there was an assortment of material circulating via oral or ephemeral-print means, which now provides a kind of index to other New Zealand singsong cultures overlapping the tramping milieu – for example:

- army ('King Farouk', 'The Soldier and the Sailor')
- scout/guide ('Be Kind to Your Web-Footed Friend', 'Woad')
- student ('Serge and I', 'Don't You Think He Looks Peculiar?')
- left-wing political ('Bandierra Rossa', 'Joe Hill')
- Māori party songs ('He pūru taitama', 'Stand in the Rain')
- drinking ('Only an Old Beer Bottle', 'Moses')
- bawdy ('The Harlot of Jerusalem', 'In Mobile').

Third, there were songs specifically about tramping and related outdoor pursuits, discussed further below.

In terms of the song genres represented, the tramping repertoires had the kind of 'hotch-potch' quality seen by Pickering and Green (1987: 12) as typifying the vernacular mode. While certain material predominated in each club, as will be seen, TTC and VUCTC trampers clearly felt unrestricted in treating the various resources available to them as a kind of 'commons' from which they could pick and choose material for its use-value. Moreover, a large proportion was 'mainstream' material, familiar to trampers from the widespread music practices noted above, as well as via commercial recordings and radio (orally transmitted items often parodied or borrowed the tunes of such songs, too). 'Mainstream' music thus facilitated tramping singsongs, providing a shared song culture and allowing neophytes a participatory toehold as they learned the more esoteric items.

Each club hotch-potch was also distinctive – only 20.8 per cent of the total collated songs are common to both clubs – thus demonstrating how the vernacular enabled these communities to actively constitute their own repertoires. Again, the research collations provide only crude indications, but they check out against trampers' own perceptions. Former members of the VUCTC, for instance, often observed that bawdy numbers, left-wing political songs and tramping-specific items were key genres. Bawdy songs dealing with sex and scatology, many introduced by ex-servicemen after World War II, comprise 29.5 per cent of the recovered student repertoire. While less numerically significant (making up 6.5 per cent), left-wing anthems carried over from the university Socialist Club were perceived to be equally iconic, especially during the 1945–55 early Cold War period, when they served as badges of independent thinking even for those with less definite political views. These emphases reflected daredevil student outlooks and a critical attitude towards the conservatism of post-war New Zealand society. Another corollary was a prohibition on Hit Parade songs being sung:

> 'No one ever dreamed of it ... because it was seen as being part of "the peasantry". The commercialized, industrial music' ;'... it was partly because of the crooning style ... it wasn't a style that a New Zealand male would adopt ... you sang and you sang properly'; '... they wanted to sing stuff that was anti-"the system". They didn't want to sing anything that was mainstream ... One of the reasons why they *got* together was because they ... refused to be part of the mainstream culture.'[5]

Significantly, 'mainstream' is here narrowly equated with contemporary popular song – material that symbolized New Zealand society's perceived conformity and consumerism. This notion of 'mainstream' was flexible, though. Songs from the Broadway musical *South Pacific* (1949), for instance, were apparently exempted because of its progressive anti-racist themes. In an ongoing series of vernacular gestures of self-definition, students constructed their own distinct sense of 'mainstream'. Eventually, as left-wing activity declined in the mid-1950s and more unconventional popular recordings (e.g. Tom Lehrer's parodies) began appearing, strong anti-mainstream sentiment waned. The vernacular dominion by which student trampers had imposed repertoire proscriptions enabled them to be dropped when no longer meaningful.

The TTC, in contrast to the student club, was a large and well-organized outfit that published newsletters, maintained many huts and was mindful of its public reputation. The membership encompassed a greater range of ages and occupations, including office workers, professionals and tradesmen; correspondingly, the club's singsong repertoire was larger and more inclusive of contemporary hits.

TTC singsongs were also more alert to the possibility of causing offence: political material rarely featured, nor did the more graphic kind of bawdy song (except on some all-male trips). Ribaldry was not excluded, though, with highly suggestive items like 'The Keyhole in the Door' becoming popular for adding a provocative spark to mixed sessions at a time when tramping itself had a slightly uncertain public reputation (see below).

Tramping Songs

The core TTC and VUCTC singsong repertoire had a special name: 'tramping songs'. This genre label is somewhat open-ended – encompassing both tramping-specific and other items – but the act of naming was an important making-our-own gesture on the part of trampers, a way of claiming items associated with their recreation, regardless of origin. Importantly, the phrase 'tramping songs' carries mild connotations of bawdy and roughhouse material that would not normally be aired in polite company, thereby fitting the self-image of trampers as adventurers prepared to have their horizons broadened.

Tramping songs about tramping, along with adjunct pursuits like mountaineering and skiing, comprise a considerable proportion of the collated repertoires: 18.3 per cent in the TTC and 8.8 percent in the VUCTC. They are filled with references to huts, rivers and mountains, and deal with topics of intrinsic interest to trampers in the post-war era: camaraderie, tramping hardships, male–female interaction and bush legends. Some items were jointly composed or acquired verses by different contributors, with some individuals becoming renowned as club songwriters. The VUCTC prized a handful of witty 'Gretton songs' written by member Harold Gretton in the 1930s and 1940s, including 'Double Bunking' and 'The Tramper's Lament', while the TTC was proud of Tony Nolan, who wrote or instigated over three dozen songs from the 1940s onwards, including the club anthem, 'The Tararua Ranges' quoted at the top of the chapter (Nolan can be seen in Figure 15.1 holding a ukulele). As songs spread by oral transmission or homemade songbooks, however, knowledge of original authorship was often lost along the way, and the songs acquired what David Atkinson (2004: 471–5) calls 'vernacular textuality'. Rather than one text being reverently treated as the definitive version, tramping songs became the common property of trampers, such that forgotten passages could be improvised, new verses ad-libbed and words adjusted to suit different club communities.

The resources of 'mainstream' music – whether specific commercial popular songs or the wider majoritarian New Zealand musical culture – were another important component of this song-making. Most tramping items adapted, parodied or borrowed the tunes of widely known songs, thus facilitating their performance and transmission among trampers. Such songs were, in effect, already 'half-learned'. Bawdy repertoire was also mined, with bowdlerization becoming a key song-making process, especially in the TTC. 'When people sang really dreadful

... bawdy words,' Don Brown told me, 'they would try and clean it up, because ... you had women present' (interview, June 2008). On the other hand, tramping parodies could add a risqué edge to fairly benign originals.

Underlying these vernacularization processes were the shifting social dynamics of mixed tramping in the post-World War II decades. Although clubs like the TTC and VUCTC had a higher proportion of males until the 1960s, many trips entailed young men and women sharing close quarters in the hills. This arrangement was considered rather unconventional in 1950s New Zealand, a decade during which concerns about teenage sexual behaviour became prominent in public discourse and censorship of popular culture was increased (Belich 2001: 504–5). But these were also the years of the post-war baby boom, a time when New Zealanders were marrying and settling down in so-called 'Nappy Valley' at unprecedented rates (489), such that tramping offered a relaxed – and, as it happened, essentially chaste – way for young men and women to meet and spend time together.

The evolution of a tramping parody like 'The Slopes of Mt Alpha' reflects something of these cross-currents. The original upon which 'Mt Alpha' is based is Jimmy Kennedy and Will Gròsz's 'Isle of Capri', a worldwide hit of the mid-1930s that recalls a romantic flirtation between the male narrator and an Italian woman. A few years later, a parody was fashioned in VUCTC circles, poking fun at the formulaic romanticism of 'Capri' in light of the realities of tramping: the 'old walnut tree' beneath which the protagonists meet becomes the skin-tearing shrub 'leatherwood', and the woman a tough tramping goddess on the hunt for a mate. The new locales – Mt Alpha, the Quoin Ridge, Kaitoke – are waypoints on the popular 'Southern Crossing' route across the Tararua Range:

'Twas on the slopes of Mt Alpha I met her,
'Neath the shade of a leatherwood tree,
She had a razor-sharp slasher beside her,
She said, 'Come down the Quoin Ridge with me.'

Summertime was nearly over,
Tararua mists around,
I said, 'Lady, I'm a tramper,
And it's for Kaitoke I'm bound.'

She had a figure like Cleopatra,
Edelweiss adorned her hair,
But I thought of the club's reputation,
And I left her a-languishing there.

(*Tararua Song Book* [*ca. 1943*])

The parody soon spread to other Wellington clubs (the tune being universally familiar), where it was embraced as an evocative lyric with wider resonance. The final lines, for instance, acknowledge the uncertain moral standing of tramping generally in the public eye. Providing another twist was a widely sung coda added after World War II, in which the narrator's alleged self-restraint is rowdily questioned:

> It's a lie, it's a lie, it's a lie!
> You know darn well it's a lie.
> Pardon me please, stop shooting the breeze,
> It's a lie, it's lie, it's a lie!

By celebrating the recreation's wilder self-image, the extended version of 'Mt Alpha' highlights how the tramping experience symbolized a more general escape from 'mainstream' New Zealand life, whether in terms of conservative social mores or the burgeoning suburban lifestyles of the post-war era. For trampers, mountain journeys – and singsongs – were a satisfying exercise in self-reliance, mixed-gender camaraderie and tough adventure beyond the horizons of everyday life – and, for younger cohorts, future prospects of settling down in 'Nappy Valley'. The students' initial parodic response to a 'mainstream' song; the tramping-specific location, characterization and narrative; the parody's easy spread into the wider tramping community; and the coda: each of 'Mt Alpha's' evolutionary stages discloses some aspect of the identities and social negotiations afoot in mid-twentieth century tramping, as well as the complicated vernacular/mainstream dynamic of the singsong culture.

Conclusion

This account of tramping singsongs has shown how the vernacular bestowed upon club communities a kind of casual dominion over their music-making. Informality was empowering. Being largely free of 'musical' expectations by way of performance standards, fixed roles, delimited repertoires and etiquette around song ownership, trampers could actively make and remake their singsong culture to suit their recreational values and interests. The chapter has also assessed the place of 'the mainstream' in tramping singsongs, describing how it variously enabled the act of group singing, resourced song-making processes and sometimes operated as a symbol in repertoire formation. An additional point that can be made here is that such vernacular–mainstream interactions were not unique in the context of mid-twentieth century New Zealand music, but can be traced – albeit unevenly – across many other singsong cultures (see Bailey and Roth 1967; Cleveland 1991), as well as domestic, school and concert music, and social dancing (see Thomas 2004). It can thus be suggested that the concept of a single 'mainstream' – rather than identifying any particular body of music – is a construct that stands for the shared qualities of numerous performance strands, each with its own vernacular inflections. In the context of mid-twentieth century New Zealand, these qualities might include an emphasis on vocal music; songs with simple melodies and rhythms not greatly dependent on accompaniment;

lyrics appropriate for a conservative society; and plain vocal styles. Like other New Zealanders, trampers – no matter how far they ventured off the beaten track – could always use the mainstream to orientate themselves.

Notes

1 Thank you to Robert Hoskins and Andy Bennett for help improving this chapter, as well as my informants and many others who have contributed to the research.
2 For a full list of research sources utilized here, see Brown (forthcoming). All interviews quoted are with the writer.
3 Space restrictions have precluded discussion of this attempt at 'mainstreaming' tramping songs.
4 From interviews with Don Boswell (February 2008), Chris Horne (August 2004), Janet King (March 2008), Wayne Griffen (May 2008), Maurice Perry (February 2008).
5 From interviews with Don Brown (June 2008), Trevor Mowbray (June 2008), David Somerset (March 2008).

References

Anon. (1971) *Tararua Song Book*, Wellington: Tararua Tramping Club.

Atkinson, D. (2004) 'Folk songs in print: text and tradition', *Folk Music Journal*, 8(4): 456–83.

Bailey, R. and Roth, H. (eds) (1967) *Shanties by the Way*, Christchurch: Whitcombe and Tombs.

Belich, J. (2001) *Paradise Reforged: a history of the New Zealanders from the 1880s to the year 2000*, Auckland: Allen Lane and Penguin Press.

Bohlman, P.V. (2001) 'Vernacular music', in S. Sadie (ed.), *New Grove Dictionary of Music and Musicians*, 2nd edn, Vol. 26, London: Macmillan.

Brown, M. (2007) ' "Earnest spade work": The New Zealand Folklore Society, 1966–1975', *Journal of Folklore Research*, 44(2–3): 127–60.

—— (Forthcoming) 'Making our own: two ethnographies of the vernacular in New Zealand music', PhD thesis, New Zealand School of Music.

Cleveland, L. (ed.) (1991) *The Great New Zealand Songbook*, Auckland: Godwit.

Cleveland, L. et al. (1963) *Bush Singalong*, Kiwi LC-11, 33#fr1/3> rpm.

Green, A. (1993) 'Vernacular music: a naming compass', *Musical Quarterly*, 77(1): 35–46.

Harding, M. (1992) *When the Pakeha Sings of Home*, Auckland: Godwit.

Hitchcock, H.W. (1969) *Music in the United States: a historical introduction*, Englewood Cliffs, NJ: Prentice-Hall.

Illich, I. (1981) *Shadow Work*, Boston: Marion Boyars.

Labov, W. (1972) 'Some principles of linguistic methodology', *Language in Society*, 1(1): 97–120.

Maclean, C. (1994) *Tararua: the story of a mountain range*, Wellington: Whitcombe Press.

Mason, R. (1958) 'Track or trail: notes on some words used by trampers', *Tararua*, 12: 22–32.

Niedzielski, N. (2005) 'Vernacular', in K. Brown (ed.), *Encyclopedia of Language and Linguistics*, 2nd edn, Vol. 13, Amsterdam: Elsevier.

Pickering, M. and Green, T. (1987) 'Towards a cartography of the vernacular milieu', in M. Pickering and T. Green (eds), *Everyday Culture: popular song and the vernacular milieu*, Milton Keynes: Open University Press.

Ross, J. (1998) 'Some songs of Wellington tramping clubs', *Music in the Air*, 6: 14–18.

Ross, K. (2008) *Going Bush: New Zealanders and nature in the twentieth century*, Auckland: Auckland University Press.

Shuker, R. (2005) *Popular Music: the key concepts*, 2nd edn, London: Routledge.

Small, C. (1987) *Music of the Common Tongue*, London: John Calder.

Solnit, R. (2000) *Wanderlust: a history of walking*, New York: Penguin.

Tararua Song Book (c. 1943), Wellington: n.p.

Thomas, A. (2004) *Music is Where You Find It*, Wellington: Music Books.

Turner, V. (1982) *From Ritual to Theatre: the human seriousness of play*, New York: Performing Arts Journal Publications.

16

MUSICAL LISTENING AT WORK

Mainstream Musical Listening Practices in the Office

Michael Walsh

Sound is all pervasive. Because of music's perennial presence, we often forego recognizing the social power of music. We forget how it provides listeners with directions, cues and in some cases a means for getting through their everyday life. However, because of this pervasiveness, listeners have developed strategies for controlling sound throughout everyday life via common modes of engaging with music – that is, through mainstream musical listening practices, or musical listening that is undertaken in everyday life, as distinct from musical listening in performance venues. I use the term 'mainstream musical listening' to denote experiences of music that are interwoven into daily life in such a way that are 'personalized'. This type of listening is seldom discussed, yet it is highly representative. It is experienced in a very personal way whereby listeners create a space that puts them in the right frame of mind. We can point to public transport situations, or within the home, as possible spaces where this type of listening occurs. This chapter, however, explores mainstream musical listening within office environments. It considers musical listening as a way in which workers respond to, and cope with, the 'noisy' open-plan office environment. The chapter argues that musical listening, enabled by portable music devices such as the iPod, is one important way workers moderate the social situation of the office environment. Musical listening provides workers with a way to control what they experience within their 'sound-space' (Goffman 1971: 46). The notion of sound-space is deployed here as being connected to the idea of musical listening as a 'framing device' (Goffman 1974). By using material developed from in-depth qualitative interviews, this chapter shows how musical listening gives rise to certain ordering strategies within the office. It provides an account of how mainstream musical listening practices tentatively construct a space of private sanctuary that allows workers to undertake their daily tasks.

Sound, Musical Listening and Everyday Life

Individuals are constantly listening. The physiology of the ear means that they are continually exposed to aural phenomena, and human beings are predisposed to perpetually experience the sounds of social life. Through sound, individuals are always connected to their social worlds. It might be said that it is primarily through listening that a person is rooted to everyday life.

Because of the relentless flow of sound, if individuals are to live in proximity to others they must learn how to negotiate and control their exposure to sound. Through social practices, individuals learn how to 'close' their ears and limit exposure to unwanted sound or to sounds that are 'out of place'.[1] Unlike the eye, which provides bodily control over how and whether visual phenomena are received, the ear has to compensate for a limited control over the sense of hearing. As the influential German sociologist Georg Simmel (1997: 155) contends, the ear communicates the 'entire polarity of subjective and objective life' governing human experience. He adds that the ear 'only takes, but does not give' (155).

Sound is particularly important for the ways in which social interaction is experienced, because it renders some situations 'public' and others 'private' (Goffman 1971: 128; Gurney 2000).[2] Here, for instance, think of how couples might engage in private conversation in a public space, such as a train, versus how a similar conversation is conducted in a domestic location. Listeners are instinctively aware that certain types of sound can conform to, or work against, the way individuals come to define everyday situations with anticipated auditory expectations. By choosing what they intentionally listen to, individuals can exercise the ability to 'close' their ears. This happens not literally, but rather through the use of communication technologies such as portable music devices like the iPod. In this sense, it is like a closing of the ear achieved through focus and attention on the music that allows one to block out other acoustic processes (Walsh 2009). I suggest that this process is a type of framing device. Framing in this sense is the cognitive ability to separate and demarcate perceived phenomena from one another – to open and close individuals to parts of the world around them (Goffman 1974; see also Zerubavel 1979b). Frames, though often associated with tactile and visual phenomena, are shown in the following to be fundamental to the ways in which the auditory dimensions of everyday life are experienced.

Notwithstanding the use of portable music devices, individuals already have the resources to construct boundaries. The most primordial and basic tendency is for the individual to try to maintain a set of boundaries around the self. The notion of 'personal space' – the immediate physical space that surrounds the body – is one such well-known instance (Goffman 1971; Hall 1969; Lofland 1973; Sommer 1969). Connected directly with personal space is the idea of sound–space (Goffman 1971: 46), or the sonic territory surrounding individuals that defines the threshold level of acceptable sound intrusion. It represents for listeners the difference between being uncontrollably exposed and comfortably experiencing auditory phenomena (Walsh 2011: 4).

Controlling sounds through listening to music is arguably an efficient way of controlling sound-space. This is because other auditory materials do not work in the same way as music. Music located throughout everyday life, though not novel in an historical sense, has had its function altered by the use of communication technology that allows listeners to experience music that they consider 'their own'. Unlike other sound (such as talk radio), listeners impose – through repeated listening – personalized qualities on to a wide variety of music. Communication technologies such as the iPod increase the ability of listeners to generate 'personalized' experiences of music (Bull 2000, 2007; DeNora 1999, 2000, 2002; Gould 2004; Hennion 2001; Walsh 2010b). They also provide listeners with the ability to use musical sounds to undertake emotional work in their everyday lives (Arnett 1995; Baker 2004; Bennett 2000; Bessett 2006; DeNora, 1997, 1999, 2000, 2002; Lincoln 2005). The prevalent use of music throughout everyday life indicates the significant role that it plays in configuring social environments, practices and even a sense of the self in listeners (DeNora 2000). It is the 'personalization' of musical listening that arguably is a key part of mainstream musical listening practices. I contend that the self-affirmation associated with listening to 'personalized' music is a telling part of mainstream musical listening. Moreover, musical experiences no longer occur in the presence of performing musicians. This change is important, as it means listening can be undertaken in 'physical solitude'. An individual can listen without others being physically present – without the presence of musicians or other audience members. This contributes to the personalization of our experiences of music. The social customs that once compelled listeners to focus on music performed in front of them cease to frame the contemporary contexts of listening in everyday life. Listeners take centre stage – or, as Obelkevich (1989: 108) describes it, rather than merely revolving in distant orbit around the production of musical phenomena, listeners are 'placed at the heart of things'.

The shifts in social practices concerning musical listening have changed what it is socially acceptable to do with music when situated with others. These changes have led to what I term mainstream musical listening practices, where music becomes increasingly pliable because of the use of portable music devices, and before that the mass production of mechanically reproduced music.[3] The use of portable music devices in everyday life has become the norm. It is the combination of proliferating spaces where musical listening is practised and the extent to which it is undertaken that is indicative of musical listening as a mainstream activity. The 'music genie' has well and truly left the 'performance space' bottle. I now turn to a case study of mainstream musical listening: musical listening within open-plan offices, beginning with an explanation of the methodology adopted for the study.

A Note on Methodology and Participants

Material used in the following analysis is derived from an in-depth qualitative study that explored how individuals regulate their proximity to others through musical listening (see Walsh 2011).[4] In-depth, semi-structured interviews were the primary mode of data collection, together with ethnographic observations. I have used a selection of data from this wider study throughout this chapter.

The interviews carried out for the study were semi-standardized. They were a mix of both structured and unstructured aspects, and therefore numerous topics were explored. The interviews ranged from 45 minutes to two hours in duration. The variability in duration related to the level of detail and the time the interviewee had available. The only restrictions placed on the selection of participants related to the ability to communicate in English. The epistemological approach was to understand the qualitative experiences of musical listening, and therefore the interviews were not concerned with statistical representation. The participants included 17 women and 12 men. The youngest participant was aged 19 years and the eldest 60 years of age. The sample contained 10 self-described musicians, who stated that they engaged in music-making activities with varying levels of proficiency. Interviewees were recruited through email advertisements sent to a variety of tertiary institutions and a variety of commercial workplaces where a number of participants volunteered their time. Half of the interviewees were full-time workers and the other half were students engaged in various kinds of casual and part-time employment. The participants all resided in Australia.

Music in the Office

Work in open-plan office environments is a public activity and requires a public presentation of a 'carefully constructed self' (Nippert-Eng 1996: 20). However, work is no longer contained within the formal physical structures of work offices (Urry 2007: 166), nor is it necessarily anchored or neatly defined by the temporality of the standard working week (Zerubavel 1979a, 1979b, 1981). Though much work is undertaken in contexts beyond the office – such as the car (Laurier 2004) and rail carriage (Lyons, Jaina and Holleya 2006), the activity is nonetheless still perceived as being anchored in one location, where we 'go to' work, 'in order to' work (Nippert-Eng 1996: 26). Due to the limited scope of the chapter, I focus here on 'white-collar' work only, though this is far from the only work environment where music frames activity.[5]

Interviewees use music as an integral part of work situations; it is a framing device that provides listeners with seclusion from 'noisy' work environments. I suggest that it provides listeners with the ability to generate solitude and manage the experience of interacting with others at work. However, this begs the question of what 'framing' is and how it relates to musical listening.

Framing Social Activity

Simmel (1994: 11) argues that framing is a cognitive process that places distance between the framed phenomenon and the person. Goffman (1974: 13–14) reinforces and extends the idea of framing by suggesting that it is any type of 'organisation of experience – something that an individual actor can take into his mind ... the structure of experience individuals have at any moment of their social lives'. Framing occurs continually in social experience, across the expanse of social life. It ensures that individuals have the means to make sense of activity by using 'mental brackets' (Zerubavel 1991: 11). In short, any of the senses and any symbolic media can be used to frame a social situation (de la Fuente and Walsh 2012).

Framing social situations through musical listening provides individuals with principles of organization that govern events and those individuals' involvement in them (Goffman 1974: 10–11). Musical listening is a specific case involving the framing of experience via sounds organized in a meaningful way (Walsh 2010a). I suggest that the framing enabled by musical listening functions in office environments by allowing listeners to seclude themselves from others – or, in other words, to achieve solitude. However, musical listening does more than just provide solitude; it sustains and in some instances helps to enable work. Participants interviewed stated that they habitually undertake work listening – that is, they intentionally listen to music while undertaking solitary work activity. For some, it assumes a central place in their experience of work.[6] Here, I consider work listening as a successful social practice that affords concentration.

Coping Strategies

Work listening is identified by participants as one of the ways in which they are able to stabilize and 'control' their experiences of work. Musical listening is a means by which listeners increase their ability to manage and regulate their work activity in the context of the office. Building on what Bull (2007: 113) suggests about iPod use in work situations as a way of managing tiredness and diminished concentration, work listening provides individuals with aesthetic materials to shape their immediate environments. This happens in a way that does not override or sideline actual work activities:

> I'll put on music I enjoy and that helps me. I find that music actually helps me concentrate. I think it's because I can often find myself wandering a lot of the time. I have trouble reading and sometimes I read a page and [when] I get to the end I realize I've been thinking about something completely different. And I think music helps me concentrate because it's not ... if I put the right kind of music on, it doesn't compete for my attention.
>
> (*David, 23, office worker, 28 June 2009*)

In this case, musical listening provides a means of organizing work activity that does not detract from the execution of work. Through intentionally listening to music, workers regulate their own sense of self and their immediate auditory environment while undertaking work activities. The situation thus provides a type of auditory scaffolding for autonomous workers. Bearing in mind that concentration levels and degrees of interaction with colleagues in open-plan office environments rarely remain static over the working day, control and the ability to experience privacy and generate social solitude are important qualities for undertaking work (Steelcase 2004: 3). In this respect, work listening stabilizes the perception of different types of work and provides listeners with the ability to set their own pace when the temporal rhythm of the office ebbs. The process of framing work activity through musical listening helps workers to cope with the shifting experiences of work. As workloads change, individuals sense a fluctuation in their own concerted efforts in relation to work. Work listening is adjusted to accommodate these fluctuations. As one of the interviewees put it:

> A lot of people at work listen to music, I hadn't really had the experience of being in a workplace where you could do that before. If you're really busy, it can be difficult because you've got to … there's too much to concentrate on. But if the day is just plodding along, which inevitably office jobs tend to do, it can make the day go faster. It puts a bit of a personal kind of bent on what's effectively a very … well, not dreary, but you know like any job I guess. You know you get to just listen to something that you like and it makes it more enjoyable.
>
> *(Alex, 35, office worker, 24 June 2009)*

Getting 'Into the Zone'

Work listening is also a way for individuals to attain a state of 'attentive focus'; however, they do so in such a manner that does not override or sideline actual work activities. Participants in these instances describe work listening as a way of getting 'into a zone' necessary to undertake work activity.[7] Work listening operates here as a ritualistic marker that symbolizes the beginning and unfolding of work activity. As Nippert-Eng (1996: 36) suggests, items such as keys, clothing and other objects specific to the work realm promote a realm-specific sense of self and, importantly, insulate us from our other-realm selves. Intentional mainstream listening and its material – music – constitute a realm-specific object (in the sense that music has a sonic materiality) that, for participants, demarcates work activity:

> Daniel: Oh look, I'll whack a CD on and often, nine times out of ten, depending what I'm doing and how involved I am in doing it [when working], I won't even hear it. I won't even hear it, apart from the occasional lapse in concentration that happens. I mean I know what's going on,

but I'm not sitting there going . . . [makes a concerted listening gesture], I'm working . . . The music is background.

Interviewer: When you're completely engaged with your work, there's no kind of distraction from the music?

Daniel: Well no, because I'm working. At other times as I say, music is beyond [my attention] and I won't be paying incredible attention to it. I mean if the CD stopped halfway through the song, I'll notice the absence. But then again, I'll be working. The CD will finish, I'll be working and think to myself, I should get up and change the CD, then 45 minutes later I still haven't done it because I'm busy working . . .

(Full-time graduate student, 45, 17 April 2009)

Work listening in this case provides a type of 'auditory scaffolding' that initiates concentration for work (DeNora 2000; LaBelle 2008). Once the CD has started, Daniel begins work and musical materials recede from his perceptual attention. The ritual for Daniel is not about music as a constant medium of musical communication; rather, it is the way in which he orients his relation to the experiential realm of work. Music therefore affords him an attentive connection for undertaking work through framing the activity. Work listening functions in this case like a frame around work. As Goffman suggests of framing:

activity framed in a particular way . . . is often marked off from the ongoing flow of surrounding events by a special set of boundary-markers or brackets of a conventionalised kind. These occur before and after the activity in time and may be circumscriptive in space; in brief, there are temporal and spatial brackets.

(Goffman 1974: 251–2)

To frame work activity in a specific way – as Daniel does with music – is to demarcate a zone that provides for the ritual of work. The 'zone' for Daniel is delineated by the frame of familiar music. Through work listening, he sets the temporal and spatial markings of work. In his case, the framing is most important at the transition point *into* work activity. Once keyed into his work activity, Daniel's initiation strategy succeeds and the music recedes in importance.

Work listening in this sense provides control by allowing listeners to delineate and anchor themselves aurally, as they see fit, within the work context. By configuring work listening, individuals can archive what they aurally expect to encounter while working because the mental horizon of listeners is defined. These ideas are reinforced by DeNora (2000: 589), who suggests that music is intrinsic to the production of environments that afford concentration and that help 'to produce the kind of focus . . . needed to carry out mental work'. As can be seen in Figure 16.1, focus is achievable through the

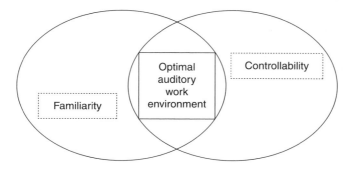

FIGURE 16.1 Achieving focus through the regulation of aural material in the workplace

regulation of the aural material in the social situation of work. However, some further explanation is required.

Work activity requires that focus and attention are given to a specific task. When musical listening is used in tandem with solitary work activity, music and its application necessarily have to be undertaken with care. Musical listening in this instance is a secondary activity, and must not dominate the attentive focus of a worker. If listening does dominate, it sidetracks the worker from his or her primary undertaking. Accordingly, the worker must retain the ability to control the music in question and regulate how loudly or at which particular moments it is to be heard. Musical works listened to in this instance are generally familiar, or at the very least are not unusual to listeners. Indeed, they are usually works that are personalized and become associated directly with the listener (hence acting as examples of mainstream musical listening practices). There appears to be a link with familiarity of the music and an ability to regulate how it is experienced in this situation. Without being able to exercise control over the music listened to, the work activity in question becomes disrupted because the music has the potential to interrupt a threshold level of focus required to undertake work tasks. In this sense, the material potency of music (which can fluctuate) has to be contained within the horizon of work if it is not to disrupt the individual's focus.

Listeners' expectations are consistently met because of the framing device of musical listening in which the sound-space of the worker is contained. Listening helps to block out all that surrounds the framed activity. With the possible exception of first dates, psychotherapy sessions and job interviews (where individuals regard all information as relevant), social activities such as work are surrounded by mental fences that mark what is included and perceptually relevant, and what is not (Zerubavel 1997: 37). By separating the things that are expected to receive attention, individuals leave behind other things that may enter their minds. Work listening affords greater concentration, allowing the listener to enter the 'zone' by providing limits on where the mind can go and what it considers relevant:

> Eliza: I listen at work, yeah, to Vivaldi, Bach, Mozart, Beethoven, Rachmaninoff, Haydn . . . you know yeah . . .
>
> Interviewer: How often would you listen to this music?
>
> Eliza: Every day. Yeah, because I stick it on when I work. If I've got to do something, where I'm writing – something that I'll need to concentrate for – I'll likely have some Baroque music in the background. It just kind of . . . I don't know, it just gets me in the zone. Classical music definitely helps me concentrate better, that's why I only put on Baroque music. I like Bach, the Goldberg variations. I just got a bunch of mp3s on my computer and I just stick it on and just play it . . . I don't tend to like vocals, the vocals tend to become a little bit distracting. I think because my brain hears the words and then I want to sing along to it and if I want to sing along to it, then I'm distracted with what I'm doing.
>
> *(Officer worker, 42, 12 April 2009)*

Music that is familiar and intentionally selected for work activity results in an experiential realm of work that does not present anything unanticipated. It does not distract and allows workers to get 'into the zone'. Framing work activity through musical listening provides listeners with the ability to experience solitude and privacy when engaged in the public activity of work.

Conclusion

By framing work activities with familiar music, listeners attempt to create idealized working environments using the inherent privacy generated by the act of mainstream musical listening. As work involves a 'cognitive distinction' whereby workers designate specific rules of interaction, the addition of solitary musical listening aids this process.

In exploring mainstream music listening at work, we can see how workers go about attaining and configuring work activity through experiences of music, specifically by undertaking mainstream musical listening. Interviewees in this sense illustrate music as an integral part of work situations. Work listening as a framing device provides individuals with seclusion from 'noisy' work environments. Importantly, though, it goes further by also providing listeners with a type of auditory scaffolding that they are able to control and manage as they see fit. Workers secluded from the auditory information system of the office are therefore partly removed from this situation. Though physically and visually remaining situated in office contexts, they are no longer aurally situated in this environment. It is this dislocation through music that provides a space for concentration.

Notes

1 See in particular Gurney (2000) and Atkinson (2007).
2 Though Goffman does not refer to sounds like coital noise, uncontrollable crying, laughter, flatulence, 'burping' and so on, these types of sounds can be extrapolated from his definition of 'backstage' and 'front stage' behaviours (see, in particular, Goffman 1971: 128).
3 See Sterne (2003) for an excellent overview of the social history of sound reproduction.
4 The larger study concerned the 'in situ' qualities of listening across a number of everyday situations (i.e. the home, automobile, public transport, work spaces and shopping contexts).
5 Music used in factories, warehouses and other situations is worthy of consideration, but unfortunately is beyond the scope of this chapter and empirical data attained. See Bijsterveld (2006) for an analysis of sound in historical industrial workplaces.
6 For some others, musical listening was found to be a distraction, and in open-plan office environments could be regarded as a direct encroachment upon a worker's sound-space.
7 The concept of 'flow' links with 'entering the zone'. For Csikszentmihalyi (1975), flow is defined as the enjoyment realized by the 'autotelic' experience while undertaking creative work. It is generally understood as a state that is experienced when undertaking an activity that requires considerable skill and represents a considerable challenge. Such experience results in a type of pleasure where the person senses they are removed from their body and everyday concerns. Timelessness is often associated with flow experiences. The focus of this section, however, is on the environmental features and use of music in achieving optimal work situations. These may sometimes result in experiences of 'flow', but to suggest that they always do so would be to misuse the term that focuses on the individual's psychic experience.

References

Arnett, J. (1995) 'Adolescents' uses of media for self-socialization', *Journal of Youth and Adolescence*, 24(5): 519–33.

Atkinson, R. (2007) 'Ecology of sound: the sonic order of urban space', *Urban Studies*, 44(10): 1905–17.

Baker, S. (2004) 'Pop in(to) the bedroom: popular music in pre-teen girls' bedroom culture', *European Journal of Cultural Studies* 7(1): 75–93.

Bennett, A. (2000) *Popular Music and Youth Culture: music, identity and place*, London: Macmillan.

Bessett, D. (2006) ' "Don't step on my groove!" Gender and the social experience of rock', *Symbolic Interaction*, 29(1): 49–62.

Bijsterveld, K. (2006) 'Listening to machines: industrial noise, hearing loss and the cultural meaning of sound', *Interdisciplinary Science Reviews*, 31(4): 323–37.

Bull, M. (2000) *Sounding Out the City: personal stereos and the management of everyday life*, Oxford: Berg.

—— (2007) *Sound Moves: iPod culture and urban experience*, New York: Routledge.

Csikszentmihalyi, M. (1975) *Beyond Boredom and Anxiety: experiencing flow in work and play*, San Francisco: Jossey-Bass.

de la Fuente, E. and Walsh, M. (2012) 'Framing through the senses: vision and sound in microsociology', in *Transvisuality: dimensioning the visual in a visual culture*, Liverpool: Liverpool University Press.

DeNora, T. (1997) 'Music and erotic agency: sonic resources and social-sexual action', *Body and Society*, 3(2): 43–65.

—— (1999) 'Music as a technology of the self', *Poetics: Journal of Empirical Research on Literature, the Media and the Arts*, 26: 31–56.

—— (2000) *Music in Everyday Life*, Cambridge: Cambridge University Press.

—— (2002) 'The role of music in intimate culture: a case study', *Feminism and Psychology*, 12(2): 176–81.

Goffman, E. (1971) *Relations in Public: microstudies of the public order*, New York: Basic Books.

—— (1974) *Frame Analysis: an essay on the organization of experience*, Harmondsworth: Penguin.

Gould, G. (2004) 'The prospects of recording', in C. Cox and D. Warner (eds), *Audio Culture: readings in modern music*, New York: Continuum.

Gurney, C. (2000) 'Transgressing private–public boundaries in the home: a sociological analysis of the coital noise taboo', *Venereology*, 13(1): 39–46.

Hall, E. (1969) *The Hidden Dimension*, Garden City, NY: Doubleday.

Hennion, A. (2001) 'Music lovers: taste as performance', *Theory, Culture and Society*, 18(5): 1–22.

LaBelle, B. (2008) 'Pump up the bass: rhythm, cars, and auditory scaffolding', *Senses and Society*, 3(2): 187–204.

Laurier, E. (2004) 'Doing office work on the motorway', *Theory, Culture and Society*, 21(4/5): 262–77.

Lincoln, S. (2005) 'Feeling the noise: teenagers, bedrooms and music', *Leisure Studies*, 24(4): 399–414.

Lofland, L. (1973) *A World of Strangers: order and action in urban public space*, New York: Basic Books.

Lyons, G., Jaina, J. and Holleya, D. (2006) 'The use of travel by rail passengers in Great Britain', *Transportation Research*, Part A, 41: 107–20.

Nippert-Eng, C. (1996) *Home and Work: negotiating boundaries through everyday life*, Chicago: University of Chicago Press.

Obelkevich, J. (1989) 'In search of the listener', *Journal of the Royal Musical Association*, 114(1): 102–8.

Simmel, G. (1994) 'The picture frame: an aesthetic study', *Theory, Culture and Society* 11(5): 11–17.

—— (1997) 'The sociology of space', in D. Frisby and M. Featherstone (eds), *Simmel on Culture: Selected Writings*, London: Sage.

Sommer, R. (1969) *Personal Space: the behavioral basis of design*, Englewood Cliffs, NJ: Prentice-Hall.

Steelcase (2004) 'Workplace privacy: a changing equation', a Knowledge Paper from Steelcase Inc., www.steelcase.com (accessed 24 June 2012).

Sterne, J. (2003) *The Audible Past: cultural origins of sound reproduction*, Durham, NC: Duke University Press.

Urry, J. (2007) *Mobilities*, Cambridge: Polity Press.

Walsh, M. (2009) 'Portable music device use on trains: a "splendid isolation"?' *Australian Journal of Communication*, 36(1): 49–59.

—— (2010a) 'Musical listening as boundary-work', in P. Murphy and E. de la Fuente (eds), *Philosophical and Cultural Theories of Music*, Leiden: Brill.

—— (2010b) 'Driving to the beat of one's own hum: automobility and musical listening', in N. Denzin (ed.), *Studies in Symbolic Interaction*, Vol. 35, Bingley: Emerald Group.

—— (2011) 'Musical listening and social boundaries: framing "public" and "private" social life through sound', PhD thesis, Faculty of Arts, Monash University, http://arrow.monash.edu.au/vital/access/manager/Repository/monash:63638.

Zerubavel, E. (1979a) 'Private time and public time: the temporal structure of social accessibility and professional commitments', *Social Forces*, 58(1): 38–58.

—— (1979b) *Patterns of Time in Hospital Life: a sociological perspective*, Chicago: University of Chicago Press.

—— (1981) *Hidden Rhythms: schedules and calendars in social life*, Chicago: University of Chicago Press.

—— (1991) *The Fine Line: making distinctions in everyday life*, New York: The Free Press.

—— (1997) *Social Mindscapes: an invitation to cognitive sociology*, Cambridge: Harvard University Press.

17

CHEESY LISTENING

Popular Music and Ironic Listening Practices

Andy Bennett

Studies focusing on the significance of popular music for audiences have tended to stress the consumption of music as a relatively 'serious' form of cultural practice, linked to a variety of socio-cultural sensibilities, including resistance (Brake 1985), identity politics (Lipsitz 1994), taste (Lewis 1992) and aesthetics (Frith 1987, 1996). Such uses of popular music are argued to cut across and complicate its economic function as the product of the cultural industries – an argument that is considered relevant not merely for niche and underground popular music but also those that characterize the mainstream. Thus, according to Negus (1992: 70), even as mainstream popular music audiences acknowledge the constructedness of their favourite music artists, 'at the same time [they] accept them as "real" '. Underlying this interpretation of popular music's cultural significance is the notion of 'authenticity' – that is, different genres of popular music, including mainstream genres such as pop, rock and heavy metal, are argued to speak in particular ways to and for particular audiences, and to inform at some level their identity and/or lifestyle. This view is supported in Frith's (1987) account of how, as a music critic, he has often received hostile correspondence from fans who believe that, in criticizing their favoured artists, he is 'deriding their way of life, undermining their identity' (143–4). In the same essay, Frith draws attention to the problems inherent in attempting to unpack and lay bare the processes around musical tastes: 'Some records and performers *work* for us, others do not – we know this without being able to explain it' (139, my emphasis). Here again, there is an implication that music that works for an individual is music regarded relatively seriously by that person – and, in many cases, as an extension of the self.

This chapter takes as its key standpoint the notion that mainstream popular music and performers that 'work for us' are not simply those in which we invest in a serious and earnest fashion. Rather, it is suggested, a sensibility of what could be termed 'ironic' listening is also evident among mainstream popular music audiences. Drawing on Ien Ang's (1982) concept of 'ironic viewing' – which she has applied as a means of differentiating between serious and non-serious viewing practices exhibited by audiences for television soap opera – it is suggested that similar discourses of irony can be observed in the listening practices of popular music audiences. The chapter then goes on to consider a range of artefacts, performance situations and reception patterns that provide evidence of ironic listening practices among popular music audiences. In the final section of the chapter, it is suggested that such ironic listening practices have more recently given rise to a new 'post-ironic' performance aesthetic – as exhibited, for example, by US experimental rock group Ween and British heavy metal group The Darkness. Through its exploration of ironic listening practices, the chapter thus contributes another dimension to our understanding of how mainstream popular music is appropriated and reframed as an aspect of contemporary popular culture.

Taking It Non-Seriously

In 1982, Ien Ang published her ground-breaking study *Watching Dallas*, the first academic book to present an in-depth, ethnographic analysis of soap opera and its audience. Lending her voice to a mounting critique of traditional accounts of media audiences, which suggested that the latter were an essentially passive and homogenous entity, Ang was concerned to demonstrate both the active and heterogeneous nature of the soap opera audience. As Ang discovered, for many viewers, their attraction to *Dallas* – the long-running US soap centred upon the oil-rich Texan family the Ewings – was framed around the way in which they could self-identify with particular characters in the series, and the fortunes and misfortunes that these characters encountered as depicted in the weekly series plots. This in itself, argued Ang, was suggestive of a more astute and critical reading of media texts on the part of media audiences than had been acknowledged by research grounded in critical theory and mass communication research (e.g. see Adorno and Horkheimer 1969; MacDonald 1957). Thus, according to Ang, although aware of the fictionalised accounts presented in *Dallas* and their often exaggerated representation, many members of the show's audience were nevertheless able to selectively appropriate and creatively rework scenes and scenarios from *Dallas* in ways that made sense in terms of their own everyday lives.

Significantly, however, Ang also identified a group of viewers for whom *Dallas* was received in a far more light-hearted way and regarded as an object of mockery. According to Ang, this group of viewers 'don't enjoy Dallas at all; what they seem to enjoy is the irony they bring to bear on it' (1982: 97). Ang refers to this as 'ironic viewing' – a practice through which individuals are able to detach themselves from the text while simultaneously engaging in an uncritical celebration of it. As Ang goes on to consider, the practice of ironic viewing allows for the negotiation of issues of good and bad taste, as these inform practices of popular culture consumption. Thus, while ironic viewers of *Dallas* are aesthetically given to understand the soap as an example of 'bad' popular culture, they are nevertheless able to justify their enjoyment of the series by citing its 'badness' as a key source of entertainment. Thus, observes Ang:

> for these ironizing fans the ideology of mass culture has become common sense: for them . . . it is self-evident that *Dallas* is 'bad mass culture'. But the very weapon of irony makes it unnecessary for them to suppress the pleasure that watching *Dallas* can nevertheless arouse; irony enables them to enjoy it without suffering pangs of conscience.
>
> *(1982: 101)*

Ang's observations are insightful in that they provide important tools for the drawing of a far more complex map of the aesthetic pleasures that audiences derive from popular cultural texts. Moving beyond the basic premise of the audience as agents active in the production of textual meanings (e.g. see Jenkins 1992), the concept of 'ironic' viewing brings a new breadth of understanding to the politics of taste exhibited by the active audience and the ways in which these are articulated through a range of different viewing practices underpinned by broad indices of legitimation. Although Ang limits her analysis to a particular form of television entertainment, the ironic pleasures she detects among sections of the *Dallas* audience can arguably be applied to the consumption of other popular cultural forms. For example, a number of 'B' movies – particularly science fiction films from the 1950s – have over the years become objects of cult fascination, often because of the ironic viewing practices that have become attached to them (Majer 1993). Similarly, 'bad taste' parties centre upon a collectively endorsed, ironically intended wearing of fashion items, typically from the 1970s (see Beattie 1990; Gregson et al. 2001). One area of popular culture that is little understood in terms of the ironic consumption practices it engenders is popular music. However, it seems reasonable to assume that if audiences for and consumers of other forms of popular culture are able to justify their attachment to objects, images and texts through practice of ironic consumption, then popular music audiences may use a similar form of legitimation in their enjoyment of what they consider to be 'bad' popular music.

Ironic Listening

As previously noted, the tendency among popular music researchers to represent popular music consumption as a relatively 'serious' form of cultural practice is particularly marked. As a fledgling academic discipline in the late 1970s, popular music studies established a series of criteria for the study and appropriation of popular music texts that saw it become entrenched in a succession of discussions and debates centring upon the political and aesthetic significance of popular music – the latter also ensuring that popular music studies became largely fixated around ostensibly more political genres, such as hard rock, punk and, latterly, rap and dance. This was achieved at the expense of any sustained discussion of other genres more associated by academic researchers with mainstream rock and pop. In many respects, popular music studies took much of its early intellectual nourishment from rock journalism, whose critical distinction between rock (intelligent – authentic) and pop (unintelligent – commercially orientated) often provided a barometer for the focus of popular music studies during its early inception (Bennett 2007; see also Catherine Strong, Chapter 7 in this book). Moreover, the dominance within popular music studies of theoretical discourses adapted from media and cultural studies resulted in a strong leaning towards textual analysis in which audience meanings were largely interpreted according to abstracted analytical readings of music genres and individual performers. This much is evident in Frith and McRobbie's (1990) reading of heavy metal. Thus, they observe, heavy metal performers tend to be:

> aggressive, dominating and boastful, and they constantly seek to remind the audience of their prowess, their control. Their stance is obvious in live shows; male bodies on display, plunging shirts and tight trousers, a visual emphasis on chest hair and genitals.
>
> *(1990: 374)*

This aligns with other similar representations of heavy metal that construe it as a genre characterized by extreme displays of male musical virtuosity (Walser 1993) and encoded messages of misogyny and male bonding that are deemed to endear it to a primarily male, working-class audience (Straw 1990). Similarly, in terms of its media representation, heavy metal has variously been linked with teenage suicide (Richardson 1991) and devil worship (Weinstein 2000) – traits that, again, are deemed to flow directly from the encoded messages in the music and style of heavy metal artists. In such representations of heavy metal, there is an underlying assumption that encoded messages are transferred unproblematically to audiences and become effectively the only way in which the latter can respond to and understand heavy metal music and its associated imagery. Yet, for a considerable heavy metal listenership, it seems clear that a significant level of ironic enjoyment is derived from what is perceived to be the excessive nature of the music and those who perform it. Like Ang's ironic *Dallas* viewers, such listeners deconstruct the scriptedness of the heavy metal performance, turning those qualities of the music and its artists that are intended to startle or offend into occasions for laughter and non-serious enjoyment. Indeed, heavy metal was perhaps one of the earliest indicators of popular music's susceptibility to non-serious and ironic modes of reception and rearticulation – a fact evidenced in the mid-1980s by the release of Rob Reiner's fictional heavy metal 'mockumentary' *This is Spinal Tap*. The film skilfully inverts a number of classic heavy metal traits and represents them in a mocking and satirical fashion, consistent with a then already fashioned counter-view of heavy metal as excessive and pretentious. *This is Spinal Tap* assumes both a familiarity on the part of the audience with those textual and performative conventions of heavy metal identified by Frith and McRobbie, among others, and more importantly, an ability to reread these in line with the film's comic interpre-tation of them. Indeed, upon its release, *This is Spinal Tap* was positively received as much by the heavy metal fanbase as by non-heavy metal fans and the group Spinal Tap's subsequent transcendence from film characters to live performance, including appearances at established rock and heavy metal festivals, paved the way for later ironic metal acts such as The Darkness.

Evidence of ironic listening practices can also be identified among audiences for other genres of popular music. Indeed, in some cases, such has been the ironic appeal of artists that they have effectively been able to relaunch their careers. A notable example here is 1970s glam rock artist Gary Glitter. Enjoying signifi-cant commercial success between 1972 and 1974, followed by a decline in popu-larity during the later 1970s, in the 1980s Glitter's music was rediscovered by both original fans and a new, younger audience. Glitter responded to this revival of interest with an increasingly elaborate array of stage costumes and a new concept, the 'Gang Show', with Glitter ironically repositioning his 1973 hit 'I'm the Leader of the Gang (I Am)' to punctuate his new-found rapport with an ever-increasing audience who revelled in the irony of Glitter's on-stage persona.[1] Other artists who have benefited from the practices of ironic listening applied to their music include Rolf Harris and Tom Jones. During the 1960s, the Australian-born Harris was a popular television personality and children's entertainer. By the mid-1990s, the primary audience for Harris' live performances were not children but young adults, including a large number of university students who were too young for Harris to have registered as a childhood icon. For these young people, Harris had become something of a cult figure; during the 1990s, Harris was a regular attrac-tion at Summer Balls and similar university functions. Similarly, Welsh pop singer Tom Jones, who scored considerable commercial success during the 1960s with hits such as 'It's Not Unusual' and 'Delilah', has also found renewed success though ironic appeal. During the 1960s, Jones' commercial success hinged upon his powerful and distinctive singing voice and the way this was accentuated through his physical appearance – a sun-bronzed, muscular body that earned him a signif-icant audience of female admirers. Jones' revived success, which began during the late 1980s, was largely down to the interest of a new, younger audience for whom the appeal of Jones was based on an ironic reading of his macho 1960s image. Jones in turn displayed a shrewd ability to read his new audience's interpretation of him, and to modify his image and song material accordingly, as evidenced though 1990s songs such as 'Sex Bomb'. Jones' self-parody also saw him increas-ingly working in the comedy genre; notable examples here include his teaming up with British comedian Lenny Henry in 1991 in a BBC *Comic Relief* sketch entitled 'Battle of the Sex Gods', which saw them wearing matching lurex jackets and pink codpieces. Similarly, in 1996, Jones performed a comic self-portrayal in the science fiction spoof film *Mars Attacks!*

In addition to individual artists, entire genres – and in some cases specific eras of popular music – have been reframed as objects of ironic listening, replete with associated patterns of tongue-in-cheek cultural consumption. A pertinent case in point here is disco. Originally inscribed with an insignia of cool, anti-rock aestheticism and working as a platform for racial and sexual politics that were systematically barred from the related spheres of rock and heavy metal, the disco audience subsequently proliferated with new conventions of ironic appreciation coming into play. Within this, disco is typically represented, alongside various other 1970s music such as glam, as an object of ironic pleasure. A pertinent example of this is the '70s Night, a club-based dance event featuring a mixture of glam rock, disco and soundtrack music from popular music-based films of the era, such as *Grease* and *Saturday Night Fever*. People attending '70s Nights are encouraged to mimic the fashion of the decade, typically flared trousers, wide-collared shirts and wigs modelling popular hairstyles of the early to mid-1970s. The appeal of '70s Nights is supported by other ironic representations of the decade, a notable example being the BBC TV series *I Love the 70s*, which reduces the popular culture of the decade to a series of stereotypical images of platform boots and sequinned jackets (synonymous with the glam rock image of 1970s groups such as Slade and The Sweet) or white flared trousers and medallions (images associated with the film *Saturday Night Fever*). The irony and humour of the '70s Night is doubly articulated, allowing participants both to make fun of the 1970s and to laugh at themselves. According to Gregson et al. (2001: 5), in the context of the '70s Night, '70s fashion[s are] constructed . . . as items of "apparel", as "outfits" that are motivated by the desire to produce bad taste'. This in turn, suggest Gregson et al., plays a key role in the way that 1970s fashions are received and understood by the clientele of such events: 'The appropriate mode of appreciation here . . . is about laughter: the wearing here is not about clever, knowing citation, but about fun, laughter and collectivity of "abject humiliation" ' (5).

Situating the Ironic Listener

As observed at the beginning of this chapter, it has been argued by theorists such as Frith (1987) and Negus (1992) that key to a popular music artist's success is their ability to come across as 'authentic' and 'sincere'. This, according to Negus, relies upon a willingness on the part of audience members to suspend their understanding of popular music artists as constructed and commodified. As the examples above seek to illustrate, however, it need not be the case that music audiences in all cases enter into or demand such a relationship with the star text. Although popular music scholars tend to argue that artists are consumed as *complete* products, the reality is often quite different. Thus, in some cases individuals follow artists not for their image *per se*, but because of the music.

In other cases, individuals do not essentially like an artist or their music in general, but rather simply select particular songs that, for whatever reason, they happen to find appealing. This is supported by Laing (1985) in his study of the UK punk scene of the late 1970s. Laing observes that at the height of the Sex Pistols' popularity, the majority of those who bought the single 'God Save the Queen' were not fans of the Sex Pistols and, given the number of units sold, probably not even punks. Similarly, Bennett (2000) notes how youth who outwardly exhibited a preference for rock and heavy metal in the later 1970s actually listened privately to a range of musical styles, including disco and soul.

Like audiences for other media, then, popular music audiences bring their own practices of consumption to bear on the way they understand and interpret music. The practice of ironic listening can be situated within this cluster of heterogeneous listening practices. If it is now a given that music audiences of all ages are able to see through the constructedness of music performers,[2] it does not follow – as Negus (1992) claims – that all members of an audience will nevertheless accept an artist as real. On the contrary, knowledge of an artist's constructedness may lead audience members to adopt other ways of consuming, and even 'appreciating', that artist. Indeed, as the examples discussed earlier in this chapter serve to illustrate, members of an audience may revel in the extreme nature of an artist's constructed image; similarly, they may 'overturn' the intended sincerity of a particular song lyric and re-represent it as fickle, over the top, and so on, thus reinscribing the lyric as an object of fun. Likewise, expressions of authenticity and sincerity that ultimately win over certain sections of an audience may be transformed by others into objects of ridicule through which they are able to devise their own ironic patterns of consumption. An interesting example of this will be discussed below in relation to Drew's (2005) work on karaoke events. As with Ang's ironic viewer, then, the practice of ironic listening allows the consumer to derive pleasure from a musical style or individual performer without buying into more accepted conventions of fandom that may demand very different forms of appreciation.

Although not directly stated by Ang (1982), there is a clear suggestion in her work that the ironic viewing practices she identifies among viewers of *Dallas* are primarily associated with middle-class viewers. This position is consistent with Peterson and Kern's (1996) concept of the cultural omnivore. Challenging Bourdieu's (1984) notion of cultural capital and its interpretation of the relationship between class, taste and lifestyle as relatively static, Peterson and Kern (1996) suggest that sections of the middle class are more eclectic in their tastes, and will often draw on cultural resources and engage in pastimes primarily associated with lower class consumers. Such a premise rests on the notion that, empowered by their media and cultural literacy, middle-class consumers are able to consume with a degree of reflexivity, and in some cases critical detachment, not available to working-class consumers. Drew's (2004, 2005) work on middle- and working-class participation in karaoke nights builds on Peterson and Kern's argument.

Thus, according to Drew (2005), whereas working-class audiences often take their participation in karaoke evenings very seriously – often becoming long-standing patrons of a particular bar where they engage with a regular 'community' of karaoke fans – middle-class individuals are more likely to treat karaoke as a non-serious activity, and as an occasion for laughter and ridicule. In the course of ethnographic research in karaoke bars in the United States, Drew (2005: 377) observed how in bars frequented by middle-class patrons singers would often effect laughter by 'put[ting] themselves in the position of performing songs that carried incongruous gender signals, or songs with inappropriate lyrics, or songs that were simply out of their vocal range'. Elsewhere, Drew's work also cites student nights as another example of the way in which middle-class values act to deconstruct the working-class perception of karaoke as a serious and status-building pursuit, this time punctuated by a particular brand of middle-class youth subversion that preys on the pretention of 'coolness' (Drew 2004).

Arguably, Drew makes too much of a distinction here between the class background of consumers and their capacity or not for ironic participation in karaoke. For example, in the United Kingdom, the long-standing tradition of fancy dress parties in pubs in working-class neighbourhoods has often prompted its own brand of ironic send-up, with overweight, senior or cross-dressed versions of popular music icons spontaneously called up on stage by the DJ to mime or sing along to a song by the artist they are impersonating. The author's own experience of performing in cover bands in working-class pubs and clubs in the United Kingdom adds further weight to this argument. Thus many venues had singers' nights where locals would routinely take to the stage and perform ironic renditions of classic pop and rock songs, much to the amusement of the audience, who were more than willing to share in the joke (see Bennett 1997). Similarly, the established send-up of popular music artists by television comedians in a global context suggests that discourses of parody and irony can be shared and understood among a broader demographic than one restricted purely to an educated, middle-class audience.

Celebrating Irony: The Post-Ironic Performer

Thus far, this chapter has been concerned with an examination of ironic listening practice as a means of broadening our understanding of the ways in which audiences can derive pleasure from the consumption of popular music, genres, texts and performers. The final section of the chapter considers how the music industry itself has responded to the desire among audiences to indulge in and effectively celebrate popular music as an object of ironic enjoyment.

The examples already drawn on in the earlier part of this chapter serve to illustrate some of the basic characteristics of ironic listening and their embeddedness in specific star texts, and also underline the growing industry awareness of the demand for ironic entertainment. Add to this the long history of novelty records that have featured in the mainstream pop charts, and the history and lineage of the 'ironic turn' in popular music begins to look more complex. Frith and Horne (1987) observe how, for many years, the music industry formula of selling 'high seriousness' to audiences – especially in genre fields such as rock, jazz and folk – proved highly successful, thus relegating novelty and comedy songs to a specific niche market. It is evident, however, that even at the zenith of such representation of popular music in some quarters of the industry, in other quarters a perceived meltdown of the audience's tolerance in this respect gave rise to new modes of presenting artists and their music. For example, Stratton (1986) suggests that part of the appeal of early 1970s British glam rock artists such as The Sweet and Slade was the way in which they injected *fun* back into rock music following the high seriousness, and ultimately failed political endeavours, of counter-cultural rock (see also Bennett 2007).

Ironic listening is thus positioned as one way in which audiences react against, and ultimately reject, the branding and marketing discourses of the music industry, replacing these with their own modes of listening and response to popular music artists, texts and genres. In recent years, the industry response to ironic demand has become increasingly nuanced, with an increasing number of new artists now being selected and marketed primarily on the basis of their assumed ironic appeal. A case in point here is The Darkness, a heavy metal band from the United Kingdom whose initial five-year career included two highly successful albums – *Permission to Land* and *One-way Ticket to Hell . . . and Back* – as well as an appearance at the Glastonbury Festival and very well-received tours of the United States. From The Darkness' first television appearances, it was clear that the band's take on heavy metal was modelled in the vein of Spinal Tap. However, while Spinal Tap songs were often an extended vehicle for the humour and irony explored in the *Spinal Tap* film, The Darkness' ironic take on metal involved a highly subtle fusion of accepted elements of the heavy metal genre combined with an ironic take on these. Observing state-of-the art standards for composition, performance and production in heavy metal, irony in The Darkness' songs was generally invoked in a subtle gloss, typically delivered through particular twists in the lyrics and visual representation in promotional videos. An example of this can be heard in the title and chorus of the track 'Is It Just Me (or Am I All On My Own Again)?' Sung with the vigour, intensity and pompous air of classic heavy metal, the clever innuendo of the chorus hook digs into and deflates a key trope of the heavy metal singer's lyrical repertoire.[3]

This and other songs operate in a context, post-Spinal Tap and other self-styled ironic artists, where the appeal of irony in rock and pop has essentially become a given and coexists alongside tropes such as authenticity as a means through which audiences find connection with popular music artists. In this respect, The Darkness can be regarded as an example of what could be termed a post-ironic popular music act. Rather than operating in a zone of ironic exploration of the heavy metal genre, The Darkness is able to target established and well-defined segments of the heavy metal and wider popular music audiences who are predisposed to the ironic intent of The Darkness concept. A similar example of a 'post-ironic' act is US experimental rock band Ween. Like The Darkness, the composition, performance and production standards applied in Ween's music are entirely comparable with the mainstay of contemporary artists working in similar styles and genres. In terms of its lyrical content, however, Ween's music often contains highly discernible elements of satire and humour. A pertinent example of this is seen in the 1996 album *12 Golden Country Greats*. In songs contained on the album, country music tropes such as rugged masculinity, religion, community and family values are often satirized. Again, it is clear that Ween is writing and recording its music with a particular audience in mind – one that is familiar with the standard country music treatment of the aforementioned issues and is prepared to critically detach itself from the latter and reappraise them through the ironic lens offered by Ween's often tongue-in-cheek take on country music.

Conclusion

This chapter has examined the concept of ironic listening and its value as a means of broadening our understanding of the ways in which audiences appropriate, understand and respond to mainstream popular music. The chapter began by revisiting and discussing Ang's concept of ironic viewing, and considering how this could be adapted to accommodate a mode of listening among popular music audiences in which emphasis is placed upon ironic appreciation of popular music genres, artists and texts. This was followed by a consideration of several popular music artists whose careers mark what could be referred to as an 'ironic turn' in the reception and appreciation of particular popular music artists. The chapter then turned its attention to ways of situating the ironic listening audience, taking to task the contention that conventions of ironic listening are open only to middle-class, educated audiences. Rather, it was argued, ironic listening practices are evident across a broader spectrum of the social strata. Finally, the chapter considered two examples of what could be termed 'post-ironic' artists – that is, artists whose music assumes a ready-made audience equipped with aesthetic sensibilities geared towards the ironic appreciation of popular music. Through its focus on ironic listening practices, the chapter has examined another dimension through which audiences appropriate and understand mainstream popular music. In rejecting the notion that audiences will, in every instance, imbue their understanding of mainstream popular music artists with discourses of authenticity, the chapter makes the point that ironic listening practices result in alternative ways of understanding and appreciating mainstream popular music and associated artists.

Notes

1 In the late 1990s, amidst a high-profile court case in which Glitter was found guilty of child sex offences, his career as a performing artist came to a dramatic and rapid end.

2 See, for example, Lowe's (2004) study of teenage, female Britney Spears fans.
3 Following lead singer Justin Hawkins' departure in 2005, the remaining members of The Darkness formed a new band, Stone Gods, while Hawkins formed his own band, Hot Leg. In 2011, The Darkness staged a reunion and in 2012 released a new studio album, *Hot Cakes*.

References

Adorno, T. and Horkheimer, M. (1969) *The Dialectic of Enlightenment*, London: Allen Lane.
Ang, I. (1982) *Watching* Dallas: *soap opera and the melodramatic imagination*, London: Routledge.
Beattie, G. (1990) *England After Dark*, London: Weidenfeld and Nicolson.
Bennett, A. (1997) 'Going down the pub: the pub rock scene as a resource for the consumption of popular music', *Popular Music*, 16(1): 97–108.
—— (2000) *Popular Music and Youth Culture: music, identity and place*, London: Macmillan.
—— (2007) 'The forgotten decade: rethinking the popular music of the 1970s', *Popular Music History*, 2(1): 5–24.
Bourdieu, P. (1984) *Distinction: a social critique of the judgement of taste*, trans. R. Nice, Cambridge, MA: Harvard University Press.
Brake, M. (1985) *Comparative Youth Culture: the sociology of youth cultures and youth subcultures in America, Britain and Canada*, London: Routledge and Kegan Paul.
Drew, R. (2004) '"Scenes" dimensions of Karaoke in the US', in A. Bennett and R.A. Peterson (eds), *Music Scenes: local, trans-local and virtual*, Nashville, TN: Vanderbilt University Press.
—— (2005) '"Once more with irony": Karaoke and social class', *Leisure Studies*, 24(4): 371–83.
Frith, S. (1987) 'Towards an aesthetic of popular music', in R. Leppert and S. McClary (eds), *Music and Society: the politics of composition, performance and reception*, Cambridge: Cambridge University Press.
—— (1996) *Performing Rites: on the value of popular music*, Oxford: Oxford University Press.
Frith, S. and McRobbie, A. (1990) 'Rock and sexuality', in S. Frith and A. Goodwin (eds), *On Record: rock, pop and the written word*, London: Routledge.
Frith, S. and Horne, H. (1987) *Art into Pop*, London: Methuen.
Gregson, N., Brooks, K. and Crewe, L. (2001) 'Bjorn again? Rethinking 70s revivalism through the reappropriation of 70s clothing', *Fashion Theory*, 5(1): 3–28.
Jenkins, H. (1992) *Textual Poachers: television fans and participatory culture*, New York: Routledge.
Laing, D. (1985) *One Chord Wonders: power and meaning in punk rock*, Milton Keynes: Open University Press.
Lewis, G.H. (1992) 'Who do you love? The dimensions of musical taste', in J. Lull (ed.), *Popular Music and Communication*, 2nd edn, London: Sage.
Lipsitz, G. (1994) *Dangerous Crossroads: popular music, postmodernism and the poetics of place*, London: Verso.
Lowe, M. (2004) ' 'Tween scene: resistance within the mainstream', in A. Bennett and R.A. Peterson (eds), *Music Scenes: local, trans-local and virtual*, Nashville, TN: Vanderbilt University Press.
MacDonald, D. (1957) 'A theory of mass culture', in B. Rosenberg and D. White (eds), *Mass Culture: the popular arts in America*, Glencoe, IL: The Free Press.
Majer, J. (1993) 'Toho's monsters speak out', *Cult Movies*, 7: 57.

Negus, K. (1992) *Producing Pop: culture and conflict in the popular music industry*, London: Edward Arnold.

Peterson, R.A and Kern, R.M. (1996) 'Changing highbrow taste: from snob to omnivore', *American Sociological Review*, 61(5): 900–7.

Richardson, J.T. (1991) 'Satanism in the courts: from murder to heavy metal', in J.T. Richardson, J. Best and D.G. Bromley (eds), *The Satanism Scare*, New York: Aldine de Gruyter.

Stratton, J. (1986) 'Why doesn't anybody write anything about glam rock?' *Australian Journal of Cultural Studies*, 4(1): 15–38.

Straw, W. (1990) 'Characterizing rock music culture: the case of heavy metal', in S. Frith and A. Goodwin (eds), *On Record: rock, pop and the written word*, London: Routledge.

Walser, R. (1993) *Running with the Devil: power, gender and madness in heavy metal music*, London: Wesleyan University Press.

Weinstein, D. (2000) *Heavy Metal: the music and its culture*, 2nd edn, New York: Da Capo Press.

LIST OF CONTRIBUTORS

David Baker teaches in Film and Screen Studies in the School of Humanities at Griffith University, Queensland, Australia. His primary research interests are cinema history and aesthetics, with a particular emphasis on popular music and cinema from the 1950s to the present, having published on such topics as Bob Dylan on screen and Hollywood youth delinquency and rebellion in the 1950s.

Sarah Baker is a Senior Lecturer in Sociology at Griffith University, Queensland, Australia. Previously, she has held research fellowships at the University of Leeds and The Open University in the United Kingdom, and at the University of South Australia. She has published widely in the field of popular music studies and is the co-author, with David Hesmondhalgh, of *Creative Labour* (Routledge, 2011).

Andy Bennett is Professor of Cultural Sociology and Director of the Griffith Centre for Cultural Research at Griffith University, Queensland, Australia. He has authored and edited numerous books, including *Popular Music and Youth Culture, Cultures of Popular Music, Remembering Woodstock* and *Music Scenes* (with Richard A. Peterson).

Michael Brown is a doctoral candidate at the New Zealand School of Music, Wellington, New Zealand. For the last 10 years, he has been researching and writing about New Zealand music, with a special focus on folk, vernacular and community music. He has also created music documentaries for Radio New Zealand, produced experimental films, written graphic novels and played guitar in various ensembles.

Denis Crowdy teaches courses in audio engineering, popular music and guitar at Macquarie University, Sydney, Australia. He is actively involved in ethnomusicological research, studio and field recording, is a co-editor of the journal *Perfect Beat*, and is the Chair of the International Council for Traditional Music's Study Group on the Music and Dance of Oceania.

Timothy J. Dowd is Associate Professor of Sociology at Emory University in Atlanta, Georgia, USA. He was the Erasmus Chair for the Humanities at Erasmus University Rotterdam, the Netherlands in 2007–08. He specializes in cultural sociology, with much of his published research focusing on music.

Mark Duffett is a Senior Lecturer in Media and Cultural Studies at the University of Chester, England. His research interests centre on Elvis Presley and fan culture. His current projects include a textbook called *Understanding Media Fandom* (Continuum) and editing a special issue of *Popular Music and Society*.

Murray Forman is Associate Professor of Media and Screen Studies at Northeastern University, Boston, USA. He is author of *The 'Hood Comes First: Race, Space and Place in Rap and Hip-Hop* (2002) and *One Night on TV is Worth Weeks at the Paramount: Popular Music on Early Television* (2012), and co-editor of *That's the Joint! The Hip-Hop Studies Reader* (2011).

Erik Hannerz is a postgraduate student in Sociology at Uppsala University, Sweden. He is currently finishing his doctoral thesis on how punks construct and make use of plural mainstreams in order to validate objects, identities and actions as subcultural. Hannerz is also a pre-doctoral fellow at the Center for Cultural Sociology at Yale University.

Alison Huber wrote her PhD, 'Learning to love the mainstream: Top 40 culture in Melbourne' (2005) in the cultural studies program at the University of Melbourne, Australia. Her work has been published in a range of international journals and edited collections. From 2010–12 she was Research Fellow on 'Popular Music and Cultural Memory', hosted in the Griffith Centre for Cultural Research, Griffith University, Queensland, Australia.

Adrian Renzo is a Professional Teaching Fellow at the University of Auckland. He holds a PhD from the University of Western Sydney. He has published on topics including 1980s medley records, Spanish megamix records and the relationship between 'handbag' dance music and gay male culture.

Ian Rogers is a Lecturer in Popular Music at the University of Queensland. His 2012 PhD thesis was titled 'Musicians and Aspiration: Exploring the Rock Dream in Independent Music'. An established freelance music writer, Rogers has been published in Australian music publications such as *Mess and Noise* (independent) and *The Vine* (Fairfax Digital).

Matt Stahl is based at the University of Western Ontario, Canada. He studies relations, representations and regulation of creative work in the cultural industries. His forthcoming monograph, *Unfree Masters: Recording Artists and the Politics of Work*, will be published by Duke University Press in 2012.

Catherine Strong is a Lecturer in Sociology at Monash University, Melbourne, Australia. Her research interests include music and cultural memory, nostalgia and the relationship between popular culture and gender. In 2011 she published *Grunge: Music and Memory* (Ashgate).

Jodie Taylor is a Research Fellow at the Queensland Conservatorium Research Centre, Griffith University, Queensland, Australia. She is the author of *Playing it Queer: Popular Music, Identity and Queer World-making* (2012). She has published widely on popular music and sexuality, queer culture and ethnographic methods, and is co-editor of *The Festivalisation of Culture* (Ashgate, forthcoming).

Michael Walsh has a PhD from Monash University, Melbourne, Australia. His work appears in the *Australian Journal of Communication, Studies in Symbolic Interactionism* and the edited collections *Philosophical and Cultural Theories of Music* (2010) and *Transvisuality: The Cultural Dimension of Visuality* (2012).

Sheila Whiteley is Professor Emeritus at the University of Salford and Visiting Professor at Southampton Solent University in the United Kingdom. She is author of *The Space Between the Notes, Women and Popular Music* and *Too Much Too Young*, and has edited numerous collections including *Sexing the Groove, Music Space and Place* and *Queering the Popular Pitch*.

INDEX

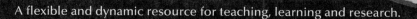